TALKING DOLLARS AND MAKING SENSE

A Wealth-Building Guide for African-Americans

Brooke M. Stephens

McGraw-Hill

New York   San Francisco   Washington, D.C.   Auckland   Bogotá
Caracas   Lisbon   London   Madrid   Mexico City   Milan
Montreal   New Delhi   San Juan   Singapore
Sydney   Tokyo   Toronto

To Baba
and
to Granddaddy Charlie Stephens,
whose infinite wisdom, humor, and common sense
taught me the simple value of a quarter.

ABOUT THE AUTHOR

Brooke Stephens, who operates her own financial consulting firm, is a 15-year Wall Street veteran, and was a weekly financial commentator on FX Cable's *Breakfast Time*. A financial planner and registered investment advisor, she has been an investment manager at Citicorp Investment Service, Inc., and an international trade officer at Chase Manhattan Bank. She has written for *Black Enterprise, Essence, Ms., New Woman, USA Today*, and other publications. Ms. Stephens received her first lesson in financial management from her mother, whose refusal to extend an unwisely used $5 allowance taught Brooke the value of "making your money last until you know where the next dollar is coming from." The author lives in Brooklyn, New York.

CONTENTS

INTRODUCTION

My first unforgettable financial lesson happened when I was 9 years old. My mother had started giving me an allowance of $5 a week. Each Sunday night as I laid out my clothes for Monday morning, the crisp new bill was put in my hands followed by the admonition, "Remember, it has to last until Saturday." A few weeks into this ritual, I was still being cautious with the responsibility of making the money last until the end of the week until one Thursday after school when I followed along behind some of my friends to the local five-and-ten department store and blew nearly all my nickels and dimes on candy, junk jewelry, and hair ribbons.

I woke up on Friday morning to the stinging reality that I had bus fare to get to school but nothing was left for lunch money or the return trip home. My piggy bank was empty. I begged for a loan from my brother, who laughed at me. I whined for an advance from my mother. She shrugged and gave me that very firm "no" with a look and a tone of voice that every black child recognizes as the final word on the subject. The only kind remark I got was that I should wear my sneakers so I would be comfortable for the 5-mile walk home. I tried to borrow bus fare from some of my classmates, the same ones who had talked me into all the silly spending I'd done the day before. No deal. During the 2 hours it took for me to make that long walk in the hot Florida sun, I was furious. With each step, I cursed my mother, my brother, the bus company, and every one of the people who had refused to help me. But I never forget the lesson. Make the money last until you know where the next dollar is coming from.

More than 20 years later when I started out on Wall Street after attending business school, I was among the first small group of women of color who weren't typing in the steno pool, serving lunch in the cafeteria, or pushing a vacuum cleaner on the evening shift. My college degrees and the affirmative action programs of the sixties had gotten me into the corporate arena, but there was still a lot to be learned about the mysteries of the financial world and how money worked. Despite courses in economics and investments, I still entertained many myths and illusions about what it meant to make money, what wealth really meant, and how money operated in my own life. The hostile atmosphere of Wall Street also led me to believe that my presence as a woman and my career as an African-American was tenuous at best and was not going to be a long-standing one, and so I was afraid of the risk of tying up money in a long-term commitment like the stock market. I also didn't know anyone who looked like me who bought and sold stock.

Earning a decent income, paying bills on time, and staying out of trouble with credit cards was the extent of my life experience with managing money. Even with my education, it was difficult for me to translate the principles and concepts of investing and risk-taking to my personal life. As I watched my colleagues, I learned that earning money was just the beginning of the wealth-building process and that a savings account was not the place to make real money. It was another 2 years before I opened a brokerage account and bought my first stock—and I worked in the business!

In the spring of 1976, as the country prepared for the Bicentennial celebration, I discovered Fraunces Tavern during a business luncheon. At the foot of Broad Street at the tip of Manhattan, the small brick two-story structure bears a plaque stating that it is both the site where George Washington met with British army officers to negotiate the evacuation of the British from New York and the place where Washington gave his farewell speech to his troops before departing New York for Philadelphia. The museum on the second floor of the building detailed the many events related to the Revolutionary War that occurred at the tavern and the facets of Washington's military life that took place within the tavern. The museum brochure made no effort to clarify the fact that Samuel Fraunces, the owner of the tavern, was a former ship's cook from the British West Indies.

Fraunces arrived in New York around 1755 and became one of the less than 2000 free black men in the city at that time. It is believed that he brought a large sum of money with him; within a year of his arrival he married Elizabeth Dalles, and the two of them bought the waterfront home of the De Lancey family, on the corner of Pearl Street, for 2000 pounds.

Despite my exposure and a liberal arts education, this was the first time I had heard of a free person of color who had been a successful businessperson during the American Revolution. This information gave me an entirely different point of view on the hidden business and financial aspect of African-American history in America. It also confirmed my belief that this was another aspect of African-American history that has been ignored or erased—our presence in the world of business and enterprise.

The following year, the death of my stepfather and the ensuing financial confusion that developed led me to question if there was a sensible approach to managing personal financial matters with the same preciseness of planning and documentation that I participated in on a daily basis in the corporate world. The death of a family patriarch should not have engendered such fear, hurt feelings, uncertainty, and indecisiveness that took years to resolve.

Twelve years later when I established a financial planning practice, I saw those same attitudes of uncertainty, fear, distrust, lack of sophistication, and intimidation among many of the people that I met. The seminars I taught might have a full house, but not everyone came with the same attitude. The African-American clientele were much more distrustful than other participants of what I had to say, much more reluctant to accept who I was as the advisor, and much more difficult to convince about the positive aspects of investing. They seemed to believe that they weren't getting the whole story. The emotional baggage of our economic history has made so many African-Americans desperately afraid of losing what they have accumulated that they seem convinced, because of risk and lack of knowledge, that there is some secret process that they are not being told about the game of investing.

So here, as best as I can share it, is the whole story. There are no hidden secrets to building wealth, no difficult principles to master, no special club you must be initiated into. Building wealth requires the desire to know and the willingness to take a chance, along with a clear understanding of the tools needed, which are more than just the cash to work with. Most of all, building wealth requires a commitment and a sense of discipline to achieve a greater goal. I have chosen many African-American historical figures as role models who took unbelievable risks and became financially successful. Like most African-American figures in history, their existence has been known to few and ignored by most. Their accomplishments are often referred to as the "exceptions." These people came out of the horrendous experience of slavery, but through perseverance and discipline they managed to find a "way out of no way" for themselves and their families. Their presence here confirms my belief that as African-Americans we have our own unique way of achieving our particular goals.

As you read their stories, you will discover that building wealth is the systematic application of a plan: a long-term plan for achieving prosperity and for building a dynasty. But the plan begins with having the right attitude. Without that attitude, most African-Americans will not attain the goal of wealth that they seek. Managing your income properly and meeting your obligations are admirable goals, but they are not the end goal of building wealth. The goal of building a financial dynasty and creating a secure financial foundation takes one generation after another of clear-sighted focus on the principles of saving, investing, dreaming, and giving back to the community that supported you in your efforts to get there.

Money management and *financial planning* may sound like intimidating terms that apply only to the rich, but if that's what you think, you're wrong. If you are earning a living, paying your bills on time, saving for the future, and investing in an IRA, you are practicing the first basic steps in the wealth-building process. I have written this book for those people who think they don't have any money to manage and aren't sure what professional help really means.

This book was written with the intent of taking some of the mystery out of the wealth-building process and bringing it down home with an African-American point of view. Our experience with earning money has been unique in the American economic system, and so our take on the wealth-building process leads us to believe that we have been deliberately locked out of the arena of competition. Racism is still rampant in the United States, but the opportunities for African-Americans to build wealth are better now than they have been in the last four centuries of our presence on these shores. Our response to the new income we are now making would be a disappointment to the ancestors who suffered such brutal lives to bring us this far. We need to make a serious shift of the African-American paradigm if we are going to change our financial direction for ourselves and the next generation. The question now is what kind of descendants have we become in the struggle for self-reliance and financial independence.

First, we will take a look at the attitudes and behavior that surround our money, which have a great influence on our financial decision making. We will also look at the basic mistakes people make with money and ways to avoid making the same mistakes over and over again. *Talking Dollars and Making Sense* has been written with a minimum amount of the Wall Street gobbledygook, which is extremely intimidating to everyone who isn't familiar with the language of "the Street." There is an emphasis on the entrepreneurial history of African-Americans who have struggled to grow beyond the stereotypical images that history would have us believe is our heritage in the financial arena. The many quotations and anecdotes are tailored toward our community and point of view to make what is often dismissed as a serious subject become basic and accessible. There is some humor, but most of all I have attempted to offer commonsense insights with a let's-get-real-and-be-honest-about-the-problems-we-had-in-the-past approach. Taking hold of our future financial well-being can be done now with the right attitude and a sense of commitment. We owe it to our ancestors to build on the wealth of hard work that has brought us this far.

The most important and difficult first step is to review the attitudes and behavior that have kept us from developing a money mentality and to begin to see ourselves as financial beings. Then we will review the building blocks of the complete financial planning process and see how it fits into your life—at all age levels. The concepts of investing, buying insurance, and planning for retirement are discussed in simple, basic terms that don't make you feel as if you've wandered into a Wall Street board room. If you think you need further assistance, I offer you some guidelines for choosing the professional help best suited to your needs.

Financial planning is simply keeping track of money's ongoing influence in your life, deciding what you want money to do for you, and figuring out the best way to bring yourself the financial stability and growth you want. *Talking Dollars and Making Sense* is intended to give you the incentive to want to know more about building wealth and to help you develop a new attitude and a fresh approach to new possibilities and the idea of being financially comfortable. I hope this book helps you on your way.

Yours truly,
Brooke M. Stephens
Financial Advisor

ACKNOWLEDGMENTS

The most important lesson for me in this process is to understand that although there is only one name on the book jacket, it is impossible for anyone to write a book alone. My heartfelt thanks go out to the friends, experts, and supporters who helped to make this book happen. The list begins with Rafee Kamaal, who gave me the idea for developing the book in this format; Cheryl Williams and Mary Robinson, good friends and professional colleagues in the Financial Women's Association of New York; Gail Miner, president of the Financial Women's Association of New York, who led me to my publisher and David J. Conti, my editor, whose infinite patience, gentle humor, and faith in my work throughout this process has spoiled me for working with anyone else in the publishing business; Ann T. Greene, who typed the initial manuscript, formatted the graphs and charts, and answered all of my clumsy word processing questions at all hours of the day and night; Mark O'Ferrall for the spreadsheets and charts; Goldie Watkins, who willingly did a masterful job of proofreading and copy editing in coffee shops and by phone at any ridiculous hour that I needed it; Loretta Britten, Frank McCoy, and Dorothy Redford for the historical research; Cynthia Ashby, Mark Ford, Martin Kelly, Bob Moss, Gary Rogowski, and the many writer friends and financial colleagues who offered words of encouragement, compliments, and pep talks at the right moment to get me back to the keyboard. With great respect and love, I thank each of you with all my heart.

WHERE WE CAME FROM, WHERE WE ARE NOW

"Up, up, you mighty race, you can accomplish what you will."
Marcus Garvey

Christopher Martin moved to Chicago in 1982 after graduating from Howard University with a B.A. in business and marketing and took a $24,000 a year management trainee position with a large advertising agency. His mother pointed out that he was starting out at a higher salary than she had seen after 19 years of teaching in the small Alabama school system where Chris had grown up. Now Chris's income has tripled, he has been recruited by several leading ad agencies around the country, he has won many awards for the marketing campaigns he has created and managed for the *Fortune* 500 clients the company represents, and he has earned a large year-end bonus. He decides to celebrate by treating his new wife, Diane, a trust officer at First Chicago Bank, and his parents to a two-week cruise in the Caribbean. During the trip he hopes to announce to them his plans for starting his own business.

By contrast, Wilma Edwards, one of the first women plant managers in the automobile industry, lives a simpler lifestyle while working a 14-hour day to keep the plant on its 110-cars-an-hour production schedule. The divorced mother of two sons began her career 16 years ago as a production assistant in the River Rouge plant outside Detroit. She now raises her children in a comfortable home in suburban Bloomfield Hills, with her boys decked out in their favorite "hip-hop grunge" look. She can afford to support them now on her $80,000+ annual salary, which gives her plenty of disposable income.

Arthur and Raylene Jackson relocated to Atlanta 5 years ago from New York with their two children after Arthur was offered a senior manager's slot in the software systems development area for Southern Bell. Raylene, who had been a research biochemist with a pharmaceutical house in Westchester County in New York, took the opportunity between jobs to start a small gift shop and bookstore until she found the right professional position with the Centers for Disease Control. She also taught part-time at the medical school at Emory University. The couple's combined income of $196,500 allowed them to buy and renovate a large Victorian home in Midwood, an inner-city neighborhood undergoing regentrification. Their two children, Leslie and Marcus, went to private schools until they graduated from high school, and now both of them attend colleges in the Atlanta area. The family still maintains the ritual of taking a vacation together each summer in some exotic locale. Next year they are planning to go to Egypt.

Gwen Walker is a 36-year-old single mother and school administrator in Oakland, California. On the second Saturday of each month when her 15-year-old son spends the weekend with his father, an engineer living with his second wife in San Jose, Gwen meets with 12 other professional women in the Bay Area. Each of them is a single or divorced homeowner with a profession, and the women alternate the location of their meetings among their homes and condos. What began as a book club 12 years ago has now developed into Les Treize Amis investment club. Gwen's $46,800 salary allows her to comfortably contribute $100 a month to the investment pool, as do all the other women in the group. The first stocks they bought were Tide, McDonald's, Coca-Cola, and Reebok's because of their children. The portfolio has now grown to over $165,000. The women have been so successful with building up their portfolio that they have been written up in two national magazines. Each Christmas, the club donates 5 percent of its annual investment dividend income to a local day-care center. As single parents, they know the importance of finding and supporting a good child care facility for other working mothers.

These people may seem to have nothing in common other than their high incomes and comfortable lifestyles, but the vital link is that they are all middle class African-Americans. They reflect a new income status that is rapidly becoming apparent to most advertising agencies and consumer marketers.

Out of the 33 million African-Americans acknowledged by the 1990 U.S. Census, more than one-third of them (38 percent, or 12.5 million) fall into the category of being middle class by earning over $30,000 a year. Not all African-Americans have money to burn, but a growing percentage of this ethnic group has a comfortable disposable income to spend, save, and invest. Over 17 percent of the African-American middle class, or 5,940,000 households, fall into the $50,000+ category. African-Americans making a lot of money, if you consider $30,000 a year to be making a lot of money, have become headline news. In June 1994, *The New York Times* reported that in 1993 income for black families in Queens, New York, was higher than the household income for white and Latino families in the same region. The University of Georgia Business School released an economic study in July 1994 stating that African-American consumers now control nearly $400 billion in income and that that figure is expected to rise by more than 30 percent in the next decade. Jeffrey Humphrey, the economist and author of the study, was quoted as saying that "doing business with this market segment may often make the difference between bankruptcy and a profitable bottom line." A year later, on Sunday, June 18, 1995, a major spread in *The New York Times* "Week in Review" section was devoted to analyzing the growth of the African-American middle class across the United States. Ten suburban communities were cited where black household incomes have now grown to exceed white household incomes.

The U.S. Census, which admits that it undercounted minority groups by at least 5 percent, projects that the African-American population will grow 50 percent faster than the white population in the United States by the year 2050. Rising income is expected to keep pace with population growth.

Now for the first time since the Reconstruction Era following the Civil War, more African-Americans are earning decent wages and steady paychecks, are able to buy comfortable homes, are able to plan for a comfortable future beyond the level of subsistence and marginal survival, and are living long enough to collect social security and some retirement benefits. *Target Market News,* an ethnic marketing newsletter produced in Chicago, indicates that African-Americans will easily control more than $450 billion in consumer dollars by the year 2000. *Essence* magazine has teamed up with Simmons Communications, a New York market research firm, and with Burrell Advertising of Chicago to produce the largest focus group/market survey of African-Americans ever produced to document our spending patterns and buying habits. Advertisers are gearing up in a big way to compete for the growing consumer dollars of African-Americans. Yet financial institutions have paid little or no attention to this market. Although the news reports of our improved income status are impressive and there is much evidence to support the argument that times have gotten better, many of us know better.

|||≡||| *The problem is not that Blacks don't have money. The problem is what we* |||≡|||
do with it, or don't do with it.
TONY BROWN

WHAT ARE WE DOING WITH THIS NEW FOUND INCOME?

The good news is black folks are making money. The bad news is what we're doing with it. Carolyn Jones, president of Carolyn Jones Advertising, stated last fall in *Discount Store News* that "very few African-Americans are poor. But we spend more than we have. An African-American family making $35,000 a year spends money at the level of a white family making $50,000." Spending like crazy is an understatement. The top 12 categories of consumer spending done by African-Americans in 1994 looked like this:

Housing	$ 88.0 billion
Food and beverages (nonalcoholic)	42.8 billion
Clothing	19.6 billion
Health care	10.7 billion
Games, gifts, and entertainment	8.8 billion
Telephone services	8.7 billion
Household furnishings	8.0 billion
Contributions	5.2 billion

Insurance (property and casualty)	4.6 billion
Travel and lodging	4.5 billion
Personal grooming and hair care	3.7 billion
Tobacco and smoking supplies	2.3 billion

A 1993 *Black Enterprise* reader survey indicated that the average household income was $73,000, but only 1.9 percent of each dollar handled by African-Americans went into financial instruments. Most of that was spent on life insurance products rather than investments. It is still not a popular concept among the younger generations of African-Americans who are beginning to earn the higher incomes to put money away for a long-term future. The importance of saving and investing is a national problem, not just an African-American problem, but goals of greater political clout and economic independence in the black community will not be developed if we give priority to buying high-priced sneakers and expensive CD players rather than blue-chip mutual funds, municipal bonds, and Treasury notes.

As we move into a new century and a new era of economic prosperity for African-Americans, we need to reexamine where we've been and how we got here. Most Americans, black and white, seem to believe that prior to affirmative action there was no work ethic or effort to achieve economic independence among African-Americans. Younger generations of African-Americans seem to have no knowledge of black economic history and are entering the job market today with the belief that the option for a middle-class lifestyle for African-Americans began with the civil rights movement. Nothing could be more false.

IIEIII *The issue is no longer, can you check into the hotel, it's whether you got the* IIEIII *money to check out. The issue is no longer whether you can go to the University of Mississippi, but whether you can pay the tuition. The issue is no longer whether you sit on the bus or whether you can drive it: it's whether you can develop the capital to own the bus company.*

WILLIAM GRAY
President, United Negro College Fund

HISTORICAL OVERVIEW

This is not the first time that we have made the effort to become financially stable and economically independent. Black folks in America have always had a peculiar relationship with money—when we did get to see it. We are the rare exception in the labor pool that shaped the American capitalist system; ours was not a voluntary participation in this economy. We were the primary work force that built the wealth of the United States through our sweat and labor as slaves, but we were in no way allowed to be beneficiaries of it. Our history is fraught with the denial of our skills and the deprivation of opportunity, which makes it irrational to compare ourselves to the white population who came here willingly and the immigrant population that has grown over the last few decades.

When the most profitable crafts jobs became dominated by black tradesmen, laws were passed prohibiting them from working at their trade. When freed blacks went north to Boston to get an education, many states—Virginia, Maryland, and North Carolina—passed laws prohibiting their returning home to share their knowledge and new ideas.

But successful blacks were not an unknown phenomenon before emancipation. The city of Chicago was established as a trading post in 1784 by Jean-Baptiste DuSable, a French-African, born in Haiti, who came to what is now the United States by way of the St. Lawrence River with a group of French explorers. The French explorers went north into Canada, but DuSable chose to stay with the Huron Indians who populated the area. He was the first foreigner to settle on the edge of Lake Michigan, where he bought 30 acres of land from the Native Americans, built a house, became a farmer and fur trapper, and began a trading post. DuSable married one of the Huron women in 1773, had three sons, and became involved in the Revolutionary War when the British suspected him of being a French spy. He was jailed briefly by the British until one of the generals decided to appoint him as liaison officer for the British army. DuSable returned to his trading post on the lake, expanded his farm to more than 400 acres, and became quite wealthy. In 1800, after the death of his wife, he sold the property and moved to Columbia, Missouri, to live with one of his sons.

Born in Boston, Paul Cuffe (1759–1817) was the son of a freed Ashanti tribesman and a Wampanoag Indian woman. Cuffe became a wealthy captain of a fleet of whaling ships in Massachusetts. He joined the Quakers and supported the abolitionist movement but decided that speeches and petitions were not enough. In 1811, he used his fortune to personally finance the first voyage of 38 freed slaves returning to Sierra Leone. He later provided two additional ships, free of charge, for 32 families of former slaves who went back to Africa. He built the first integrated schoolhouse in Westport, Massachusetts, called Cuffe's School, near his farm because none of his white neighbors wanted his children to attend their school.

In 1857, when her master died in the goldfields of Colorado and left her emancipated in his will, Clara Brown (1801–1877) found herself in a situation in which she was free, black, over 21, and broke. Stranded in Colorado, far from the St. Louis home she had known, where her children had been sold from her before she was taken to Colorado, she did the only thing she knew how—laundry, cleaning, and cooking; but this time she was getting paid for it—50 cents a shirt, 50 cents a hot meal. She worked out of a tent that she paid rent to share with a gold assayer. She got paid in gold dust and gold nuggets and saved every penny of it. She also took payment in shares of gold stakes and even financed a few miners in their prospecting ventures. Within a year she set up her own tent. Two years later she built a hotel and a restaurant and had a staff of five people working for her, doing the laundry she still took in from the growing community. Her business served the territory, but her primary goal of saving money was spurred by her desire to find and buy her children and relatives who were still enslaved in Missouri. She was successful in purchasing the freedom of 23 relatives but was only able to find one of her five children during her lifetime. The Colorado Historical Society Museum has on display a box seat from the Denver Opera Company which is thought to have been her regular seat.

James Forten, Sr. (1766–1842), established the first black-owned sail-making business in Philadelphia. He contributed heavily to the radical abolitionist movement and was one of the organizers of the American Antislavery Society founded in 1833. He left a large portion of his fortune, over $100,000 when he died at age 76, to his daughters Sarah, Margaretta, and Harriet and to his granddaughter, Charlotte Forten Grimke, in support of their efforts to educate freed blacks before and after the Civil War.

John Mashow (1805–1864), born in South Carolina, was the son of a slave woman and a white planter. Freed in 1815, Mashow and his mother moved to New Bedford, Massachusetts, where he apprenticed as a shipwright for $1 a week. At 27, he established his own shipyard and eventually designed and built 60 ships, including 14 whalers.

CeeCee McCarty (1806–1866) was a mulatto woman trader in New Orleans in 1835 who ran a successful dry goods trading business buying and selling fabric and housewares with a small army of 32 slaves who managed her "tinker" wagons that traveled through the parishes of Louisiana for 30 years. Upon her death, she left property and cash valued at more than $250,000 to her three sons, who continued to develop the business.

In large cities, some free blacks became livery stable owners. Others became business owners in the service professions of catering, barbering, and wigmaking. Joshua I. Smith opened a thriving catering business in Boston, Massachusetts, in 1854. Robert Bogle, another caterer, opened a similar business in Philadelphia in 1843.

William T. Shorey, a ship captain who was originally based in New England, moved to San Francisco in 1890 and eventually became the captain on 14 voyages financed by his private group of investors, traveling to China, Japan, and the whale grounds of Alaska and Siberia.

|||≡||| *We must take the profit out of prejudice.* |||≡|||

COLEMAN YOUNG
Former mayor of Detroit

After Emancipation, many freed slaves had no choice but to remain on the plantation and become sharecroppers. The legendary 40 acres of land, the mule and the supply of farm tools, and the $50 promised by Lincoln were quickly vetoed by his Vice President and successor, Andrew Johnson. The sharecropper system developed out of a lack of opportunities for most freed slaves to go elsewhere. Sharecropping became a denigrating way of life, a life of "making do," getting by, hanging on, praying for a way out of no way, and settling for less as a means of survival. Blacks stuck in the sharecropper system rarely saw cash for their labors. They had no choice in shopping for food, clothing, seeds, fertilizer, or tools, instead having to use a "credit system" imposed on them at the "company store" that was controlled and operated by the landowners. Getting receipts was unheard of and questioning the credits and debits on the books that they were never allowed to see could get a family evicted from the property. If it was possible to get out of the debt column on the company books, cash still was not paid to them. A due bill was provided at the store for future credit rather than cash. This practice led to a deep distrust of the whites who managed and controlled the unseen financial records and who thereby controlled their daily lives.

Some freed slaves did manage to build successful businesses without waiting for the opportunity to present itself. Isaac Myers (1835–1891) organized the Chesapeake Marine Railway and Drydock Company of Baltimore, Maryland, on February 12, 1866. It was the first major black shipfitting company developed by and for black workers. His employees were the black longshoremen, sailmakers, carpenters, and caulkers forced out of the white shipyards of Baltimore and Philadelphia.

|||≣||| *People ravin' about hard times./Tell me what it's all about?/Hard times* |||≣|||
don't worry me. I was broke when they started out.

MUDDY WATERS
Blues lyric

Prosperous black communities did come into existence during the Reconstruction Era following the Civil War. Blacks owned businesses in Durham, North Carolina, establishing their own banks, insurance companies, funeral homes, schools, barbershops, and hospitals. Durham was a tobacco town for decades, with many black farmers growing and selling their crop to the new cigarette manufacturers developing there. Durham was also the home base for the North Carolina Mutual Insurance Company, the Mechanics and Farmers

Bank, and the North Carolina Central College for black students. A small black elite grew up around these institutions and created a considerable cultural influence. It was not unusual for the local Negro newspaper to carry frequent announcements about meetings of the ladies' reading club, sewing circles, and bridge parties.

Wilmington, North Carolina, with its busy waterfront and brisk trade with the West Indies allowed many blacks to become financially successful. Cotton, sugar, tobacco, and the slave trade were instrumental in a fast-growing shipping business, and let blacks develop a strong political base beginning in the late 1840s. So many free blacks who were educated professionals had settled in Wilmington that by the 1880s more than half the population was black. Free blacks controlled nearly all of the state and local political offices in the area during Reconstruction. But much of that progress was wiped out when white hostility erupted in the 1898 race riot that destroyed the homes and businesses of all the prominent black citizens.

During the oil boom of 1910 in the West, the Greenwood section of Tulsa, Oklahoma, became known as the black Wall Street of the South, sharing in the wealth that developed in the area. The members of the black community were financially independent as a result of their excellent farming and agricultural skills and their profitable interaction with the white community and with one another. They kept the flow of capital within their own small town until the race riot of 1921 began and wiped out the community.

Atlanta, Boston, Philadelphia and New Orleans grew in economic power as middle class blacks grew in prosperity. The Atlanta State Savings Bank was the first chartered black banking institution in the state of Georgia in 1898. Among the first depositors to support the bank were the Atlanta Mutual, North Carolina Mutual, Pilgrim Health and Life, and Standard Life insurance companies—the largest black life insurance companies in existence at that time.

In 1900, a major drought and a plague of boll weevils destroyed the cotton crop throughout the South. Shortly thereafter, Henry Ford sent labor recruiters to southern towns to hire men for his automobile plants in Detroit. The promise of $5 a day sounded like a fortune to cotton-pickers who were still working from sun-up to sunset for $1 a day. The Great Northern Migration started as blacks headed for the cities of Pittsburgh, Detroit, Cleveland, Chicago, and Gary, Indiana, to accept the back-breaking dirty work of the stockyards and steel mills and auto assembly lines. Black men and women worked at legally sanctioned lower wages of $2 or $3 an hour less than white workers, who protested the presence of black workers and insisted on higher pay for the same work. The white workers also demanded separate facilities for lunch rooms and rest rooms and insisted that blacks be kept out of union jobs.

Life in the North offered a better income but a harder time getting it. Black families crowded into less than human living conditions in the slums of large cities. Survival strategies adopted by some families included the weekend rent party or waistline party to pay the $5 that kept them from sleeping in the park or having six people share a two-room apartment with a bathroom down the hall. The Depression, starting in 1929, brought bank failures, race riots, labor strikes and evictions and was harder on black workers than white workers. During this time, even in northern cities, welfare and unemployment compensation for blacks was not an option.

World War I gave many black men a chance to get out of the cities and the rural South. However, after returning from the battlefields of Europe, they were still unable to get jobs and yet did not want to return to the exploitation of the sharecropping system of the South. The Army became the salvation and lifetime careers for a select few. In the 1940s when World War II began, there was a major influx of black soldiers who volunteered for service and mastered whatever skills they were allowed to develop.

James O. Plinton (1914–1996) of Westfield, New Jersey, was one of the first Tuskegee airmen. He became an army flight instructor and remained in the Army to develop his skills as a pilot, eventually becoming a lieutenant colonel. In 1948, Plinton was the moving force behind Quisqueya Lte., in Port-Au-Prince, Haiti, the first major airline outside the United States established by a black man.

THE BLACK-WHITE WEALTH GAP

In December 1989, *Money* magazine released an in-depth story, "Race and Money," written by Walter Updegrave, comparing the incomes and net worths of black families and white families. The impact of racism and segregated

STEVE L. SANDERS
FINANCIAL ADVISOR AND CEO

Sanders Investment Advisors
Philadelphia, Pennsylvania

Steve Sanders founded his company 10 years ago to bring competent financial services to the African-American community. As a young lending officer at Mellon Bank, he had observed the need for such services, so he took the plunge and started out in his parents' basement with a phone, a file cabinet, and a vision. He quickly realized that the most important ingredient that he had to develop in his business was a financial education component. Fin-Ed-Co. (for Financial Education Company) grew out of this need to teach, and it has become the foundation for Sanders's practice as a financial advisor.

Sanders now devotes a considerable amount of time to working with "at risk" youth groups and explaining the basic concepts of budgeting, saving, investing, and being financially responsible for one's future. He is determined to make an impact on African-American youth coming into the job market before they make financial mistakes that will take precious years of earnings to correct. For the last 6 years he has traveled the country teaching over 200 seminars a year and bringing his message to over 20,000 students in 25 major cities, working with various community groups such as "To Our Children's Future with Health," where he is also a member of the board of directors. He has appeared on CNN, CBS, and CNBC and has done a seven-part series on personal finance for the Turner Broadcasting Network.

The five-point message Sanders offers is so simple that it's easy to miss. (1) Recognize that having more income does not mean that you will be able to manage money better. If you can't do it on a few dollars a week before you have a big paycheck, it won't get better. You'll just be living at a higher level of poverty and financial distress. (2) Start budgeting early with the first paycheck you get and put something away for the future, even if it's only $1 a day. (3) Learn the difference between a need and a want and eliminate the unnecessary spending. (4) Make a plan that includes some goals to have a reason for saving and investing and start with paying yourself first. (5) Avoid using credit to pay for luxuries that you think you need to be happy. Adding 20 percent—the interest charged on your credit card bill—to the cost of eating dinner out is not sound money management. Offering this kind of basic advice, Sanders writes a weekly column in the local African-American newspaper and appears regularly on CNBC's *The Money Club* and *Mutual Fund Investor*. His investment firm, with over $20 million under management, has attracted more than 350 clients—individuals and small-business owners throughout the country.

*"*Everybody in America is a victim of the "spender's disease," but there's a much more acute case of it in the African-American community. So many of our kids are being given the message that financial success is about wearing the sharpest clothes, the biggest earrings and driving the coolest car in the parking lot when they should be trying to build up the biggest savings account and investing in a mutual fund. I've vowed to make them aware of that insight and the many other options that come from being a financially educated being. The more you learn, the more you'll have.*"*

housing, job opportunities, and financial lifestyles was evident in the numbers. At that time the average black family in America earned $38,585 and had $4,112 in net worth. The typical white family had an income of $51,518 and a net worth of $16,415. Despite our new earning capacity, most African-American families have not reached economic parity with white families. We are more than a century behind other groups in the wealth-building process of earning, saving, investing, owning property, and passing on assets to the next generation. We know that a major gap still exists between black and white income in America, but some of that lack of net worth is our own fault, the result of excessive and reckless spending and marginal financial values.

A recent report on the black-white wealth gap, updated and released in January 1996, by the Joint Center for Political and Economic Studies, an African-American think tank in Washington, D.C., confirms the facts that we are all aware of. The wealth gap is still there, and the slow economy and job layoffs of the last 3 years have taken their toll, but by the year 2000 African-Americans will still control over half a trillion dollars.

Our income may be increasing, but we are not building wealth. There's a difference between making money and building wealth, and we have never had a chance to discover what that means. Our financial education is more severely underdeveloped than that of most Americans. The lack of financial education is an overall American problem, but it is magnified by the lavish consumption prevalent in the African-American community. The U.S. Department of Education stated in 1994 that only 18 percent of all U.S. schools systems have classes in personal finance for high school students. Less than 25 percent of U.S. colleges have money management courses in the curriculum. Only 2 percent of United Negro College Fund schools teach any money management courses, and they are usually confined to the business and accounting departments. African-American students are coming out of college with some of the largest student loans in history, but they are also being offered credit cards much quicker than ever before, with little or no preparation for the responsibility of managing the debt. Most young African-Americans are directionless and clueless about how to handle the new-found income and sudden wealth that is coming into their lives. Witness the recent financial debacle of the rock group

TLC out of Atlanta, who sold 12 million copies of one album but found themselves filing bankruptcy in the same year with $3 million of consumer debt! At the other extreme, African-American high school graduates complete job-training programs with the illusion that all they need to be financially well-off is to get a good job paying $35,000, two major credit cards and a new car. Our financial opportunities have changed, but our financial mindset has not.

Using these new-found dollars to build and maintain financial independence has to become a personal responsibility as well as a community goal. African-Americans must begin changing behavior and attitudes about what money really is and how to use it well if there is going to be any serious economic empowerment in the next millennium.

|||≡||| *Civil rights laws are not enough. The emergency we're facing now is economic.* |||≡|||
DR. MARTIN LUTHER KING, JR.
1967

2

WHAT HAS KEPT AFRICAN-AMERICANS FROM BUILDING WEALTH?

"The fundamental difference is the attitude white people have about acquiring wealth and the attitude black people have. White people know that wealth brings power, so they do everything possible to gain more wealth and thus more power. Black people, too often, seek wealth to have enjoyment, to buy pleasure. There's a big difference between power and pleasure, and since power lasts longer than pleasure, whites have gained control of practically everything."

Raymond St. Jacques
Actor, 1968

October 16, 1995, was a monumental day in African-American history when men of African descent assembled on the mall in Washington, D.C., to participate in the Million Man March, a remarkable event that will not be forgotten by anyone who witnessed it. It was not surprising to hear that a chief concern of most of the men was a desire for economic opportunities and financial self-sufficiency. Regardless of your opinion of Minister Farrakhan's religious beliefs, political statements, or economic strategies, African-Americans must acknowledge the pertinent part of his message about our lack of financial success. Racial oppression is a reality that all African-Americans have endured, but beyond the scars of racism we have to look at some wealth-building obstacles that cannot be blamed totally on the white man. Some of these financial inequities are our own fault.

Call it the nasty emotional baggage of slavery, decades of deprivation and poverty, years of fighting over the few resources that were tossed our way, or whatever, but African-Americans have more money hang-ups than any other ethnic group in America. The psychological legacy of racism—self-hatred, denial, deprivation, petty jealousy, backbiting, and poverty—gets manifested in our money behavior. The way many African-Americans handle money, and often treat each other in financial transactions, is far more damaging and detrimental than anything that could be conceived of by white racists. Unless we change the negative attitudes and self-destructive conduct that gets acted out around money, it won't matter how much income African-Americans have.

III≣III *Poverty is not about color.*   III≣III

QUEEN LATIFAH
Detroit Free Press *interview, 1992*

ATTITUDES

Start a discussion about money with a group of African-Americans and you unleash an emotional firestorm of highly charged and impassioned rhetoric about what we don't have, don't do, and don't understand. The views will range from exasperation and pessimism to secrecy and dread, but the strongest emotions are fear, envy, and distrust. The bottom line is that most black folks are scared of money. Scared to talk about it. Scared to admit that they don't understand it. Scared to take responsibility for financial decisions. Scared to acknowledge their ambition to have a lot of money. Scared to admit that they've made some dumb choices with it. Scared to take risks as entrepreneurs. Scared to let go of some of the old ideas that have kept us stuck in poverty. Scared to trust and respect each other as professionals and in business deals. Scared to challenge outdated beliefs about prosperity and economic well-being. Scared to stop blaming racism for all the financial problems that exist in the black community.

FEAR OF HAVING MONEY

This fear and anger gets translated into myriad layers of convoluted excuses and concepts that add to the baggage and become burdensome in the pursuit of wealth. Issues of class, gender, skin color, and social status also compound the problem of financial well-being—the field hand versus house slave competitiveness still haunts our collective consciousness, particularly when we approach the idea of doing business with each other. Some of the naysayers who oppose the idea of wealth building offer cleverly disguised statements of fear wrapped in phrases that downplay the idea of having money. "The world would be a better place without money." Or "Rich people are all dishonest." Or "The only way to get rich is to cheat your way to the top." Another fearful approach comes from a self-righteous point of view cloaked in a disdain for money. "No one is ever really honest about money." Or "Money can't buy love." Or "If I were rich, I would lose all of my friends." Or "My spouse would leave me if I made more money than he does."

The worst money fear among African-Americans is a fear of failure—the "what will people say about me if I don't make it?" syndrome. The segregated society that shaped most African-American social circles formed some very conservative and restrictive perceptions about class consciousness and social status fraught with resentment and competitiveness. It was more important to conform to the conventional expectations of the group and protect one's image in the community since there was no escape from the group norm. African-Americans can be so unforgiving in ridiculing each other when it comes to succeeding or failing in business that our emotions get inflamed to a greater degree than the situation merits in many cases. Many African-American dreams of prosperity get lost in suspicion and paranoia.

|||≡||| *When we are noted for enterprise, industry, and success, we shall no longer* |||≡|||
have any trouble in the matter of civil and political rights.
FREDERICK DOUGLASS
1869

Any other ethnic group—Asians, Russians, or Latinos—consistently seek out lawyers, doctors, accountants, and business owners from their own ethnic group to do business with. They cling to a communal sense of identity and practice wealth-building habits that keep their cashflow in the community and support each other economically. John Wray, an economic development specialist in Washington, D.C., did a study that traced the flow of dollars through comparative ethnic communities. Wray found that in the Asian community a dollar circulates among the community's banks, brokers, shopkeepers, and business professionals for up to 28 days before it is spent with outsiders. In the Jewish community, the circulation period was 19 days; in the WASP community, 17 days; but in the African-American community— 6 hours! African-Americans are still waiting to be rescued, accepted, and approved of by white America and paying for the privilege of being neglected, ignored, discounted, and mistreated. But it doesn't have to be that way. At the beginning of the twentieth century, even after the devastating political and economic losses that followed the Reconstruction Era, the black community of Tulsa—Greenwood—had extremely limited contact with the white community of Tulsa, but the black community was still able to build considerable wealth. Any dollars that came into the black community would circulate there for a period of up to 3 years before being shared with the white community.

Some ingrained fears in the black community are based on habits and attitudes that were inherited from our parents, but these habits and attitudes must be reexamined, adjusted, and eliminated. In the past, African-American parents rarely spoke to children about money because they were too busy worrying about how to get it and keep the bills paid. But these parents didn't have the educational opportunities and career choices, access to government loan programs and scholarships, computers, and the vast amount of information available in libraries, in magazines, and on the Internet that are now available to African-American college graduates. Don't waste those choices on something that your ancestors would not be proud of. Prove to them that you are worthy of the dreams they had and the sacrifices they made to clear a path for you to get this far.

|||≡||| *Black folks buy what they want, and then beg for what they need.* |||≡|||
DR. MARTIN LUTHER KING, JR.

BEHAVIOR

Living beyond our means is the most self-destructive habit that plagues African-Americans. Purchasing a BMW when the paycheck says buy a secondhand Taurus is totally irrational behavior. No white man puts a gun to your head and makes you spend $2000 on a 48-inch big-screen TV/stereo system/home entertainment center when your budget says you can only afford a $300 display model on a clearance sale. Too many African-Americans knock themselves out chasing tangible symbols of success—cognac and cars, clothes and credit cards, anything that is a visible statement of the image of success. Trying to buy recognition, esteem, and respectability with material goods is a ridiculous waste of precious assets and will never achieve the goal of wealth that most African-Americans purport to be seeking.

These conspicuous-consumption patterns are also encouraged by our own media, which should be in the forefront of developing the idea of financial independence. Financial advice columns are absent from most African-American publications. *Ebony* magazine, the oldest national magazine targeted at the African-American community, constantly promotes the idea of material goods as images of success, but it offers no regular financial column or any hands-on information about personal financial advice. Most other African-American publications are guilty of the same limitation or total lack of regular information about personal financial topics, with the exception of *Black Enterprise* which was created to encourage black entrepreneurship.

Very few African-American newspapers have regular personal finance columns or business news pages. With rare exception, most radio stations serving the African-American community do not offer any talk shows that advise their listeners about saving money, buying a home, or investing for retirement. A money conversation on black radio seems to be as taboo as a Victorian era public discussion of sex, politics, racism, and religion. As our social behavior with politics, religious practices, and sexual patterns have changed in the last few decades, our financial behavior must also change.

||≣|| *At the bottom of education, at the bottom of politics, even at the bottom of* ||≣||
religion, there must be economic independence.

BOOKER T. WASHINGTON
c. 1903

If you're still buying money orders to pay your bills because that's how your mother did it, then you're about as out of place in today's market as a horse and buggy at the Indianapolis 500. African-Americans cannot continue to operate under the same outdated concepts that motivated their parents and grandparents. There has been a quantum leap forward in job opportunities and educational attainment, and the nature of the financial marketplace has changed tremendously. Along with learning new job skills and taking on new professional roles and career paths, African-Americans must make the effort to develop a new perspective on money and how to use it in their lives. Some of the old myths just don't work anymore, but they still cloud our minds with fuzzy thinking and paralyze us when it comes to financial decision making.

‖☰‖‖ *Jesus never made a sweeping indictment against wealth. Rather, he con-* ‖☰‖‖
demned the misuse of wealth. Money, like any other force such as electricity,
is amoral and can be used for either good or evil.

DR. MARTIN LUTHER KING, JR.
Strength to Love, 1967

AFRICAN-AMERICAN MONEY MYTHS

1. The Lord will take care. The Lord also provides the opportunity for you to get a good job, and to learn how to manage your finances better by being realistic about what you can and cannot afford. God also created the public library, which everyone has access to, where you can learn about improving your opportunities to have a better life and pick up some guidelines for the right way to manage your assets. Reread the Bible story of the three servants who were given the various talents to develop in the Gospel of St. Matthew, chapter 25, verses 14–30. If you squander the chance for abundance that is given to you through access to knowledge, then that opportunity will be taken away from you.

2. Money is evil. From the days of slavery, African-Americans have bought into this bizarre fallacy that there was something noble about poverty and suffering and that the only comfort we should expect will be in an afterlife. What the Bible verse really says is, "The love of money is the root of all evil" (1 Tim.

6:8), which gives a totally different meaning to money and how it is used. Money is an innocent tool. Like a knife that can be used to slice bread, chop vegetables, or stab an enemy, money is not guilty of the action for which it was used. Too many African-Americans want to blame the money itself, like blaming alcohol for the bad habits of a drunkard, rather than examining the internal attitudes that encourage the irrational behavior. Here is another Bible verse, which is more appropriate to the reality of wealth building: "Money answereth all things" (Eccl. 10:19).

The church has been the primary organizing force in the African-American community and has spawned many social and political movements that have created new opportunities for wealth building, but it has also been the source of some of the most outrageous exploitation that has taken place in the black community. Witness the many ministers who encourage lavish anniversary programs, live in extravagant homes, encourage expensive birthday gifts, and accept new cars every year, all at the expense of members of the congregation who tithe to support the church when they cannot save for retirement or pay college tuition for their children.

3. Investing is for white people. Less than 2 percent of middle class African-Americans have money in the stock market. The only color that matters in the wealth-building process is green. Believing that all this financial stuff about investing in the stock market does not involve you is a head-in-the-sand approach to life which will keep you poor. If you live in America and get paid in dollars which you use to buy goods and services, whether you like it or not, you're affected by the stock market. Trying to ignore it is like trying to avoid a dead cat in your living room.

4. High income equals great wealth. If you think this is true, check out Kareem Abdul Jabaar, Sammy Davis, Jr., Redd Foxx, Flip Wilson, and any number of African-American performers and athletes who made millions and ended up broke. M. C. Hammer, the rap singer who has sold millions of albums and has done concert tours, films, and television shows over the last decade, recently filed bankruptcy for $10 million. His financial story is a typical example of irrational money behavior.

5. Looking rich means being rich. Gimme a break, please! Does this really need to be discussed? Is this how you justify being in such debt? You can lie to yourself if you want to, when you spend so much to look good, but when you do a budget or a net worth statement and look at the numbers, you can't deceive yourself any longer. Doing a budget is a financial reality check.

6. The only way I'll get rich is to win the lottery. Suppose you won the lottery tomorrow for $20 million. What would you do with it? If you don't have any financial goals and an idea of what you want to accomplish in your lifetime, then it won't matter how much money you have, now, next year, or ever. A financial plan makes you focus on what is sensible and possible. Refusing to plan will guarantee failure, no matter how much you earn or inherit.

7. Capitalism is corrupt, and I don't want to be corrupt. If this idea keeps you from taking money seriously, then you better get over it, real quick! This capitalist society that you live in is the only one available to you at the moment to make the social and political changes that you want to see happen. If you want to feed the hungry, heal the sick, improve the school system, start a day-care center, go back to Africa and support a third world political movement—whatever—you will need capital to do it.

8. White people won't let us. Most white people don't really care what African-Americans do, as long as it doesn't get in the way of their economic well-being. To go on blaming society, the white man, recent immigrants, Congress, the "establishment," for one's lack of prosperity is good for venting one's frustration, but what are you going to do about the situation once you get past the talking stage? Conspiracy theories are far-fetched, irrational, and absurd. They are just another category of black paranoia and a set of excuses not to make any effort to change and stop being a willing victim. Our ancestors bought and paid for our success—it is time to claim it as being long past due.

9. What else can you call an attitude like this but downright laziness. *The few dollars I make don't mean anything, and I'll never have anything, so why try?* This is a self-fulfilling prophecy that needs no explanation. If you make no effort to help yourself, then you get what you deserve out of life. African-Americans can find the time and money to buy the latest stereo, or big-screen TV, or car, or to take expensive vacation trips to Nassau or Jamaica or Mexico if we want to. Or we manage to find the cash or an increase in the credit card limit to buy a new computer or dress or shoes, or to attend a convention or class reunion where conspicuous consumption is the requirement for registration when we want to make a visible statement and impress relatives, classmates, ex-lovers, or professional colleagues. If we really wanted to find $50 or $100 to invest each month, we could.

10. Advancement is betrayal. This is the big guilt trip that gets dumped on anyone who has become financially successful and made the effort to do something different. Behind this accusation is an acute case of the "crabs-in-a-barrel" syndrome. "If I can't make it out of the trap of poverty, why should someone else?" Or "If anybody is going to make it big, I want to be the only one who does." African-Americans also have such a strong historical identity with poverty that we seem to define ourselves by what we don't have rather than what we do have. If and when a brother or sister finds a way to create a profitable life, that person is immediately looked upon with suspicion and condemned as having "sold out." These financially successful people are accused of betraying their heritage, background, and community and are denounced as "trying to be white" when they have simply learned the rules of wealth building and applied them realistically to their lives. If Ron Brown, the recently deceased secretary of commerce, had subscribed to this philosophy of never trying anything new, never taking a risk, he never would have become chairman of the Democratic party or a member of the President's cabinet.

III≣III   *I can't tell a solid gold coin from a gold-plated penny. I also have never learned*   III≣III
to tell the difference between time told by a $40 Timex and a $6,000 Rolex.

SUSAN WATSON
Detroit Free Press *columnist, Oct. 26, 1988*

DESIRE AND DISCIPLINE

Getting by on a day-to-day basis and ignoring the future will not build wealth! If you have an inside track on the state lottery numbers, or own a Las Vegas casino, or have an irrevocable trust with a couple of million dollars in it, then you can skip this part of the planning process.

Regardless of racism, poverty, and lack of education, there have been many successful African-American survivors who developed into wealthy pioneers and blazed trails for themselves and others. None has become more famous and laudatory than Sarah Breedlove (1867–1919), who had to overcome every obstacle and stumbling block before she became known as Madame C. J. Walker, the hair-care millionaire. Sarah started life as a sharecropper's daughter in the fields of Louisiana, living in a weather-beaten shack, picking cotton each day with her parents and her sister. At 7, when her parents died, she moved to Mississippi with her sister, who married a man who was cruel and abusive to Sarah. Sarah had no idea what she was going to do to change her life, but she knew there was something better for her in the world. At 14, she married Moses McWilliams to escape her abusive brother-in-law. Four years later, when her husband was murdered by a lynch mob and she had a 2-year-old daughter, Sarah took in laundry to support them until she could afford to move to St. Louis, where she became a cook for a wealthy white family. Despite these hardships she kept searching for ways to improve life for herself and her daughter. In 1904, Sarah discovered Annie Turbo Malone, the creator of a hair-care system for African-American women. Malone had just opened her first store in St. Louis and hired Sarah as a door-to-door salesperson.

A year later, Sarah met and married C. J. Walker, a newspaper man from Denver, who taught her about advertising, marketing, and promotion techniques. In Denver, they continued to sell Malone's products, making $75 to $100 a week, quite a lucrative income in 1906. Mr. Walker was content to have the extra income, but when Sarah decided to develop her own product line, her husband was reluctant to support her. Ignoring his warnings that she was too pushy and ambitious, she opened her own company. The marriage ended within a few years as the business grew and she built her first manufacturing plant in Indianapolis. Walker, who officially changed her name to "Madame" because she knew that whites would not address her as "Mrs.," sent her daughter to New York to open an East Coast office for her company and create a school training beauticians and saleswomen in the use of the product. By the end of her life in 1919, Madame Walker had created a multimillion-dollar empire, employed an army of more than 3000 saleswomen, and sponsored the opening of more than 300 hair salons around the United States for African-American women. She also used her wealth to support black artists, black writers, and other black professionals and businesses of her day.

Madame Walker didn't have a financial road map to guide her to her financial success. What she did have was a desire to grow and take the risks of creating something new and different for herself and the people who supported her. Taking risks and trying new ideas—in other words, being a pioneer—these are the things one needs to do to build wealth. Learning the financial principles are vital, but a sense of adventure is what is necessary to create wealth.

||≡|| *The way an individual or group perceives itself is a critical determinant of* ||≡||
their drive and goals.

CLAUD ANDERSON
Black Labor, White Wealth, 1995

DEVELOPING A MONEY MENTALITY

Each of us, at one time or another, has the vague fantasy that some day a miracle will occur and the big pot of gold at the end of the rainbow will fall into our laps (see Figure 2-1), and we will never have to work again. S. B. Fuller (1905–1988) knew better. He didn't wait for the miracle or the pot of gold but instead created his own miracle. Still he is one of the least-known African-American entrepreneurs, even though he was the role model and mentor for John Johnson (*Ebony*) and George Johnson (Johnson Products). Fuller arrived in Chicago from Memphis in 1928, hungry and broke, with only 27 cents in his pockets. Following his mother's death, he had dropped out of school after sixth grade to support his seven siblings. He took a job in a coal yard until he found work selling life insurance for the Commonwealth Burial Association. He kept that job until he discovered that he made more money making and selling soap. With $25, a determination to be independent, and a wife who supported him, he made $1000 profit over a 6-month period and never looked back. By 1935, Fuller had created 30 new hair- and skin-care products and built a small factory on the South Side. His most controversial

EUGENE MORRIS, CEO

E. Morris Communications, Inc.
Chicago, Illinois

Gene Morris has been a veteran observer of African-American consumer behavior and buying habits for more than 25 years. Nine years ago, he opened his own advertising agency and has achieved award-winning ad campaigns for such notable companies as Wal-Mart Stores, Kraft General Foods, Coca-Cola, Carnation, Alberto-Culver hair care, and Tribune Entertainment. His agency was chosen by the *Today Show* to design their logo for following the campaign for Bill Clinton when he was a presidential candidate.

Morris is a native Chicagoan, born, bred, and still residing in the Hyde Park region. He received a B.A. degree in business science and an M.B.A. in marketing from Roosevelt University. Despite his busy schedule, he finds time to serve on several corporate boards in the African-American community, including those of Junior Achievement and the Mary McLeod Bethune Archives Museum in Washington, D.C., and does fund-raising for the Midwest Association of Sickle Cell Anemia.

Gene is honest enough to admit that when he started working 25 years ago, his only clear goal was to make money. Even though he had a degree in business administration, he did not really begin to apply the tools and principles of wealth building to his own life until he had to fill out a loan application and see his assets listed on paper. Facing the numbers on the page gave him an insight into how he should begin to build personal net worth as well as value for his business. He finds that it is a daily requirement, like eating a proper diet, getting exercise, and watching your weight, to be consistently committed to the practice of staying with a budget, saving for specific goals, and putting something away on a regular basis for retirement.

Morris is serious about taking care of business—personally and professionally. He supports his employees in the process of wealth accumulation by encouraging each of them to continue their education and job-skills development. He also urges each of them to participate in the company payroll savings plan and has set up a SEP retirement plan for the company. His second commitment to African-American wealth building is to insist that, wherever possible, his company use other African-American suppliers and vendors.

"Unless you have a rich uncle who will leave you a fortune or win the lottery, you have to take charge of your own destiny. Wealth accumulation is so easy if you make the effort to do just a tiny bit on a daily basis. It may be a simplistic statement, but wealth building requires altering attitudes and behavior for a people who have done little or no saving and have never thought it possible, and that isn't a simple process. Slavery has been over for more than a century but we just don't understand how much of a massive change in behavior and thinking is required to develop wealth. Many of us get in each other's way. The anger and hostility that exists among African-Americans makes us feel ugly, dumb, and distrustful of each other. White people continue to put obstacles in our path, but even if that stays the same, there is so much we could do. If we just put together the few little dollars that each of us has, there is so much more that could be accomplished."

GOALS EQUAL $1,000,000

Figure 2-1. The financial roller coaster: fantasy versus reality over a lifetime of earnings.

business decision was when he secretly purchased Boyer Laboratories in 1947, a white firm that had two successful product lines: Jean Nadal Cosmetics and H.A. Hair Arranger; both were quite popular in the segregated South.

Fuller expanded into real estate including the Regal Theater, started the Fuller Insurance Guaranty Corporation, purchased a major share of the Pittsburgh Courier newspaper, and opened the Fuller/Philco Home Appliance department store. His was the first black-owned company to advertise on television in 1956 and at Wrigley Field, supporting the Chicago Cubs. Sales rose to over $10 million a year by 1960 when the bottom fell out. White Southerners discovered that a black man owned the Jean Nadal company and boycotted the product, which was 60 percent of Fuller's bottom line. Within a month Jean Nadal sales were down to zero. A New York liquor company gave a letter of intent to buy Fuller out at $1 million; Fuller used the letter to finance his department store, which had just opened, and a new factory that was being built. The liquor company reneged on the deal, which forced Fuller to quickly sell his most lucrative properties at a loss. The Securities and Exchange Commission began an investigation to see how he was financing his business ventures and ruled that his methods were not legitimate. The fines against him added up to nearly $1 million, and his department store had to be sold at a loss. By 1978, sales of Fuller Products had fallen to less than $100,000. With the help of the people that he mentored over the years and a keen sense of discipline, Fuller rebuilt his business to a reasonable level before his death, but he never attained the financial success he had realized in the early 1960s.

‖≣‖ *Our crown has been bought and paid for, all we have to do is wear it.*   ‖≣‖
                                    JAMES BALDWIN

Developing a money mentality requires thinking, planning, and doing more than the required daily minimum effort to get a paycheck. Finding a "good job," with a comfortable salary, benefits, and perhaps a good union, does not guarantee the right path to building wealth. The recent wave of corporate layoffs should burst that bubble in a hurry. Getting serious about financial habits, attitudes, and choices is the only way to get the money you desire for a comfortable future. Set up a plan and stick with it. Establish priorities that give you some degree of financial control in the uncertainty of the financial world. Develop a daily and weekly routine that includes reading a financial periodical and/or listening to a financial talk show. Think about your daily actions in terms of expense items and income items. Does doing the laundry constitute an expense activity or an income-generating activity? Do you use the time during the spin cycle to watch some dumb cartoon on television, or do you read a book like this one which gives you some intellectual enlightenment? The learning process for life management does not end when you leave the classroom.

Do you earn enough money to be careless with it? Do you expect somebody else to plan your financial life for you? Are you waiting for reparations for slavery, or are you hoping for a national referendum to eradicate the problems of financial illiteracy that plague our educational system? Don't wait for a government program to create a national movement to enlighten you about how to manage your money better. You can get ahead on your own if you make the effort to find out how to do it. Look back at some of the historical role models included in this book. They didn't wait for anyone to show them how to make it happen.

Is it a wise use of your time to have Sunday brunch with an old classmate who wants to borrow money that you won't see again? Are you looking forward to going to a party where most of the people will bore you with the same tired gossip and complaints about job politics, boyfriend problems, new cars they bought, etc. Does this information add to your professional knowledge? Can it help you understand more about personal finance or the way to start a business or offer some economic awareness that will help you get ahead in your career? There are just so many hours in a lifetime, and you must decide if your time is being used wisely by other people when you share it with them.

Oprah Winfrey developed a money mentality long before she accumulated the millions that she now controls through Harpo Enterprises. It is rumored that when all her friends went out to buy Reebok's sneakers, she went out and bought Reebok's stock. As a young television personality in Baltimore, she made a speech to a group of high school students who were surprised to see her driving a 3-year-old Honda and asked her about it. Her answer was that this was the car she could afford and this one was paid for.

Alphonse Fletcher, Jr., understands the function, power, and purpose of money far better than most African-Americans. He rides around New York in a Lincoln Town-Car limo, favors Armani suits, and sports a large diamond ring on his left pinkie finger, and he can afford to without worrying about next month's American Express bill. "Buddy," as he prefers to be called, is not a rap star, football player, film idol, or even Denzel Washington's manager. This 30-year-old millionaire is one of the newest wizards of Wall Street. A stockbroker, investment advisor, and securities analyst, Buddy is respected as one of the most successful pension fund managers of the year. In 1994, he pledged $1 million to the United Negro College Fund. When the NAACP fell on hard times in 1993, he donated another million to the organization's coffers to keep it afloat. He can afford it. Four years ago, he won a multimillion-dollar settlement against Kidder-Peabody, his former employer. He used the proceeds to start his own money management firm, which now attracts some of the largest institutional investors on Wall Street. He enjoys making money, but he also knows the need for giving some back to the community that created him.

At 28, Kirbyjon Caldwell was on the brink of a promising career as an investment banker after getting an M.B.A. from the Wharton School of Business at the University of Pennsylvania. After honing his skills and developing a sophisticated knowledge of finance, Caldwell felt a need to take a different path. When he announced to close friends and professional colleagues that he was going to the seminary, they were convinced that he was crazy. When he took over a struggling church in Houston with less than 25 members, he was dismissed as an impossible dreamer wasting his training.

Seventeen years later, his colleagues are happy to see how wrong they were. The Reverend Kirbyjon Caldwell did not discard his knowledge of money management and capital markets as he studied scriptural text. He has used his skills, training, knowledge, and contacts to spearhead the development of the 104,000 square foot complex dubbed the "Power Center." The center was once an abandoned department store in a shopping center. It has been renovated and now houses 27 office suites, a bank branch, a pharmacy, a day care center, a health clinic, a banquet hall, and the Houston Community College, which specializes in business and computer courses. The church, which has grown to over 9000 members, owns, manages, and develops the property and provides jobs for 120 people from the community. The Reverend Mr. Caldwell formed a partnership with a Minnesota investment group that specializes in working with nonprofit groups to develop viable community businesses. He expects the Power Center to generate about $27 million within the next 3 years and to eventually employ 200 people. None of this would have been possible if the Reverend Mr. Caldwell had ignored the power of money in his personal and professional plan for success.

Financial success in the next century starts with knowing what you want to accomplish and where you want to go in the financial life cycle. In the same way that there are stages of career development, there are several levels of money management that should be followed for financial success and future financial well-being.

‖☰‖‖   *If you can count your money, you don't have any.*   ‖☰‖‖
DON KING
Sports promoter

DEFINITION OF MONEY

What is money? The dictionary definition you learned in school is that money is a means of exchange to buy goods and services, right? If you believe that, then you see money as a way simply to buy things. The simple truth is, money is a reflection of how you spend your time and energy to fulfill the personal, spiritual, and material needs that reflect how you feel about yourself.

Adapt this perspective and measure the hours and days of your life to develop a money mentality. Look at it this way. How many hours do you commit to the experience of getting that money on a daily basis? What time do you leave home each day headed for work? When do you get home? Do you bring work home on weekends? Add these hours together, and you'll discover that you've got more than a nine-to-five job; it's probably more like a nine-to-nine schedule, which means that you really are putting in around 60 hours a week. About 70 percent of working Americans devote at least 11 waking hours a day to getting income.

Compare the hours you work and the money in your paycheck. Assume that you earn $600 a week. Divide $600 a week by 60 hours a week, and you get $10 an hour before taxes. After taxes, FICA, and deductions for insurance and benefits, you probably have about $6 an hour left over. Now calculate the number of hours you work to pay rent. To pay the phone bill. To pick up a pizza and rent a couple of videos. A $40 trip to the supermarket equals how many hours? The clothes you left at the dry cleaners that cost $15 equals 2½ hours of work time for that service. Now you will understand the true meaning of the old adage, "Time is money." Once you absorb this definition, you will be much more serious about honoring your goals and using your money wisely.

In addition, when you use your credit cards, you put a "time mortgage" on your future earnings to pay next month's bill. How much of your future earnings have you "mortgaged" with credit card debt? With so much of your time and earnings already committed to debt, when do you start paying yourself? Who are you really working for? Your landlord? The credit card companies? Or yourself?

III≣III *Money isn't everything but I rate it right up there with oxygen.*   III≣III
TONY BROWN
1995

CHANGING ATTITUDES AND OLD HABITS

Taking control of your money is the final step toward gaining financial maturity and independence and realizing that your money choices dictate the life that you lead. Taking control means being fully responsible for your life without spending time apportioning blame for the past and fudging excuses for irresponsible behavior in the present. For the first time in our history more African-Americans have financial and career chances that place them far ahead of their parents. With the large amount of dollars—$450 billion of projected income by the year 2000—that we control, imagine what a difference there would be in our economic and political power if we spent just half of those dollars among ourselves. Not helping each other is the major drawback to the personal and communal goal of wealth building. Whether you want to start a business or just buy a new car, it is up to you to start with your own financial situation in order to have some effect on the whole community.

When you look for a new opportunity you will need savings, a good credit report, and the right attitude to take advantage of that opportunity when it presents itself. Preparation must occur before opportunity presents itself. Anthony Overton (1865–1946) knew the secret of such planning and preparation when he decided to change his career despite the protests and lack of support from friends and family. That forthright attitude made Overton the first black man to create a conglomerate at the turn of the century. Overton's parents moved to Kansas City shortly after he was born at the end of the Civil War. It was there that he attended public schools, graduating with a law degree in 1888 from the University of Kansas. After a brief career as a municipal court judge, Overton became bored with the bench and searched for something more interesting to do.

He used his $2000 savings to start manufacturing baking powder. Two years later, after surviving a near-bankruptcy, he began experimenting with food flavorings, toiletries, and cosmetics. He hired door-to-door salesmen, but his most innovative move was to export his products to women of color in Egypt, Liberia, India, and the Philippines. In 1912, Overton relocated to Chicago and had a 52-item product line including shoe polish, hair-care products, and perfume as well as a 400 man door-to-door sales force in 36 cities. By 1926, Overton had expanded his empire to include a newspaper, the *Chicago Bee*; the Douglass National Bank; the Victoria Life Insurance Company; and the Great Northern Realty Company, which had vast real estate holdings on Chicago's South Side. Although the bank and the insurance company both failed during the Great Depression, Overton continued to operate the newspaper and the manufacturing company until his death.

Overton saved and planned for wealth and based his effort on faith and hard work, the same way our ancestors had faith that one day things would change and the world would get better for them. They didn't know when it would happen, but they didn't stop trying just because they didn't have a road map to the future. The habits and attitudes of a lifetime are difficult to change and will not change overnight, but it isn't impossible. Here are some guidelines that can help you.

1. Start educating yourself about money. Money will be a part of your life for the rest of your life, so you should make an effort to get to know each other very well. If you think of money as an employee, a person you're hiring to work for you, you must consider that "person's" skills and the duties you expect the person to perform. Begin educating yourself about how to be a good boss and create a job description and a set of tasks of what you want money to accomplish for you. Allocate 15 minutes a day to reading the financial pages in the newspaper. Watch one of the financial news shows on television. Leaf through a personal finance magazine at the library. Make a list of questions that you have about money. Set a timetable for getting some answers. Reading this book is a good beginning. Look for a one-day seminar on finances or an evening course at a community college or adult high school.

2. Think positive. Focus positively for one day at a time or, perhaps, for an hour at a time. A pessimistic attitude can be more destructive than a stock market crash. If you see yourself as a loser, then you always will be. Use positive affirmations that will help you change how you see your situation.

3. Examine your money worries. What is realistic, and what is not? What can you control and change, and what is beyond your reach? What are your alternatives for resolving your problems? Often the lack of knowledge and effort to find another way limits your opportunities to grow and change financially. Don't be afraid to ask for help.

4. Set a goal that seems realistic and approachable. Dealing with money is like going on a journey. You get to your destination by making a reservation, looking at a map, and planning the best way to get there. If you never decide what you want to achieve with your money, then how will you know if you are a success or a failure? Give yourself a dream to achieve, but put a date on it.

5. Stop misusing credit and make a budget to get out of debt. How you handle your money is a reflection of how you feel about yourself, and too many African-Americans are much too willing to be victims of the media message of instant gratification by overspending. More and more money is devoted to spending on clothes, cars, jewelry, and expensive vacations in a desperate desire to achieve some pathetic idea of social status and public recognition, which cannot be bought in a store or ordered from a catalog. If you have a compulsive shopping problem, go to Debtors Anonymous or Shopaholics Anonymous, two organizations that can assist you. There are also psychotherapists who specialize in treating money problems.

6. Choose a role model. Throughout this book, there are historical anecdotes about successful African-Americans who developed prosperous lives long before there was an affirmative-action program to open doors for them. Their life stories can assist you in developing a money mentality and seeing yourself as a financial being.

7. Stop taking the crisis management approach. Do you wait until April 13 to call an accountant or pick up tax forms? If you didn't file the year before, then you're begging for a problem from the IRS, and the IRS is all too willing to accommodate you and collect the extra fees and penalties for late filing or not filing at all. If you think ahead, you can avoid most financial crises with careful planning and paying attention to the calendar.

8. Examine your money habits and expectations. Are you being irrational about what is affordable and necessary in your life? Do you spend $45 on designer sunglasses when your budget says get a $6.95 pair from Kmart? Are you trying to satisfy some emotional emptiness with overspending? Are you staying in a bad personal relationship because of the financial arrangement? Romance without finance becomes a nuisance, but a relationship based on financial need and lack of respect becomes a nightmare if the only reason you are there is for status or money.

9. Practice patience. Wanting too much too soon guarantees financial chaos. Putting a lot of dollars into weekly lottery tickets in hopes of becoming an overnight millionaire is highly unlikely when there is only a 1-in-6-million chance to win. In fact, you rarely, if ever, make back what you laid out. Check out the stock market if you want to do some educated gambling. You can start by investing as little as $25 or $50 a month with a better chance of building some security. Remember, though, that patience here is important, too. Trying to win a quick high return on investments can run the risk of sudden dramatic losses. Still, it's also important not to go to the opposite extreme by investing only in "safe" programs that provide little or no growth.

10. Get professional help. Your brother-in-law can fix your car, but can he pick stocks? Doing it alone is like trying to be your own dentist. Most people have been sold insurance by an insurance agent, stocks by a stockbroker, and CDs by a banker, but they have no consultant to coordinate all their financial objectives. Like a baseball team without a manager, this "strategy" creates confusion. You may wish to invest $100 to $200 for a consultation with a financial advisor who can help clarify your goals and offer guidance and objective insights. However, don't expect the advisor to be a mind reader and solve all your problems in one short session. Prepare a list of questions before you make the appointment.

11. Invest some time. Give yourself at least a year to learn the language and concepts of money. You didn't learn to ride a bike the first time you got on it, did you? After you fell off and skinned your knees, you got up and tried it again and again until you got it right. Apply the same discipline to building wealth. Cut out the use of credit cards and put away at least $100 a month. Then recalculate your net worth. Time will tell.

12. Practice emotional self-control. You may have feelings, but money does not, and the money game is the most unimpassioned game you can play. Investing by "gut feel" is often the worst way to make a financial decision. Though there are times for gut feelings, it is unwise to let your emotional life rule your financial life. Ask yourself the following questions when considering an investment: What is the potential reward? What is the risk? Is the reward worth the risk?

The most lasting vision of hope for African-American financial independence at the Million Man March was symbolized by the thousands of black hands waving dollar bills to cover the cost of the assembly. It is optimistic to believe that each man returned home with a commitment to restructure his life, personally and collectively, and a desire to develop a plan for personal financial well-being and communal economic development. Whether you practice the principles of Kwanzaa or decide to follow your own plan, you are responsible for making the effort to change your life; nothing will happen until you do.

|||≣||| *To get where you want to go, you can't only do what you like.* |||≣|||

PETER ABRAHAMS
Tell Freedom, 1954

3

‖‖‖ ‖‖‖‖ ‖‖‖‖ ‖‖‖‖ ‖‖‖‖ ‖‖‖‖ ‖‖‖‖‖ ‖‖‖ ‖‖‖‖ ‖‖‖‖

SETTING GOALS–
BUILDING A DYNASTY
IN STAGES

"Politics don't control the world, money does. And we ought not to be upset about that. We ought to begin to understand how money works and why money works.... If you want to bring about ... feeding the hungry, clothing the naked, healing the sick—it's going to be done in the free market system. You need capital."

Andrew Young
"Words of the Week," JET, Oct. 14, 1985

As African-Americans, our freedom and our finances have always been connected, and this is extremely clear in the life history of "Free Frank." When Frank McWhorter was born in the Piedmont area of South Carolina in 1777, he had little to look forward to as a slave except a life of endless drudgery, which began for Frank at 8 years old. His mother, Juda, a West African woman, was one of four slaves on the McWhorter farm, and she was responsible for all the cooking and cleaning for the eight-member family. When Frank was 17, George McWhorter, who was also Frank's father, pur-chased 57 acres of raw land in the virgin forests of Pulaski County, Kentucky. Frank was sent to live in a tent in this wilderness to clear the land and build a home for the family to move there the following year.

At 22, Frank met Lucy, a slave woman belonging to William Denham, George McWhorter's brother-in-law. She lived half a day's journey from the Kentucky farm, and the couple were only allowed to visit once a month. A year after their meeting, Frank and Lucy were married, although as slaves, they were considered property, not citizens, so their union was not recognized as legal. Their brief monthly visits continued and produced 12 children, only 4 of whom survived until adulthood. It was another 20 years before the two slaves were allowed to live together under the same roof.

George McWhorter found Frank to be so reliable that he moved to Tennessee and left Frank to manage the Kentucky farm and to "hire himself out" as long as half his earnings were given to McWhorter whenever he returned. On a portion of the property designated for his garden, Frank discovered the various minerals needed for making saltpeter and set up a manufactory. Saltpeter, used for making gunpowder, was in great demand because the United States was fighting the War of 1812 and because many pioneering settlers passed through the area on their way to the new Illinois, Nebraska, and Kansas Territories. Frank's saltpeter operation was profitable for himself and for his owner. It took 4 days to make 1 pound of saltpeter, and he sold it for 75 cents a pound. Frank's share of each pound he sold was 37 cents (half the market price), and he saved every penny to achieve a dream he had harbored for the 24 years. Frank wanted his freedom and his own land.

By 1817, Frank had saved enough money to buy Lucy's freedom for $800. Denham had originally asked for $500, but he suspected that Lucy was pregnant again. Five months after her manumission, Frank's fourth son, Solomon, was born, making him the only free black male in Frank's family. All Frank's savings went into buying land and building a home for Lucy and his son, although he was still a slave himself. With Lucy now able to "hire herself out for wages," they both worked diligently to save every penny. Two years later, in December 1819, for the sum of $800 Frank purchased his own freedom. He was 42 years old.

Over the next 5 years, Frank and Lucy worked steadily to meet their second goal of purchasing their children from Lucy's former owner. In 1826, Obediah Denham threatened to sell Frank, Jr., "down the river" for $1000. Free Frank did not have enough money saved to buy his son's freedom, so he tried to convince Denham to accept his saltpeter manufactory in exchange for his son, but Denham rejected the offer. Frank, Jr., ran away from the Kentucky plantation and escaped to Canada. A fugitive warrant for his arrest and capture was issued by Denham. Three years later, Denham dropped the fugitive claim against Frank, Jr., and accepted Free Frank's business. Without the salt-peter manufactory, Frank and Lucy decided to move to Illinois, which was a free state. Frank, Jr., returned from Canada in 1830 and helped the family to relocate to Illinois.

At 53, Free Frank and his family moved to another virgin territory and started over again. They purchased 820 acres of land in Pike County, Illinois, on the eastern bank of the Mississippi River. The first legal right that Free Frank exercised when he moved to Illinois was to marry Lucy legally in a court of law after being together for 40 years.

Free Frank divided his acreage into lots and sold them to other free blacks who wanted to live in a free territory. They created the first free black town in America in 1833 and called it New Philadelphia. When Free Frank built the family's new house in Pike County, Illinois, the cellar, which was blasted out of solid rock, contained a hidden room that they used to shelter runaway slaves who were trying to escape to Canada.

In 1853, the Illinois legislature prohibited the migration of any more free blacks into the state. This stopped Frank's efforts to bring together the rest of his family. During his lifetime Frank spent over $14,000 (this was when the cost of dinner for four at a good restaurant in New York was $5!) and made nine trips back to Kentucky to buy his children and grandchildren so that his dream of a united family could become a reality. At the time of his death in 1854, two of Free Frank's grandchildren were still enslaved in Kentucky. In his will, Free Frank specified that whatever money he had should be spent on purchasing those remaining family members whenever the law permitted.

Frank and Lucy couldn't read or write, did not have special government grants to support their effort, and could not apply for a minority set-aside program. They had the harshness of the Slave Codes, the brutality of segregation, and the evil intimidation of racism to stop them at every point along the path to freedom. But they also had a clearly focused idea of what was important to them and were committed to the discipline of sticking to a principle regardless of the hardships and setbacks they encountered.

IIIEIII *Freedom has always been an expensive thing. History is fit testimony to the*   IIIEIII
fact that freedom is rarely gained without sacrifice and self-denial.
DR. MARTIN LUTHER KING, JR.

SETTING YOUR OWN GOALS

A goal has to be some inner desire that drives you to want to accomplish something greater than owning a tangible asset like a car or a house. There has to be an inner need that must be fulfilled so that you are satisfied that you are spending your life in a meaningful pursuit. Setting goals takes research, some commitment and forethought, and a willingness to constantly learn and explore new ideas and opportunities.

Your goals may not be as lofty or ambitious as Free Frank's, but whatever you choose to focus on can be accomplished if you emulate some of the same dedication and discipline that helped Frank and Lucy to achieve their goals. Each of us has some ancestor who made a similar sacrifice for some purpose. You owe it to yourself and your ancestors, who struggled more than most of us will ever know or remember, to achieve financial success and well-being. Although racism is still rampant within American culture, the economic exploitation of slavery has ended and the harsh deprivation of segregation that limited financial opportunities has diminished considerably in the last three decades. Frank and Lucy could have spent their earnings on new clothes, a hat for Lucy, and new shoes for the children. Their savings could have been invested in a new wagon or an extra horse, but Frank and Lucy were motivated by a dream that was greater than any of the material goods that were available to them.

When it comes to examining life from a financial perspective, most African-Americans now have far more options than their parents were ever able to consider. Like Free Frank and Lucy, we are exploring new territory and discovering new options. The steady increase in income and financial opportunities has made it possible for many African-Americans to develop a more comfortable lifestyle, yet the choices that are being made often do not contribute to wealth building. Many African-Americans have become afraid to dream big or are reluctant to express a desire for something greater than what is available within their social circle for fear of being looked upon as being too ambitious or greedy. But for the first time in our history more African-Americans have financial choices and career paths that place them a quantum leap ahead of their parents. Don't waste those choices on something that your ancestors will not be proud of. Prove to them that you are worthy of the dreams that they had for you. You have more control than you think over the answers to the question of what you want to accomplish.

‖☰‖‖ *Unless a sense of service and duty is instilled, our upward mobility will only* ‖☰‖‖
be measured by cars and styling.
DR. NIARA SUDARKASA

THE "BLAME AND EXCUSE" GAME

Some African-Americans are reluctant to take full responsibility for their financial futures and have perfected the art of looking for reasons above and beyond the usual ones to avoid making a decision about their future. Blame the system, blame the boss, blame the bank when your deposit doesn't clear on time, blame the post office when payment is late. The amount of time that is given to apportioning blame would be much more productively spent looking for an answer to how it is possible to change one's attitude and behavior to improve one's situation. Ultimately, it is up to you to change your life, your habits, and your attitude toward money.

THE EXCUSE CYCLE

We are all good at making excuses to not plan for ourselves. How many friends do you know who have been promising to lose weight, go back to school, get out of debt, find a new job, leave a bad relationship, but never seem to do it. Making a decision to change one's financial life falls into the same category. How many excuses have you given yourself when it is time to confront the checkbook? Here are a few creative ones you can borrow to entertain yourself. They will amuse you, but they won't help you.

1. I'd rather change the cat's litter box than balance my checkbook.

2. Getting a root canal is more interesting that reading the financial pages.

3. After I finish my nails, sweep the sidewalk, clean out the closets, and solve the problem of the ozone layer, I'll think about getting some life insurance.

Every excuse is a missed opportunity to be responsible for one's well-being. Earning money and knowing what to do with it are not the same thing, and the trial-and-error method of learning can be extremely expensive and depressing.

IIEII *You can live your fears, or you can live your dreams.* IIEII
JEFFREY VINCENT NOBLE
African-American psychologist

As noted before, in the same way there are career development stages, there are also levels of money management and financial development that should be followed for financial success and future financial well-being.

Financial awareness is not taught in college or high school unless you are in a business school class, and even many of them don't teach the basics of commonsense money management. *Except for the "school of hard knocks," making the effort to learn on your own before you get into trouble is the only way to make sense out of how to use money in your life.*

START SEEING YOURSELF AS A FINANCIAL BEING

How many Monday mornings have you punched the snooze button on the alarm clock to steal another few winks and thought, "If I were rich I wouldn't have to do this"? As you sit in rush-hour traffic or stand on a crowded subway platform, what fantasy do you harbor about having a million-dollar lottery ticket? Is the major purpose of your work life to support your landlord, pay the auto mechanic, pay the phone bill you've run up, and get your nails done every week?

The average employed African-American spends 70 to 80 percent of his or her waking hours involved in the arduous process of earning and accumulating money. Getting up at 6:30, suffering through the 7:30 rush hour, bringing home the files to work on over the weekend—the job does not end at 5 o'clock even though you may refer to it as having a 9-to-5. Many management trainees and small business owners quickly discover that building a career or a business requires working 12-to-14-hour days, as well as putting time in on weekends to catch up on professional reading or to finish a proposal or a report. When you

Forty years before the Civil War, several African-American businessmen found a way to fulfill their dreams of owning a business, despite the restrictions of Slave Codes and the harsh resentment of white competitors. Two of the most successful were Henry Boyd of Ohio and Thomas Day of North Carolina.

Boyd moved to Cincinnati in 1826 and tried to find work as a carpenter. When racial prejudice prevented him from earning a living, he went into partnership with a white man and established a home construction business. As they became more successful, Boyd invented a new type of bed frame, patented it under his white partner's name and built a factory making the bed frames, employing 50 workers, black and white in four large buildings. As news of their success began to spread, their buildings were vandalized several times and ultimately destroyed by fire. They rebuilt the business three times but eventually sold out when their insurance company refused to cover them again.

Thomas Day was more fortunate with his furniture-making business in Milton, North Carolina. Day employed more than 60 craftspeople, black and white, in his shop known as the Yellow Tavern. In 1829, when the state passed a law forbidding the migration of any more free people of color into North Carolina, Day threatened to close his business and relocate to Virginia since he was engaged to marry a free mulatto woman who lived 30 miles away in Danville, Virginia. The mayor and town residents of Milton petitioned the governor and the legislature and obtained a variance for Day and his bride. The Yellow Tavern is now a national historic landmark, and any remaining cabinets made by Thomas Day are considered priceless antiques today.

devote that much time and energy to earning money, you deserve to get the most out of it. Yet very few of us have been taught how to use money wisely, because there was usually so little left over after the basic needs were met.

Like most other Americans, African-Americans have had little or no financial education as a part of their upbringing. Public school systems do not offer classes in drawing up a family budget, making good consumer spending choices, staying out of trouble with credit cards, or setting up an investment portfolio, even though more than half your adult life is dedicated to earning and managing money.

In fact, money operates as a major force in your life from birth to death. The choices you make will determine the life you lead and how your descendants will grow and develop into the next century. Succeeding in the next century requires that you start learning how and when to make the most of each dollar. You can begin by seeing yourself as a financial being.

||≡|| *I wanted to become rich and famous simply so no one could evict my family* ||≡||
again.

JAMES BALDWIN
Author

All of us have a life-long relationship with money that influences our behavior on a daily basis. Look at these money milestones and learn how you have developed a relationship with money throughout your life.

CHILDHOOD—(BIRTH TO 6 YEARS OF AGE)

From the day you are born, you are a tax exemption on your parent's Form 1040 and an expense item in the family budget. As a child you have no idea about the cost to your parents of keeping you healthy, well fed, and comfortable. As you grow up, you see money merely as a way to get an ice cream cone when the Mr. Frostee truck stops on your block or as a means to see a Saturday afternoon movie. Perhaps you are rewarded with a quarter for helping with a few small chores around the house. Maybe you are given a piggy bank to put your pennies in.

STARTING SCHOOL—AGES 7 TO 12

You begin to see what other kids have for clothes, toys, and entertainment privileges, and you harass your parents for the same items without the vaguest idea about what they cost. Perhaps you begin to get a small allowance and learn what $2 or $3 a week can or cannot buy. You probably get a quarter or, if your grandmother is generous, a dollar for getting good grades on your report card. Maybe you break a neighbor's window or lose your glasses, gloves, or schoolbooks and have to find some part-time work to replace these items. You might have a paper route, and begin to feel the peer pressure to have the same bike, clothes, and games as your friends, siblings, and neighbors.

ADOLESCENCE—AGES 13 TO 17

You want to impress your friends with your braided or beaded hair-do, buy the hottest new compact disc, wear the hottest brand name sneakers, start wearing makeup, and find out the high price of the "gotta-have-it-all" stuff you think you need to blend in with the right crowd. Your parents probably insist that if you want more than they can afford, you have to get a part-time job. You begin to explore opportunities to make money outside your home and to discover what it is like to have a minimum wage, part-time, or summer job or realize how little you could make from baby-sitting.

YOUNG ADULTHOOD—AGES 17 TO 25

You finish high school, go into the military, get into a job-training program, or, if you are lucky, attend college. If you are still living at home with your parents, they expect you to contribute to the rent and the living expenses. You want to use the family car or get your own set of wheels, and they inform you of the increased cost of auto insurance because of your age. You think about getting your own apartment and discover how much you will need to make your move to independence. If you start your first job, you open a bank account and start saving money and you encounter your first credit card application.

Up until now the financial milestones have simply been sketched out. Since this book is aimed at readers 18 and older, the sketches from here on are fleshed out with choices and questions you need to consider as you reach each milestone.

If you attend college, you are concerned about the cost of your education and the reality of managing money on your own. How much are you borrowing in financial aid, and when will you have to start repaying student loans? This will be your first credit reference, and it is critical that you follow through on regular payments.

If your parents did not open a savings account for you while you were in high school, this will be your first trip into a bank to establish an account. Open both a savings and a checking account and make regular deposits of part of your income into some interest-bearing account each month. Ask your employer if you can sign up for payroll savings deductions. If you can join a credit union do so. If you will only be writing four to five checks a month, choose a budget checking account. Compare at least two banks and their fees before you decide on one. Does your first job require any major purchases before you begin—a business wardrobe, a car, or a computer? Make a budget and plan for these expenses.

You probably have established some intimate relationship with someone and are thinking about marriage. You have to decide how to merge two lifestyles and share your new financial responsibilities, including getting an apartment or a house and combining incomes, savings, health and life insurance, and disability coverage. You will begin keeping joint financial records and filing joint taxes. If one of you wants to return to graduate school or get further job training, can you afford to live on one paycheck for a year or two? Will that extra education really enhance your future income? Who is going to pay for the tuition? Should you take on another student loan?

Midlife I—Ages 26 to 39

You have set and reached some personal and career goals. Perhaps you are married, have a couple of children, and have been able to buy a house. Or maybe you are single, live in the city, and still have an independent lifestyle. You begin to ask yourself if this is what you really want out of life. Have you maintained a good credit record? Considered a career change? Perhaps a new job or job relocation could offer a career boost. How would your lifestyle be affected by a new job or a move? Do you have sufficient savings for 3 to 6 months of living expenses if you want to make a career switch? Do you have adequate life insurance?

If you have children, you should be concerned about how to plan for their college education. If you have not yet bought a house and you want to, you have to put money away for it. But if you are concentrating your efforts on saving for the down payment or putting money away for you child's education, planning for retirement may be the last thing on your mind. Just the same, you should begin to think about saving for retirement. So if you have a 401(k) available through your job, join it.

If you're married, you and your spouse should discuss and agree on some financial goals, to be reevaluated every other year. You and your partner may or may not still be in agreement on what your professional, spiritual, and financial goals are. If you have gotten a divorce or ended a long-term relationship, how have your living expenses changed? By now, your parents are aging and may be asking you for assistance with their financial responsibilities.

Midlife II—(Ages 40 to 49)

Remarrying, saving for your child's college education, helping your aging parents, and makng a career move are situations that can dramatically affect your finances. You should focus on career growth and investments for the future. A major health problem, like hypertension and heart disease, particularly for minority men, may affect your income and savings. How secure is your company? Is there a chance that you will be laid off, downsized, outplaced, or fired? Do you have sufficient savings to cover your living expenses if you do not have a paycheck for 6 months? Have you thought about leaving your job and starting a business? Review your benefits and expected retirement income with your benefits counselor. Project what you need to be saving for retirement. Begin investing in mutual funds for long-term growth. Complete a will and keep accurate financial records. Does your spouse know where all the records and documents are? Do you both have access to the safe deposit box?

PRERETIREMENT—(AGES 50 TO 64)

Planning for retirement should be at the top of your financial list now. Every dollar you can spare should go into a 401(k) plan or a tax-deferred annuity. This is also the time when many African-American males experience some health crisis, like diabetes or prostate cancer. Review your financial records and all forms of insurance. If the children are out of the house and the mortgage is paid off, then reduce your life insurance coverage. Physical changes in your health and well-being should make you consider how your lifestyle will change. You may begin thinking about selling your house and moving to a different location. Reviewing your will and checking your legal responsibilities as well as your financial assets should be a major concern. Have you thought about the tax implications of retirement? Meet with a financial advisor and your benefits counselor to clarify your pension options. Visit or call your local Social Security Administration to anticipate your retirement benefits. How will Medicare affect you? What will it cost? What is not covered?

If you are offered early retirement, don't jump into it until you know exactly what benefits you may keep and what ones you will lose. What will be the cost of replacing the health coverage your employer has formerly paid for?

RETIREMENT—(AGES 65 AND UP)

Now at last you should be able to begin enjoying fully all that you've worked for. If you don't have sufficient retirement income, you may *have* to work and participate in one of the training programs for senior citizens to serve fries at Burger King. Figure this out and then find out how your income from the job will reduce your social security payments. Remember, that nursing home insurance is available. If you are in good health, you can participate in a second career developed from a hobby or some volunteer work. Some careers may allow you to still have a part-time job to keep active and healthy.

Discuss your plans with your spouse and children. In case you fall ill, decide who should hold your power of attorney. Review your will and see if all your assets have been accounted for. Discuss or make plans for funeral arrangements. Do you own a cemetery plot? Decide how long you want to continue working.

Total financial planning is an ongoing, lifelong process. Once you accept this fact—and see yourself as a financial being—you can begin to create financial freedom in keeping with what you want to do, to be in charge of your own life. It's your life, and it's your money!

FOUR LIFE EVENTS THAT INFLUENCE YOUR FINANCIAL LIFE

Not all financial decisions are as clear-cut as opening a savings account and putting money into a retirement plan. At one time or another, you will be faced with one of the following life events which will have a serious impact on your financial well-being. There is no set timetable for when they will occur, but the issues still need consideration as you approach these horizons in your personal and financial life cycle. (See Figure 3-1.)

1. MARRIAGE

Rahim and Khadijah met in college 5 years ago as they were working their way through school, and they are now engaged to be married. They have set a date for next spring. Khadijah is a social worker who still lives at home with her parents, goes to school at night studying for her M.S.W., drives a 5-year-old car, and has saved $12,000 out of her modest salary of $26,500. She pays cash for everything, rarely uses credit cards, and carefully budgets for all major expenses like vacations, appliances, and the house she wants to buy in 3 years.

Rahim laughs at the idea of saving, claiming that the capitalist system is not to be trusted, banks cheat you anyway, and it's a dumb idea to put money into institutions that are so racist and don't support the community. He is 4 months behind on his student loan payments, is always late with the rent, has charged up to the limit on four Visa cards, and is thinking about filing bankruptcy "to get a fresh start." He has changed jobs three times in 2 years and is avoiding a tax audit because he can't find any receipts or canceled checks. This is a marriage that will be headed for chaos unless these two do some serious negotiating about money habits and expectations.

Rahim and Khadijah represent two basic money personality types: spenders and savers, and these extreme opposites often end up married to

NOTE: Total financial planning is an ongoing process that touches every aspect of your life. When one aspect changes, remember to notice how such changes ripple throughout.

Figure 3-1. The financial life cycle.

each other. Extreme opposites or not though, most couples march down the aisle blissfully ecstatic about starting a new life together but totally clueless and completely dense about what to expect from each other in the money matters department. But when you plan to spend your life with another, you should discuss how you plan to handle money, credit, and savings before you tie the knot. Premarital counseling doesn't give sufficient time to discussing finances, and once the problems start, anger, blame, and frustration usually get in the way of problem solving and can lead to serious misunderstandings, unnecessary emotional problems, and divorce. African-American women in particular are quite used to the responsibility of working and making many of their own decisions and frequently have their own ideas about saving, investing, and sharing money.

Discussing how you are going to handle money is more important for a second marriage. In addition, a second marriage likely will require a serious decision about the expense of child support as a part of the monthly budget. You may also wish to consider a prenuptial agreement that will specify how certain assets will be passed on to your children. Living happily ever after means talking about and agreeing on financial priorities that are comfortable for both of you. Setting some ground rules before you marry will give you some guidelines to refer to when problems arise.

1A. LIVING TOGETHER

Some couples who prefer not to marry still have a legal commitment to each other. In certain states, common-law marital arrangements are recognized as being legal after a couple has established a living-together situation for more than 7 years. Many gay and lesbian domestic partnerships are also being recognized as legal living arrangements. But whether or not there is a legal commitment, other legal and financial issues must be sorted out and agreed upon when you begin to think of a long-term commitment. The following guidelines outline 10 important issues.

TEN GUIDELINES FOR COMMUNICATING ABOUT MONEY

1. *Budgeting.* Make time to talk about budgeting once or twice a month, or more often if necessary. Rent or mortgage payments and utilities should be no more than 25 percent of your gross income. Use this percentage as a guideline to decide what you plan to do.

2. *Responsibility.* Decide how you will share the work of bill paying. Who will take care of writing and mailing the checks each month? Your marriage is really a small business enterprise. Don't you want it to be profitable?

3. *Debt.* How will you merge your debts? Do either of you have high credit card balances, school loans, or car notes? Decide if both of you will assume responsibility for each other's debts. If more than 20 percent of your income is used to pay off loans, you can't afford to take on more debt or do much saving until these are cleared up. This can also delay your plans for buying your first home.

4. *Credit.* Resist the temptation to have a joint credit card account just to save on a credit card annual fee. Husbands and wives should maintain separate credit ratings, but each of you should be aware of the other's credit cards.

5. *Handling the checkbook.* Separate accounts may work for you if you are used to having your own money. Establish a joint account to share household expenses, contributing to it based on income—60 percent from him because he earns more, and 40 percent from her because her check is smaller. Do what is comfortable for both of you. Try both kinds of accounts to see what works.

6. *Taxes.* Joint filing is the best way to get the highest refund, but be sure you understand your mutual liability. Before December 31, have a tax preparer do a sample tax filing to see what steps you should take before year-end. Combining two paychecks may have put you in a higher tax bracket and could require additional tax payments. Decide how you plan to invest the refund before you receive it. The "marriage penalty" for joint filing can increase your tax bill by 11 percent.

7. *Record storage.* Where do you keep the apartment lease? Marriage license? Car title? Bank books? Shared information avoids headaches. A major mistake many husbands make is not telling their wives about their business affairs; this can lead to major financial problems in an emergency. Wives need to ask more questions about what is happening with the family finances. Start with a small file cabinet to keep receipts, bank statements, insurance policies, and tax returns. To protect valuable irreplaceable records, get a safe deposit box—and get it in both names so each of you has access access to it.

8. *Shared goals.* Decide what your priorities are and how you will use any extra money you have. Set a savings goal that you both share: a vacation, a new car, graduate school. How much do you want to put aside for long-term investing, and how do you both feel about taking risks? Financial education should be a shared goal.

9. *Professional guidance.* A financial planner or some third party to advise you can take the emotion out of the decision-making process as well as provide professional recommendations. The cost of a written financial plan is worth the expense since it will give you a timetable and help you clarify some goals.

10. *Insurance policies.* These include health, homeowner's, disability, life, and auto. Concentrate on merging health plans and having adequate disability protection. When you do buy life insurance, a low-cost term policy equal to 5 times your salary is a good beginning.

2. CHILDREN

Babies are beautiful, cuddly, tiny, and fragile, and are often the most over-whelming experience a woman can have and frequently the most expensive one. The infant mortality rate among African-Americans is 27 percent higher than the national average. Many of these problems can be alleviated by getting good prenatal care and medical advice during pregnancy. As soon as you discover that you're pregnant, after you adjust to the idea, you should start considering the financial issues that are going to change in your life.

1. *Medical care.* The cost of vitamins during pregnancy, periodic checkups for the baby, and immunization shots should be covered, at least somewhat, by your health insurance. Without insurance, well-baby care can be as much as $700 your child's first year. Speak to your health insurance company and find out what the company covers and what you must pay for yourself. If you don't call your health insurance company and report your baby's birth within the first 30 days, you may find that you have to wait another year to enroll him or her in your medical plan.

2. *Income.* Do you have enough money in savings to sustain you during the time that you will be out of work? Will you be allowed to return to work at your same salary level? Losing income during pregnancy and staying at home with the new baby can add to the pressure of adjusting to the responsibility of having a new life to care for. Some states allow you to collect worker's compensation during pregnancy, or your employer may have a short-term disability insurance plan that will cover your time away from the job.

3. *Furnishings and formula.* Baby's first year can easily wreck the family budget and eat up any savings you have accrued. Added together, the cost can be overwhelming. For example, a car seat costs $39 to $99 (most states require proof that you own one before you can even leave the hospital); a new baby bed can cost anywhere from $200 to $600; disposable diapers average about $28 a week; and formula, if you are not nursing, is about

$78 a month. Add in the cost of clothes, which have to be replaced every 4 to 6 months as baby grows, and the costs can total up to $5000 in the first year. Shopping at garage sales, thrift shops, and flea markets can reduce the costs for a new bed or a high chair by half. Just remember to check that all items meet the necessary safety standards. Remember, your baby will not care if these items came from a secondhand store or are brand new from a department store.

4. *Child care.* The cost of taking care of your baby when you return to work has to be added to the family budget. The average cost for a day-care center varies from $75 to $200 a week. If you want to qualify for the child-care tax credit, which gives you a maximum deduction of $960 per year, you must use a licensed day-care center that provides you with a tax identification number. Using a neighbor who keeps children in his or her apartment may be more convenient, but the neighbor may not wish to provide a social security number to assist with taking this child-care credit.

3. DIVORCE/BREAKING UP

Forty-five percent of all marriages break up because of money problems. And divorce compounds those money problems. Community property is still the law in nine states, and the laws of equitable distribution apply in most others. The fees for an attorney, the complications of divorce law, the expense of joint child custody, and problems dividing shared assets and pre-owned property have created financial nightmares for many people. Spouses may suddenly start hiding financial assets, close joint accounts, overcharge on credit cards, and secretly sell jointly owned property.

Even if you both want to end the relationship amicably, money discussions can turn the most civilized situation into an expensive bill for arbitration or litigation. Premarital agreements have become more popular with people who are going into second marriages.

4. DEATH

The emotional trauma that occurs when a loved one dies makes it difficult at that time to reach realistic financial decisions. If decisions have not been made about burial versus cremation, people caught in this moment of great stress and anxiety may not realize that the costs can become astronomical. An average funeral runs between $4000 and $8500. Cremation and a memorial service can be done for less than $1500. African-Americans seem to prefer large, showy funerals as a demonstration of respect, esteem, and family pride. The cost of unplanned travel, lodgings, and legal fees for probate of assets can add to the costs of a painful family loss.

When Biddy Mason (1818–1891) left Logtown, Mississippi, in 1847 with her owner, Robert Mason Smith, she and her three children, each fathered by Smith, had no choice but to follow Smith to Utah after Smith decided to convert to Mormonism. Biddy and her children walked the 2000 miles, organizing the cooking in the camp each night; supervising the herd of cows, mules, and oxen; and serving as midwife to three women who gave birth during the 6-month trek.

For 3 years, Biddy and her children lived among the Mormons, enduring the daily insults and outspoken degradation spurred by the Mormon philosophy of black inferiority. In 1851, Smith decided to move to San Bernardino, California, to join a new Mormon community where the weather was more amenable. What Smith did not know until he, Biddy, and the children arrived was that California forbade slave ownership, but that state's law against slavery had never been tested in a court. When Smith learned of the law and the status of his slaves, he hid Biddy and her family in a cave in the Santa Monica Mountains near Los Angeles and kept them isolated until he could make plans to move to Texas, a slave state.

Biddy managed to escape one day and met Robert Owens, a free black man who rescued her family and hid them in his home until he could file a court petition demanding that Biddy and her children be given their freedom. This became the first test case for the new law, which upheld the freedom of Biddy and her family. Biddy remained in California without Robert Smith where she worked as a midwife for several years. She used her savings to buy property and offer decent housing to other free blacks in her neighborhood and made major contributions to establish the first AME church in Los Angeles. In 1872, she opened the first day-care center and community school for African-American children in her neighborhood. She did not open her first bank account until 1880 and always paid cash for each of the properties that she purchased. She had no promises or guarantees offered to her in her life, yet she kept moving toward a goal and ended up as the richest black woman in California.

HOW TO SET FINANCIAL GOALS

A goal is a dream with a date on it.

ANONYMOUS

Where do you want to be in 5 years? In 10 years? Familiar questions that you often hear and ignore since you don't want to consider the answers—or the lack of answers. Too many of us confuse setting a goal with having a guarantee. If we cannot find a promise from someone that we will achieve what we're after and not risk a failure or a shortcoming, then we refuse to even try something new and different. Here are some goals you might consider:

Short-term goals—Anything you want to accomplish within 1 year

- Pay off your credit cards.

- Buy a car.

- Attend the Essence Jazz Festival in New Orleans.

- Treat yourself to a day at Naomi Sims.

- Improve your business wardrobe.

Medium-term goals—What you want to do 2 to 5 years from now

- Go to law school.

- Get married and start a family.

- Buy a house, co-op, condo.

- Plan a family reunion.

- Spend a week shopping in Nassau/St. Thomas.

JOSHUA I. SMITH

CEO of Maxima Corporation
Lanham, Maryland

"When I started teaching high school biology in 1966, I loved the students and was happy with the experience of making a difference in the classroom. Then one day I saw the salary chart. I realized that no matter how good I was, somebody else who didn't know me had already decided how far I could go and how much I was worth. I didn't like that and I got angry." One of eight children, Joshua Smith was born in Kentucky in 1941, shortly before the family moved to Loveland, Ohio. Smith graduated from Central State University, where he got a teaching job and became a counselor in the men's dorm. College teaching didn't satisfy him either. "Tenure is another way of saying, guaranteed to have a job, but guaranteed to stay poor. I knew I wanted to do something else, but I didn't know what."

Smith and his wife moved to Washington, D.C., where he hoped to go to dental school, but Smith gave it up and went back to teaching high school when his marriage developed problems and he was not able to get financial aid. He kept teaching high school, but he was continually searching for new opportunities by doing what everyone now refers to as networking. He joined professional associations, got involved in meeting other professional colleagues of all colors, and discovered the growing new field of computer sciences and information management. Several interviews with headhunters and the support of some of his professional colleagues led to a position as director of one of his professional associations. He was challenged and satisfied for the moment, but not yet fulfilled by his daily work life.

In 1978, when his marriage broke up and with $10,000 from the sale of his house, Smith started Maxima Corporation. What started out with two employees and "more ambition than organization" has now grown into one of the largest black employers on the East Coast in the information services business. Maxima specializes in computer facilities management and systems engineering and has more than 800 employees on its payroll. Maxima has offices in 14 states and services many *Fortune* 500 companies as well as government organizations. Smith didn't wait for a special government program to build his business. "I didn't know there was a minority vendors program until two years after I started Maxima. When we applied for assistance we were immediately accepted because we were well established and clear about the service we were providing. We were in such great demand then, I wasn't ready for how fast we grew, but we adjusted and kept making it happen."

Despite his busy schedule, Smith still finds time to be a frequent speaker to promote economic development and minority business education. As a trustee on many corporate boards, he is a never-ending voice for economic development and black entrepreneurship.

"We all recognize that we have been wronged, but to stay angry is like driving down the road looking through the rearview mirror. The day you get angry is the day you have lost the deal. Getting angry means that you have blown your strategy, and giving in to anger means you don't really have a strategy."

Long-term goals—What you want to do in 10 years

- Pay for a daughter's wedding.
- Learn to do calligraphy and start a greeting card business.
- Take a heritage tour of West Africa.
- Write a book.
- Buy a vacation home.

Now it's time to set some goals.

III≡III *Anytime you see someone more successful than you are, they are doing some-* III≡III
thing you aren't.

MALCOLM X

WHAT DO YOU WANT TO DO BY WHEN?

Choose the goals you want to accomplish from the following list of common goals. On the worksheet in Figure 3-2, write each goal you've chosen and identify when you plan to reach your goal; what it will cost, if anything; how much you've saved toward it to date, if applicable; and how many months remain before you reach your original target date.

Common Goals

Have retirement security	Save for a home
Saving on taxes	Do estate planning
Buy less expensive insurance	Improve current income
Invest	Start a business
Invest for college	Go on vacation

Our ancestors had few choices in what happened in most of their lives, but we do. Take charge of what you want to accomplish and start defining it in ways that you can see. Put a pencil to each of these goals, look at a calendar, and take out your checkbook and savings account books. List some figures next to your choices and begin to explore your financial prospects for making them real.

If you have to, create a goal-reward system as you had when you were a child and worked at getting an A on a spelling test to get an extra dollar to buy an ice cream cone. This time choose a reward that doesn't require you to spend money to feel a sense of accomplishment, like taking a mental health day off from work and going to the park with a friend or browsing through a museum at an exhibit you want to attend. Stay away from bookstores, shopping malls, boutiques, and flea markets!

When you finish filling out Figure 3-2, go on to Figure 3-3.

WORKSHEET

Goal	Target Date	Cost	How Much Saved So Far?	Number of Months to Meet Goal	Must Save Each Month
Vacation	9/98	$1,350	$285	8	$133

Figure 3-2. Tracking your progress toward reaching your goals.

WHAT ARE YOUR FINANCIAL CONCERNS?

Evaluating general financial concerns:
- ( )   Simplifying your budget
- ( )   Stretching your present cashflow:
  - _____ for ordinary expenditures
  - _____ for unusual expenditures (e.g., college)
- ( )   Creating an emergency fund ($_____)
- ( )   Getting out of debt
- ( )   Saving from current income
- ( )   Handling tax matters from prior years
- ( )   Reducing income taxes
- ( )   Keeping financial records

Examining insurance needs:
- ( )   Determining the need for life insurance
- ( )   Buying life insurance economically
- ( )   Determining the need for health insurance
- ( )   Determining the need for disability insurance
- ( )   Buying property and liability insurance economically

Selecting investment targets:
- ( )   Creating an investment portfolio
- ( )   Increasing net worth
- ( )   Evaluating new investment opportunities
- ( )   Managing existing investments
- ( )   Doing succession planning for your business
- ( )   Increasing personal benefits from your business
- ( )   Finding appropriate professional advisors
- ( )   Coordinating the work and communications between your advisors

Accumulating funds for specific purposes:
- ( )   Buying a home
- ( )   Sending a child to college
- ( )   Living during the retirement years
- ( )   Starting a business
- ( )   Making a wedding for child

Figure 3-3. Here are some areas that concern most people at one time or another. Indicate which issues you need to tackle for your financial well-being. If applicable, make a separate copy for your spouse, and each of you complete the form separately. You may have some interesting issues to discuss after you compare your responses.

|||≣||| *You get out what you put in.* |||≣|||

TRADITIONAL SAYING

||||| ||||≣ ||||| ||||≣ ||||| ||||≣||||| ||||≣ ||||| ||||≣ ||||≣||||

4

PUTTING IT ON PAPER—RECORD KEEPING, BUDGETING, AND DEALING WITH TAXES

"Start from the bottom up and work like a son of a gun."

Fats Waller
1950

Harold and Samantha were close as brother and sister as they were growing up in Atlanta, Georgia sharing a comfortable lifestyle and being an emotional support for each other after their parents died. Through various life circumstances, the two siblings had grown apart over the last 20 years. Samantha married a Navy officer, had two children, and moved to San Diego where she taught school and had a busy social life as a working parent. Harold went into the Army, got his education on the GI bill, became a college professor at the University of Pittsburgh, was married briefly and divorced, and had one son. Christmas cards, a few phone calls, and a brief meeting at Harold's son's wedding were all the contact the two managed to have over the years. Harold and Samantha never seemed to be able to spend time together.

An automobile accident put Harold into a coma for several months, and Samantha was contacted as next of kin and told that she would have to manage her brother's affairs until he was well again. After arriving in Pittsburgh, Samantha had no idea where to start and felt like an intruder as she entered

Harold's apartment looking for papers and documents that would help. Fortunately, Harold was a pack rat and held onto every piece of paper that ever passed through his hands. Without too much effort, Samantha was able to find his file of bills and bank accounts and knew when to pay the mortgage on Harold's townhouse, where to make his life insurance payments, what credit card bills had to be taken care of, and which professional advisors to contact about handling his affairs. Six weeks later when Harold finally recovered and returned home, Samantha had been able to maintain the major aspects of his life and keep his affairs in order for him.

Like it or not, your whole life can be documented on paper, and we all leave a paper trail of our affairs as we move from one end of this mortal existence to the other. Every aspect of your life, from your birth certificate and baptismal certificate to your high school diploma, driver's license, social security card, passport, marriage and divorce decrees, and deeds to your house and your cemetery plot, can be traced, documented, analyzed and reconstructed from all the forms of paper that we now have in this computerized society that we live in today. Canceled checks and credit card statements provide the details of where you went for vacation last year and how much you spent, which restaurant is your favorite place to stop off and have dinner at after work, where and when you buy your groceries, where you service your car, and even when you send flowers to a friend or loved one. Records are also critical to allow someone like Samantha to take over and manage your life for you in a crisis.

KEEPING TRACK OF RECORDS: USING FILES AND SAFE DEPOSIT BOXES

A good home record-keeping system should be complete enough to be useful, but simple enough for you to use on a regular basis. Your accountant will also love you, and it will probably save you money if you can go to him or her every year with organized files and receipts in neatly arranged categories. A good record-keeping system can also accomplish several other things.

- It gets important information out of your head and into some organized format that you and your family can find in an emergency.

- It eliminates the stress and aggravation of searching for little bits of paper.

- It simplifies the day-to-day process of keeping records.

- It gives you the satisfaction of knowing that everything is within easy reach and you can get a document at a moment's notice.

- You can save time and money on expensive legal and financial procedures. For example, if you want to sell your house or your car but can't find the deed or the title, it may be very expensive and time-consuming to try to replace it.

First, think of all the documents that are important for you. Everyone knows about keeping records for income tax purposes. But you should also document your bank accounts, credit cards, insurance policies, marriage licenses and divorce papers, birth certificates, wills, and mortgage documents. Vital family and financial records usually fall into three categories:

1. Permanent papers that you should keep all your life

2. Temporary receipts that will be needed for a few months or for a year or two

3. Long-term semipermanent records that you will probably need for about 5 to 10 years

You need four items to make your record system work:

1. A desk ledger or file for active current papers and receipts that you may receive on a regular weekly or monthly basis and have to refer to quite often. This is your active file.

2. A notebook for keeping a summary of important records and documents.

3. A file cabinet for any out-of-date records, old canceled checks, back tax statements, or paid-up loan agreements that are more than 5 years old. This is your inactive, or dead, file.

4. A safe deposit box for one-of-a-kind documents—passports, stock certificates—and irreplaceable items, including old photographs of great-grandparents and family jewelry. Keep in the safe deposit box photographs of the contents of your house along with the fire insurance policy. For any original document that you do not want to keep in a safe deposit box, buy a fireproof storage box with a good lock on it.

The diary of William Johnson (1809–1851) is a meticulous record of the life of a free Negro businessman in Natchez, Mississippi. Johnson was a freed slave whose mother, Amy, was a peddler selling trinkets and dry goods from a street cart. He grew up assisting her with the daily rounds of managing her wagon. In 1829, Johnson started an apprenticeship as a barber and began recording the details of his life in a series of daybooks, ledgers, and journals that documented an active and successful business life. He opened the largest barbershop in Mississippi and became successful at many forms of trade. The entries for a vacation in New Orleans in 1831 read:

> *July 14—paid $10.00 for steamboat passage to New Orleans.*
>
> *July 15—bought fruit, lottery ticket, cloth for shop, soda water. $14.00.*
>
> *July 19—hired two carriages for $12.00 and drove the 'Ladys' to the 'Lake' for dinner. Paid $3.00 and bought two watermelons on the way home.*
>
> *July 21—went to the Lake again with 'Ladys.' Met Miss Mary Gatewood. Spent $3.00 for dinner.*
>
> *July 23—bought liquor, soda water, oranges, paid a 'bathing fee' at lake and played billiards. Won $3.00.*

Aug. 5—spent $1.25 for a silk handkerchief for Miss Gatewood.

Aug. 11—crossed the river, with the 'Ladys' spent $9.50 on playing billiards, bought whiskey, wine and music box gift for Miss Gatewood.

Aug. 13—took steamboat back to Natchez, $10.00. Hired drayman to haul trunk up hill to house, $2.00.

Total month in New Orleans cost $135.87½.

A long correspondence with Miss Gatewood continued for more than a year, but Johnson married Ann Battles on April 21, 1835. When he first met her, he recorded in his journal that she did laundry and earned $4.00 a week. His wedding coat cost him $48.87½. The new experience of marriage distracted Johnson for several months because there were no entries in the journal again until October 12, 1835, when he purchased 162 acres of land at $4.12 per acre.

SETTING UP FILES

Begin by setting up an active file of current records. This file will include anything that has to do with your current budget and your present financial life. Start simple. Get a record-keeping book from a stationery store. You can also get a budget book and set up a list of your current accounts. While you are at the stationery store, you can also pick up about 20 small file folders and labels or perhaps a cardboard box file. You can use some files for your current unpaid bills. And you can store receipts in others.

Now there is no point in keeping all receipts indefinitely for everything that you've purchased. However, some department stores won't take anything back, ever, unless you have the receipt. So if you've ordered furniture, or any large items to be delivered, keep the receipt until the item has been delivered. In case there's damage, you have to prove when you bought the item and when you received it. Be sure, though, to save the instruction booklets and warranty cards on any appliances that you purchase. Not only do they tell you how to operate the appliances, but the addresses and phone numbers of repair centers are usually listed there.

All your insurance policies should be documented in a notebook and kept in one place. Homeowner's and auto insurance policies should be kept on file in an obvious place. You may receive a new policy each year, but save the old ones for reference. Health insurance, life insurance, and disability policies should always be kept in a safe but accessible place so that you can easily refer to them and know what coverage you have. Personal liability policies are usually a part of your homeowner's policy. Keep them in an obvious place, too.

Your employer is supposed to supply you with an employee benefits booklet. This booklet includes information about your retirement plan, any health insurance that is provided by the job, and benefits records. The documents should be kept in a strong box, along with information on where your other assets are invested. All retirement accounts, anything having to do with annuities, and pension profit-sharing plans, should be kept in a file regarding retirement.

Employee and education records should be kept in a separate file. These include transcripts from college, graduation diplomas, certificates, professional permits, business licenses, résumés, and any union memberships. Set up a file recording all the personal loans and mortgage agreements you may be paying. School loans and installment purchase agreements should also be kept in your current file. When you have made all the payments on a loan, you should have a copy of the statement from the creditor proving that it has been paid and keep this on record for at least 3 to 5 years.

Finally, any documents of ownership regarding your home, the title, the survey, the deed, and a copy of the name, the address, and the telephone number of the title insurance company should be kept on record in a separate file.

III≡III *By patience and hard work, we brought order out of chaos, just as will be true*   III≡III
of any problem if we stick to it with patience and wisdom and earnest effort.
BOOKER T. WASHINGTON
Up from Slavery

MAKING A NOTEBOOK

Start a notebook that summarizes all this information. This notebook can be useful for several purposes. It will be your master list of important account numbers and policy numbers that you can find very quickly if you have to. It's also much easier to replace a lost insurance policy if you have the policy number at your fingertips. Using a notebook also makes it possible to update and change the information quickly, because you can just remove one page at a time. Your notebook should contain the following information:

1. Each family member should be listed with his or her social security number, date of birth, driver's license number, and any special health information that would be critical to know about that person, perhaps indicating blood type, recent medical history, past operations, and any allergies. You may also want to record where each person works and how he or she can be reached in case of an emergency. This is an especially good idea if some of the family members live in different cities.

2. Bank accounts and investment accounts should be listed in the notebook along with the name of the banks, their locations, the account numbers, and each branch manager's name if possible. Do this with each and every account—savings accounts, checking accounts, investment accounts. Keep the passbooks in a safe but obvious place.

3. Insurance policies, including the policy numbers and the name and phone number of each insurance agent, should be itemized.

4. A recent net worth statement listing all your assets and how they are owned would also be useful in this book. This can help you if you ever want to apply for a bank loan or a credit card. If you need to discuss some aspect of your financial status with your accountant or your attorney—the notebook would be easier to carry to the meeting than a large file of documents. Your family will also know where to look in case you're suddenly hit by a car and disabled.

5. CDs, money market accounts, mutual fund accounts, and all brokerage accounts can be listed on one page. The account numbers and the phone number of your broker should also be included there. If you wish, you can also itemize the securities or bonds you own.

6. Credit and charge card account numbers should be itemized on a page. The account numbers and the telephone number of each creditor should be listed in case the cards are lost or stolen. If the credit cards are held in more than one name, that should also be noted.

7. Magazine and newspaper subscriptions should be listed, with the phone number of the publication's circulation department in case you have to cancel.

8. Business and financial advisors can be included on a separate page. List the names of your accountant, your attorney, your medical doctor, and perhaps a minister or priest. List the name, address, and phone number of anyone who should be contacted in case of an emergency. This may be a best friend or a business associate.

How do you get all this done without driving yourself crazy? Well, don't try to get it all done at once. This is a job that can take several months, so approach it in small doses. Include this task as one of the special things that you do for yourself on a regular basis, just as you would get a haircut or do your nails. Decide that once a week for an hour you'll sit down and go through that box that's been in the closet for the last few years and see what's there that should be kept. Don't get sidetracked by looking at old photographs and reading old love letters. You'll never finish once you start that. Remember, try to have fun with this, and add whatever categories you feel would satisfy your own needs. It's your money. They're your papers. It's your life. Putting your records in order allows you to begin to put your finances in order.

SAFE DEPOSIT BOX

Safe deposit boxes are convenient and inexpensive storage facilities provided by banks and savings and loan associations. The cost of the service varies according to the size of the box, and the rent is billed to you once a year. In most banks the fee varies from $25 a year up to $95. If you keep large balances in the bank, you may even be lucky enough to get a box at no charge. The rental fee is deductible each year on your tax return as a miscellaneous item if you keep investment records in the box. Two keys are needed to get into the box. You keep one and the bank keeps one. Whenever you need access to your box, you go to the bank and sign in. The bank clerk will verify your signature and record on the ledger sheet the date and time that you were there. Next the bank clerk will use your key and the bank's key to open the "door" to the safe deposit box and then will give you your box. Several rooms are available for you to choose from, where you can open your box and go through the contents in privacy.

The safe deposit box should contain the following items: birth certificates, adoption papers, marriage licenses, divorce papers, passports, military discharge papers, citizenship documents, trust agreements, and duplicate copies of wills. Your attorney should keep the original copy of any wills. You could also include in the safe deposit box the deed to the house, the car title, any stock and bond certificates you may own, and an inventory of the contents of the house. You should get a certified appraisal from an art dealer of any special items that you own, like antiques or coin and stamp collections, that you may have at home or even keep in the safe deposit box. Make a photographic record of all the contents of your house. You will definitely be glad you have this if you have to file a claim with your homeowner's insurance company. Include photographs of valuable items such as antiques, paintings, jewelry, furs, and anything else that may have to be documented to prove ownership for insurance purposes. If anyone owes you money, then, by all means, keep a record of that IOU in the box. You should record the terms of the loan, the amount of it, the payment dates, the interest, and the name and address of the person who owes you.

|||≡|| *Save money and money will save you.* |||≡|||

JAMAICAN PROVERB

YOUR SPENDING PLAN
(AKA THE "B" WORD: BUDGET)

If the word *budget* makes you nervous, call it your *monthly money plan*. Call it a *spending plan*, a *financial road map*, or a *money diet*—whatever you can swallow—but this is where you have to start. This is not an exercise in deprivation, but rather an opportunity to make intelligent choices. Your budget allows you to work toward getting rid of the illusions and mysteries about where your money goes and why you don't have any. The purpose of a budget is to see clearly where your money is coming from and where it is going. It will allow you to set some savings and investing priorities.

Another major purpose budgeting serves in your life is to let you anticipate future expenses and prepare for them. If you know that you have to pay your homeowner's insurance of $400 once a year in June, then you should be putting aside money for that at least 6 to 8 months ahead of time. It's easier to set aside $50 a month for 8 months rather than have to scramble for it at the last minute and risk having your policy canceled for late payment.

Do whatever you have to in order to get started. It will cost you about $10 for the basics—a pencil or a pen, a yellow pad or a $3.98 budget book from a stationery store, and a $5 pocket calculator. Or you can get fancy with a new $40 software program from Quicken, Microsoft, or IBM. One of the best and simplest to use is *Anybody Can Do It: Home Budgeting* by Rex Johnson. The book and software are $16.95 from King Lizard Publications, (800) 327-5113.

Do whatever works for you but you have to lay it out on the page so you can see exactly where you are before you can decide where you want to go. You cannot set or complete any financial goals until you can face the numbers on the page. Meanwhile, your life is stuck in financial chaos with no clear direction or determination about how to clear it up.

|||≡||| *Success in life revolves around recognizing and using our abilities, our 'raw* |||≡|||
material.'

DR. BENJAMIN CARSON
Gifted Hands

CREATING A SUMMARY OF ASSETS

Start by making a list of everything you own that has a dollar value. Putting it on paper makes you get honest with yourself. Begin by listing your bank account. How much cash do you have there as of today's date (or your last bank statement)? Next list what you have in savings. Write down everything including credit union accounts, CDs, money-market accounts, savings bonds, mutual funds, and government securities.

In listing the assets you have, place a check next to the ones that earn interest or dividends and include the interest rate earned on each account. If you hold securities, include each annual dividend rate.

Look at your life insurance policies. If you have a whole-life or universal-life policy, call your insurance agent and ask for a current statement of its cash value. How much money would be returned to you if you canceled the policy today?

If you own a house, co-op apartment, or condominium, what is the current value of the property? A real estate broker can give you an idea, or you can look in the classified ads for similar real estate for sale in your neighborhood.

As for your car, boat, or computer, find the trade-in value by calling a bank or the dealer you bought it from. Check the classified ads for similar items.

Don't forget about IRA accounts, annuities, and the current value of your company retirement plan. Your employer should give you a copy of your pension statement each year, including the current value and how much has been earned.

Next, make a list of all your personal property. Include your clothing, furniture, books, stereo, kitchen equipment—everything in the house. Don't list the purchase price of the items, though; personal items like these are worth less than half of what you paid for them—even though you may have bought them just a month ago. They decline in value each year and generally must be replaced every 3 to 5 years. If you want to find out the truth about what that diamond bracelet and fur coat will get you in a crunch, go down to the local pawnbroker and see what he or she will offer you for it in cash.

Pawnshops, or "collateral brokers" as they now call themselves, are the fastest-growing cash businesses in the United States—they even have stocks trading on the American Stock Exchange and NASDAQ. The interest you must pay to retrieve what you've pawned varies from state to state, but runs from 3 percent a month in New York State to as high as 21 percent a month in Texas, and the average "loan" is $60. Make sure that you are desperate for cash when you go into one of these places and that you won't feel disappointed if you can't get the cash you need to redeem the items they are holding.

Continue this personal inventory until you have included everything you can remember. After you put a dollar figure next to each item, add the list up. This is your *summary of assets*. Which items do you think will continue to increase in value? Look over the list and divide your assets into two categories: those that are growing in value and those that are losing value each year.

To reveal exactly where you've been putting your money (a frightening but liberating revelation), answer the following questions:

- Where are most of your assets?

- How much income or value are they earning for you each year?

- Are your assets keeping up with inflation?

- After you pay taxes on dividend and/or interest income each year, does the income exceed the inflation rate?

This is the real total return on your investment.

‖≡‖ *If it's on your back, it's not in the bank. If it's on your ass, it's not called an* ‖≡‖
asset.

JOSHUA I. SMITH
Maxima Corporation

CREATING A SUMMARY OF LIABILITIES

Let's bring a picture of your debts into view. It's probably not as grim as your anxieties tell you, and even if it is, before you can reduce your debts, you must recognize them and, hopefully, save yourself from making the same mistakes again.

Your debts are your liabilities. Answer these questions as completely as possible:

- What are the current balances on your credit card accounts?

- Have you borrowed against your life insurance?

- Do you still have student loans outstanding?

- What do you owe Uncle Sam? Don't forget to consider accrued interest and penalties for overdue taxes.

Just as you did for your assets, make a list of your liabilities. To the left of each debt item, note the current interest rate. If you have cosigned a loan for someone close to you, you should consider this potential debt. Don't forget about car loans, your mortgage, and leasing payments. One last item: Remember loans from the family. Your family came through for you and trusted you to pay them back when you asked for that emergency money, so even if they're patient and haven't asked yet, put them on the list of debtors and respect their support for you.

Okay, add it all up and subtract this amount from your summary of assets. The remaining figure equals your *net worth*. This is what you would have if you suddenly had to liquidate all your belongings to pay all your debts. How does it look?

If it's a negative figure, you are living beyond your means, using credit to finance your lifestyle. Like too many other Americans, you may find that you're working hard each day to support banks, department stores, and the federal government. Use the balance sheet in Figure 4-1 to list all your assets and liabilities.

‖≡‖   *Everything costs a lot of money when you don't have any.*   ‖≡‖

JOE LOUIS
c. 1965

WHERE DOES YOUR MONEY COME FROM AND WHERE DOES IT GO?

Use the budget worksheets in Figures 4-2 and 4-3 to set up the categories to see where your money is coming from, but most of all you want to

BALANCE SHEET

_____ _____ 19 _____

ASSETS Everything you own that has cash value.

CASH Money you have on hand. Include cash at home, today's checking and savings account balances. $ _____

TIME DEPOSITS Funds deposited for a specified period of time, such as a certificate of deposit (CD). $ _____

STOCKS, BONDS, OTHER SECURITIES U.S. Savings Bonds, Treasury issues, other money market and stock market investments. Check your records for documentation of current holdings. Current market value for some types of securities may be found in newspaper financial pages; for others, contact your broker. $ _____

CASH SURRENDER VALUE LIFE INSURANCE Investment or equity built up in your life insurance policy; not face value. Find the cash surrender value from the chart on your policy. $ _____

ACCOUNTS RECEIVABLE Money owed to you for goods and services. Check files for items outstanding. $ _____

NOTES RECEIVABLE Money owed to you and documented by promissory notes. Check your records for the balance of any note due you. $ _____

REBATES/REFUNDS Money owed to you for refundable deposits, sales or tax refunds, or rebates. Check your files for receipts and your most recent 1040 income tax form. $ _____

AUTOS/OTHER VEHICLES Trucks, trailers, motorcycles, campers, boats, and airplanes. Vehicle dealers and some libranes carry special price books such as the Kelley Blue Book for new and used automobiles. If no published information is available, dealers may be able to estimate the current market value. $ _____

REAL ESTATE Any land and/or structures on the land. Also, legal rights you may have to resources in the land: growing crops, water, minerals, etc. For an estimate of the current market value, contact a local real estate agent or hire a professional appraiser. $ _____

VESTED PENSION Nonforfeitable rights to benefits you accumulate after a certain time under your employer's pension plan or your own pension plan (Keogh), if you're self-employed. If you're covered under your employer's plan, ask the plan administrator for the current amount of your vested benefits. $ _____

INDIVIDUAL RETIREMENT ACCOUNT An account you establish that provides retirement benefits for you. Record your account balance. $ _____

OTHER ASSETS Any property other than real estate that has cash value, estimated in terms of what it is worth today. To find an item's value, check classified ads for comparable items or get estimates from dealers or special appraisers.

Home furnishings/household goods/appliances $ _____

Hobby/sports equipment $ _____

Art/antiques/collections/jewelry/furs $ _____

Trade/professional tools and equipment $ _____

Livestock/pets for show or breeding $ _____

Trusts/patents/memberships/interest in estate $ _____

Interest in business/farm/commercial operation/investment club (whole or part ownership) $ _____

TOTAL ASSETS $ _____

LIABILITIES What you owe: your debts.

ACCOUNTS PAYABLE Total balance of what you owe today on bills for goods and services (such as doctor bills) and credit card and charge accounts. A credit card company or store usually lists your account's total balance due on the monthly statement mailed to you. If you do not have these records, contact the credit department of firms where you have accounts. $ _____

CONTRACTS PAYABLE Total remaining balance on installment credit contracts for goods such as a car, furniture, appliances, or services of someone working for you under contract. To figure the total amount due, multiply your monthly payment by the number of months remaining on the contract. $ _____

NOTES PAYABLE Total balance due on cash loans, both secured and unsecured. Contact the office where you received the loan if you don't have these figures. $ _____

TAXES Federal and state income taxes or property taxes due now (including any that are past due). Do not list property taxes if they are automatically included with your mortgage payments or income taxes if they are automatically withheld. If you're self-employed, you should include any Social Security taxes due. Check your income or property tax statements. $ _____

REAL ESTATE LOANS Balance you owe on deeds of trust (mortgages) on your property. Contact the office where you received the loan if you don't have these figures. Also list any liens on property that you are liable for and must pay. $ _____

OTHER LIABILITIES Court-ordered judgments of payments you must make, lawsuit settlements, past-due accounts, etc. $ _____

TOTAL LIABILITIES $ _____

CONTINGENT LIABILITIES Debts you may or may not owe sometime in the future. If you cosigned a note and the other signer doesn't pay, you may be responsible for paying the debt. If a suit is pending against you, you may be liable to pay a settlement. $ _____

NET WORTH Your assets minus your liabilities.

ASSETS $ _____

MINUS LIABILITIES − $ _____

NET WORTH $ _____

To check your figures, make sure:
Assets = Liabilities + Net Worth

Figure 4-1. Balance sheet.

Primary income

Paycheck (after taxes)	$_____
Self-employment income	$_____
Unemployment	$_____
Off-the-books	$_____

Secondary income

Interest from savings	$_____
Dividends on investment	$_____
Credit card cash advances	$_____
Rental property return	$_____
Insurance claims	$_____
Pension	$_____
Social security	$_____
Annuities, IRAs, etc.	$_____
Gifts	$_____
Other	$_____

Figure 4-2. Where does your money come from each month?

see where it is going on a monthly basis and also on a yearly basis. To see where your money is coming from, list your various sources of income. Start with your paycheck; that's the obvious one. Also include your interest income, any dividends, and income you collect from rental property that you own. Don't forget to add in your year-end bonus if you get one. Do you do any freelance work? Do you get child support? Well, include those too. Add them all up and see what percentage is coming from where. The average working person has at least 90 percent of his or her income coming solely from a paycheck.

Where does your money go? Think of the major spending categories:

- Housing (include utilities and telephone)

- Food

- Clothing

- Transportation

- Insurance

Fixed payments: Payments for the same amount which must be made each month (or quarterly, annually, etc.) with or without income.

Rent/mortgage payments $_____
Car payment $_____

Loans:

Personal loans $_____
Student loans $_____
Other $_____

Insurance:

Health $_____
Disability $_____
Homeowner's $_____
Other $_____

Payroll deductions:

Insurance $_____
Pension $_____
Savings $_____

Flexible payments: Necessities that vary in cost from month to month, year to year

Food $_____
Clothing $_____
Laundry/dry cleaning $_____

Utilities:

Telephone $_____
Electricity and gas $_____
Personal grooming $_____

Transportation:

Gas and oil $_____
Taxis, bus, subway, railroad $_____

Medical Expenses: (not covered by insurance)

Dentist $_____
Therapist $_____
Other $_____
Savings $_____
Real estate/property tax $_____
Other $_____

Discretionary spending: Modifiable luxury items

Eating out $_____
Vacations/weekend trips $_____
General entertainment:

Movies $_____
Books/magazines: $_____
Courses, seminars, workshops $_____
Maid service $_____
Charitable contributions $_____
Other $_____

Figure 4-3. Where does your money go each month?

Of these primary expenses, some are fixed and some are flexible. Fixed expenses are those that must be paid whether or not there is income, e.g., your rent or mortgage payment, car loan, child support. The amount is the same each month.

Flexible expenses include those that need regular attention, but the amount varies. These expenses can be divided into two types: basic lifestyle spending and discretionary spending. Basic spending includes the telephone bill and utility bills, plus food and transportation costs. Of course, there's also parking and day care, and don't forget the kids' allowance.

The chiropractor, dentist, or therapist fees, not covered by your insurance, are also considered basic flexible expenses. So are laundry and dry cleaning expenses and property taxes.

Your discretionary expenditures are recurring expenses over which you have a good deal of control. These include expenses for eating out, vacations, gifts, etc. The amount and the timing of these expenses offer you an opportunity to cut back when necessary.

Now turn to the worksheets "Where Does Your Money Come From?" and "Where Does Your Money Go?" in Figures 4-2 and 4-3. Pick up a sharp pencil, find your calculator—and your patience—and begin doing some figuring and setting some guidelines.

If your discretionary spending totals more than 30 percent of your net monthly income, then you can reduce some of your spending and maintain your lifestyle. The difference can be best used for long-term goals and investments.

If you want to look at the trend of your spending over a longer period of time, you can use the same format to review your expenses for the last 6 or 9 months. Take out your pay stubs, canceled checks, credit card statements, and bank statements for the last 6 to 9 months. Use the worksheet in Figure 4-3 or a standard ledger sheet and record the various spending categories.

Your credit card statement will tell you what you have charged and what was really a necessity. Your bank statement will tell you how many times you went to the cash machine and what you withdrew on average. You will also see if you have written too many checks and if your account is frequently overdrawn. Do you see a pattern here? Have you been spending too much money repairing your 6-year-old car when it may not be worth saving? Are you depositing money in your savings account only to withdraw it to keep up with your credit card bills?

To see exactly where your money goes every day, keep a money diary. Pick up a pocket-size blank book to keep a record of each expense: cab fares, newspapers, lunches, haircuts, movies, even that Snickers bar or after-work cocktail. Here's a typical example of a single day's spending.

Brooke's Money Diary

Subway/bus fare to work	$1.50
Newspaper	$0.50
Magazine	$1.95
Coffee and muffin	$1.75
Postage stamps	$6.40
Lunch	$5.75
Drugstore—shampoo, pantyhose, aspirin	$9.53
Birthday card	$1.75
Subway/bus fare home	$1.50
Dry cleaning	$8.50
Groceries	$9.71
Total	$48.84

Don't be discouraged. You can look at your budget as a road map to guide you where you want to be. Fill out Figure 4-4. Remember, the way to increase your net worth each year is by budgeting for future wealth. The return on investing for your future will allow you more freedom to experience what brings you joy.

Where Will My Money Be a Year from Now?

Income	Jan.	Feb.	March	April	May	June	July	Aug.	Sept.	Oct.	Nov.	Dec.	Total
Salary													
Consulting fees													
Bonus													
Profit sharing													
Commission													
Stock dividends													
Interest (all sources)													
Rental income													
Capital gains													
Other													
Total income													

Figure 4-4. Money planning chart.

How Will I Get There?

Uses of Income													
Saving/investment													
Mortgage/rent													
Utilities													
Insurance premiums													
Loan payments													
Credit card payments													
Taxes													
Food													
Transportation													
Clothing/personal													
Medical													
Child care													
Entertainment													
Vacations													
Meals													
Cleaning													
Repairs													
Other													
Total expenditures													

Figure 4-4. (*Cont.*)

81

CAZEMBE BEKTEMBE, CPA

Partner, Bektembe & Bediako
New York and New Jersey

Sitting in his office in the City Hall area of Manhattan, surrounded by computers, tax forms, and ledger sheets, Bektembe looks younger than his years behind the beard and bright smile. Bektembe has been serving African-American clients as a certified public accountant for more than 15 years after graduating from Baruch College and spending several years doing his initial professional training at Peat-Marwick, one of the Big Eight accounting firms in the United States. He went into private partnership with his colleague Barudi Bediako, another Peat-Marwick veteran, in 1980. When he isn't staring down a spreadsheet, Bektembe is teaching future accountants at a local university and doing volunteer work with a Junior Achievement program in Harlem—Cazembe's way of supporting the financial education needs of young African-Americans.

Most African-Americans look upon financial planning as what should we do once a crisis occurs, and the crisis is usually too much debt or a letter from the IRS asking for an audit. We are so terrified of anything to do with the government that we go out of our way to avoid any contact with the IRS, assuming that avoiding them will keep you out of trouble. By then, it's too late to do much except figure out how you can negotiate a payment plan or avoid having your paycheck garnisheed. Some clients have unrealistic expectations of being owed a refund even when they aren't because everyone else they know is getting one and they got one last year.

Bektembe's five tax recommendations for African-Americans are:

1. Be more proactive in learning what your rights are in dealing with the IRS. Paying more than you should does not win you any brownie points or save you any aggravation if you do make a mistake next year.

2. Stop waiting until after December 31 to plan for filing. It's too late to make any useful decision that will have an impact on your situation by then.

3. When you file each April, find out what you could have done differently to get more back from the IRS.

4. Stop using the IRS as a forced savings plan and stop looking at the refund as a gift. It's your own money and you're giving a free loan to Uncle Sam. They wouldn't do the same for you, so stop being so generous with the government.

5. Hire someone to do your taxes who will educate you and be there for you to explain the deductions. Remember, you are responsible for the final numbers although the accountant put them together.

"Show me a person's financial situation and I can tell you what their family background is. The numbers on the balance sheet, the budget and the tax forms reflect the behavior and the choices made. Saving and investing, even on a small scale has never been a big thing for us, but the high credit card interest paid shows that spending is the biggest financial investment we make. We have to learn to be financially accountable one person at a time for the decisions we make with money, for our children's sake and for the future of any economic development. Until we absorb that idea, we're lost."

DEALING WITH TAXES

In 1976, the *Guinness Book of World Records* listed Annie Turnbo Malone (1869–1957) as the world's first self-made woman millionaire, yet most African-Americans have no idea who she was and what she accomplished. Malone was the tenth of eleven children, born in Metropolis, Illinois, and orphaned shortly thereafter. She was raised by an older sister in the town of Lovejoy, Illinois. Malone dropped out of high school after tenth grade because of an extended illness and never graduated. During her illness, she became fascinated with finding a way to treat her sister's hair; her sister, like most African-American women of the period, used harsh soaps, goose fat, and heavy oils to smooth out the kinks and treat dry scalp.

Malone found a way to make hair preparations that were lighter and cleaner than what was available and that gave a nice sheen and texture to the hair. In 1900, she rented a small room in the back of an office building, paying $5 a month for the space, and started selling her "Wonderful Hair Grower." She had also worked with a blacksmith to make an iron comb she had read about that was being used by French women to straighten their hair. Public demand for the product was so great that within two years Malone moved from Illinois to a storefront on Market Street in St. Louis and hired three assistants to go door-to-door demonstrating the use of the comb and selling her products.

In honor of the St. Louis World's Fair, Malone expanded her business by initiating a national advertising campaign in black newspapers throughout the country, and she undertook an extensive marketing tour of the South demonstrating her products and her hair-care technique. In 1905, she expanded her warehouse and took on five times as many sales assistants, including a Sarah Breedlove, who later became known as Madame C. J. Walker, another hair-care millionaire and chief competitor of Malone.

There were so many imitators of her products over the next few years that she finally copyrighted her system and her products under the name "Poro," which is a West African word meaning a discipline devoted to physical beauty and well-being. In 1910, Malone's beauty product line included cosmetics and skin-care products. She opened the Poro College of Beauty and Culture in St. Louis at 3100 Pine Street, which grew into a complex of buildings where students trained in hair and skin care for women of color. The Poro Complex, constructed at a cost of $1 million, was a social and entertainment center for black St. Louis. It included a bakery, a restaurant, an auditorium, guest rooms, and a dormitory for students who came from all over the United States to learn the Poro System.

Malone also became famous for her generosity by giving lavish donations to hospitals, churches, schools, and other organizations such as Howard University Medical School, the NAACP, the St. Louis Colored Orphans' Home, and the Phillis Wheatley Branch of the YWCA. Her employees received expensive Christmas gifts from her, and it was not uncommon for a 5-year employee to get a diamond watch as an anniversary present. At the peak of her business empire in 1924, Malone had 75,000 agents affiliated with her through the Poro College of Beauty in the United States and the Caribbean islands. In 1926, Malone paid $38,467 in personal income taxes. This was at a time when the average schoolteacher was working for $100 a month. All of the real estate, the businesses, and the product line she owned were valued at over $14 million in 1932—during the time of the Great Depression!

The hard work and ingenuity that Annie Malone had put into building a successful business empire eventually came to nothing when her empire fell apart because of three incidents of litigation and financial conflict: (1) The first incident involved a dishonest business manager, whom she had hired without a written agreement. She had caught him stealing business funds within a few months of putting him on her payroll and fired him. The manager sued her and presented a fraudulent contract claiming that he had been given a 2-year contract and a percentage of the business. Malone settled out of court for $50,000. (2) During divorce proceedings, her husband, Aaron Malone, whom she married in 1914, tried to claim that he had started and built up the business. The divorce became a national scandal in the Negro press and took 2 years of litigation to be resolved when Malone bought him off for $200,000. (3) The final blow was dealt by the IRS. Malone would not pay any of the federal excise taxes that were levied against her products until she was taken to court several times. Every year, from 1933 until 1951, Malone was in and out of the Federal District Tax Court in St. Louis and Chicago because she would not pay her taxes. By 1951, her legal and financial affairs had become such a bungled mess that the Internal Revenue Service attached her property and sold it at auction for back taxes. The previous year the buildings had been valued at $5 million, and it is rumored that the tax bill was less than $500,000. At the end of her life, Malone had less than $100,000 left in her estate.

|||≣||| *There are only two things to fear in this life. God and the IRS. God will forgive* |||≣|||
you but the IRS won't.
ANONYMOUS

A WORD ABOUT TAXES

A common tax mistake many people make is to pay too much money to the IRS through payroll withholding taxes each year. Some people do this by accident. Some do it deliberately using the IRS as a savings account and looking forward to a huge tax refund of $1200 to $1500 every April to pay for a vacation or summer event. *Dumb!* You're giving the government a free loan of your money—do you think the government would do that little favor for you?

Taxes have been around since the beginning of recorded time—even the Bible documents the existence of the tax collector. And after all is said and done, the IRS will still be around collecting a portion of whatever little estate that we will have to leave to our heirs. We cannot escape taxes, but we can learn about whatever legal means there are available to hang onto as much as possible of our hard-earned dollars. This is called tax planning. It is the job of the IRS to get the money out of you, not to educate you when you overpay. It is your responsibility to learn your legal rights and remedies.

The Tax Reform Act of 1986 changed many of the rules, eliminated familiar deductions, and redefined income. Income now has three categories:

1. Active income—salary, commissions, and tips

2. Investment income—dividends and interest

3. Passive income—income from limited partnerships and any business activity in which the taxpayer performs no active management role

Regardless of the source, all income is now taxed as ordinary income. A lower capital gains tax is still being debated in Congress, but that discussion has gone back and forth since the last tax reform bill of 1986, and so far the rules still have not changed, so don't wait for it to happen any time soon. If you're in the 31 percent tax bracket, from January through April you're under Uncle Sam's thumb. And for state and local taxes you continue to work until approximately May 5, labeled by accountants as Tax Freedom Day.

TAX PLANNING RECOMMENDATIONS

The two major tax planning recommendations to every taxpayer are retirement planning and tax-free investing.

1. Retirement plans, such as 401(k)s, SEPs, Keoghs, and profit-sharing plans.

Take advantage of any form of deferred income that can reduce your current income tax liability and build a future nest egg. IRAs are still a good idea if your employer doesn't have a pension plan. You may still be eligible for the IRA deduction. If you are eligible, ask your accountant about keeping separate records for the deductible and nondeductible IRAs.

2. Tax-free investing, such as taxable yield versus tax-free income. This is a good idea if you are in a high enough income bracket that it matters to you to get tax-free income.

Keep in mind that tax-free income is not growth-oriented. You save on taxes, but you don't exceed inflation with the return that you receive on tax-free investments. Keeping good records such as canceled checks, credit card statements, and charitable contribution receipts is your responsibility, not your accountant's. These records should be saved for up to 5 years—in case of an audit.

	Equivalent Taxable Yield		
	Tax Bracket		
Tax-free Interest	**15%**	**28%**	**31%**
6%	7.06%	8.44%	8.96%
8%	9.41%	11.11%	11.94%
10%	11.76%	13.96%	14.93%
12%	14.12%	16.67%	17.91%

The best investment you can make to learn about taxes is to call the IRS and order a copy of Publication 17, a free guidebook (your tax dollars have already paid for it!) that is published each year. It explains the changes that have been made, the new forms that have been created, and they way each form should be filled out. The toll-free number for ordering from the IRS is in Appendix B.

Finally, here is a list of frequently overlooked deductions to consider when you do your taxes.

Abortions	Estate administration expenses	Support hose (prescribed)
Accounting fees		
Acupuncture treatments	Electrolysis	Safe deposit box fees
	False teeth	Special diets (prescribed)
Addiction/alcohol therapy	Investment expenses	Telephone calls to psychologist
	Legal fees (medically related)	
Birth control pills		Therapy
Contact lens insurance	Medical supplies	Vitamins (prescribed)
Dues and subscriptions (work-related)	Nursing fees	Whirlpool baths (prescribed)
	Special mattresses (prescribed)	

SMART TAX MOVES TO FOLLOW ALL YEAR LONG

1. Review your taxes early. Start in June, September, or October, but don't wait until January to think about what you need to file for the previous year. Marriage, divorce, self-employment, unemployment—all these events affect your taxable income as they occur, so don't wait until after December 31 to find out how they affect you. By then it's too late to make any helpful decisions about how to handle income and deductions.

2. Keep accurate records for your donations. The rules have changed on taking tax deductions for charitable contributions. Canceled checks alone are no longer adequate proof if the amount you contributed was $250 or more. You need a signed receipt from the charity stating the amount you gave and whether you received something—theater tickets, a benefit dinner—in exchange for your donation. You must reduce your write-off by the value of whatever you received. If you do monthly tithing to your church in $50 a month installments, then your canceled checks are acceptable. Raffle receipts, theater stubs, and money order carbons are not accepted as proof of payment.

3. Do your state taxes before the end of the calendar year. Meet with your tax preparer in December to see if you will owe any state or local taxes from interest income, self-employment income, or a change in marital status, and pay them before December 31. Then you will have a deduction on your federal taxes when you file in April. If you were lucky enough to get a tax refund on your state taxes the previous year, guess what? Yep, that refund is now taxable income on your federal return.

4. File jointly if you are married. Many African-American couples choose to file separate returns in the same way they may keep separate checking accounts, but this is usually the most expensive way to go. Almost always, filing jointly will save extra dollars. Still you should review your filing status each year as your income changes. If one spouse has a very low income and extremely high medical deductions, it may be wise to file separate returns, but get advice before you do this. Medical expenses must exceed 7.5 percent of the adjusted gross income in order to be taken as a deduction.

5. Review your FICA payments. If you have several different jobs during the year, you may have overpaid your social security taxes. Each employer must withhold 7.65 percent on the first $61,200 in wages. But if you're lucky enough to make more than that in one calendar year from two separate employers, you may be entitled to a refund. The excess tax can be claimed as an extra tax payment on your 1040.

6. Resist the "rapid refund rush." It isn't worth it to do the loan on a tax refund when you see that it is costing you as much as 15 percent of the amount you expect to get. Fees for electronic filing, usually $35, are deductible, but the loan interest isn't. And although it's not "instant," you will receive your payment within 3 to 4 weeks. If you must have the money yesterday, then let the IRS do a direct deposit of your refund check into your bank account. The IRS can do this if you file a Form 8888 along with your Form 1040 giving the IRS the appropriate information, i.e., bank account number, bank routing code, your social security number, etc. If you file only a 1040-EZ, then do it by phone and get the process going much sooner. This is a new service started in 1996 to cut down on the delay and the paperwork that has to be processed. You must have a preprinted computerized mailing label with an IRS code number for you on the sticker and a touch-tone phone. You will be given a confirmation number, and you should receive your check within 2 to 3 weeks.

7. Sign and attach everything. The one mistake most people make most often is forgetting to sign the return and to attach the W-2 statements. Make sure that the name and social security numbers on your W-2 statements match those on your tax form. The IRS computer will kick out anything that is even vaguely different. If you got married or divorced, attach a letter explaining the name change. If you've forgotten to do this, everything you sent the IRS will be sent back to you, and if you are past the April 15 deadline, this could trigger a penalty for late filing.

8. Redo your W-4 form. The average tax refund in 1995 was $1149.50. This was a "free loan" to the IRS of $100 a month which the average taxpayer could have used for saving and investing. If you received a refund greater than $300, then you are overpaying.

9. Don't try to hide income. If you're collecting alimony and/or child support or have a scholarship for college, it's taxable. If you don't report it, the source of the income will.

10. Don't exaggerate your deductions. The IRS uses some average guidelines for what it considers reasonable amounts to be deducted in each category on Schedule A. If you make only $25,000 and you list deductions of $15,000 spread out among the different categories, unless you can prove some extraordinary circumstances, that will be a red flag that will kick your return and trigger an audit.

5

CREDIT AND BORROWING– USING OTHER PEOPLE'S MONEY

"Buying on credit is robbing next year's crop."
African proverb

Financial institutions are the gatekeepers to the funds required to support the wealth-building process, and, historically, African-Americans have been shut out of them except as occasional depositors. In 1833, Thomy Lafon, a wealthy mulatto merchant in New Orleans, initiated the practice of pooling his funds with those of several other black businessmen to provide loans and mortgages to other free blacks who wanted to purchase property and build businesses. Lafon and several of his prosperous colleagues had been entrusted with the savings of friends and neighbors who had asked Lafon and his colleagues to invest their money for them. Before the Civil War, small groups of free blacks in major cities like Philadelphia, New York, Richmond, and Atlanta duplicated this effort of cooperative capital to provide loans and mortgages to other blacks and small businesses. These small attempts at private financing never developed into legally established lending institutions, although the idea was proposed on several occasions.

Three separate military banks managed by the Army were created during the Civil War for black soldiers in Norfolk, Virginia; Beaufort, South Carolina; and New Orleans. At the end of the war more than $200,000 had been accumulated in savings by the troops, who had earned a salary of $10 a month. The military banks were absorbed into the Freedmen's Savings Bank and Trust Company. It was established in Washington, D.C., by a group of abolitionists and free blacks to support newly emancipated slaves in their effort to save money and develop an economic base. The military banks had confirmed the need for the bank. Congress approved the Freedmen's bank charter in 1865. John Mercer Langston, a former slave and a trained attorney from Arlington, Virginia, was appointed as bank manager of the D.C. office and eventually became a member of the board of trustees.

Although the bank was headquartered in Washington, between 1865 and 1871 thirty-four branches opened throughout the South—one in each major city—largely managed by whites. The bank's relationship with the Freedmen's Bureau led many people, black and white, to believe that it was a government funded institution.

Frederick Douglass was elected president of the bank and wrote many columns about the need for a financial institution that would assist blacks in developing financial independence. At the end of 7 years, over 72,000 accounts had been opened, and the deposit base had grown to over $7 million. A European visitor commented that while traveling through the South it was possible to find the bank open for business on a regular basis. Each day there would be a group of African-Americans depositing or withdrawing small sums of money or forwarding drafts to family members in other parts of the country.

When the economy changed, due to a national banking crisis, Douglass invested $50,000 of his own money to keep the bank open. A decision by Freedmen's management to invest in the First National Bank of Washington was the turning point for the bank's financial future when First National Bank of Washington failed in 1870. Other bad loan decisions and the overall hostility to the bank as a black institution eventually destroyed the support for and confidence in the institution. Douglass appealed to the Senate Finance Committee for aid, but Congress withdrew its support in 1874, leaving 61,000 black depositors to lose over $3 million after 9 years of being in business. The demise of the Freedmen's Savings Bank and Trust Company was a detrimental blow to the confidence blacks felt for lending institutions for many years to come.

Following the failure of the Freedmen's Bank, blacks were on their own when it came to a resource for financial assistance. White banks were not interested in having Negro depositors and discouraged them from opening accounts because the amounts they deposited were small and the cost of maintaining such small accounts was unprofitable for them. Negro churches and fraternal organizations such as the Grand Fountain United Order of True Reformers in Virginia tried to fill the gap created by the Freedmen's Bank in April 1888 by establishing a bank in Richmond. Capital Savings Bank, an independent bank without fraternal connections, was established six months later by seven black businessmen in Washington, D.C. It began with initial capital of $6000, which grew to $50,000, and managed to survive the banking panic of 1893.

Over the next two decades more than 75 black banks came into and went out of existence. The Mutual Trust Company, organized and owned by local black businessmen in Chattanooga, Tennessee, opened its doors in 1889. It was the first fully owned black bank to be established in the South. Robert R. Church, Sr. (1839–1912), born a slave, founded the Solvent Savings Bank and Trust Company of Memphis in 1893 and is believed to be the first black millionaire who built his wealth from banking and real estate. The most notable institution, and the only one still in existence today, was the St. Luke's Penny Savings Bank of Richmond, established by Maggie Lena Walker in 1903—and now known as the Consolidated Bank and Trust Company of Richmond.

Many banks, black and white, failed in the Great Depression of the 1930s because of the loose-knit, poorly regulated financial system in America. The Federal Deposit Insurance Corporation (FDIC) came into existence as a result of the failure of so many banks during this time. The FDIC was created by several major life insurance companies and was finally taken over by the federal government in the late 1930s.

The Community Reinvestment Act (CRA) was passed by Congress in 1973 to prohibit the banking practice of "redlining" a neighborhood. Many large white financial institutions would accept the cash from neighborhood minority depositors in checking and savings accounts but would not make business loans or give mortgages to the residents in that neighborhood. CRA was designed to force banks to give back a portion of their earnings in loans and services to the local depositors in minority neighborhoods. Enforcement of the law has been slow, tedious, and difficult to monitor since there are so many ways in which banks can satisfy this requirement without making loans or mortgages. Services include grants to church groups, donations of used equipment and office furniture to day-care centers, or the transfer of the deed of a closed branch building to a community group, such as the building provided to the Central Brooklyn Federal Credit Union for the price of $1.

||≡|| *When they count the money, they do not know Negro money from white* ||≡||
money.

Mrs. Georgia Gilmore
During the 1956 Montgomery, Alabama, bus boycott

BANKING IS BASIC

Building financial credibility and establishing a relationship with a bank are two steps that go hand-in-hand and form the major basis in the wealth-building process, but these steps are becoming more and more difficult for many African-Americans. Nearly 15 percent of working African-Americans do not have checking accounts. There are two reasons for this: (1) Large commercial banks charge high fees for maintaining most checking accounts, and (2) The merger mania gripping the banking industry has forced the closure of many branches, resulting in a lack of bank branches in many African-American neighborhoods.

WHERE TO OPEN A CHECKING/SAVINGS ACCOUNT

Where you do your borrowing has a lot to do with the bank you do business with. Many of the early entrepreneurs that you will read about in this book built their businesses using a black financial institution because they were not able to get the loans that supported them for start-up or growth capital from white institutions. Keep that in mind when you choose to do business with any financial institution. What is its track record for lending to minorities? Ask the bank about its CRA report, which is supposed to be available to the public on request, or check with the state banking commission to find out if the bank you're considering has been sued or cited for redlining in the African-American community.

The first question a lender wants to know when you apply for a loan is: Do you have a checking account and how long have you had it? If you keep all your money in a savings account and pay your bills with money orders, you are wasting money. You also don't qualify as a good credit risk. A money order receipt is not always acceptable by the IRS or in small claims court as proof of payment. The common proof of payment is a canceled check. If you don't have a checking account, verifying your payments becomes nearly impossible.

All banks are not the same. Before you race down to the nearest bank to open a checking account, think about what sort of bank you need and the cost of such a bank's services. Here's the breakdown:

1. Large commercial banks. These are full-service banks that offer checking, savings, mortgages, money-market accounts, credit cards, traveler's checks, and a variety of loans. Fees can be very high and are based on balances. Nationally chartered member banks are covered by the Federal Deposit Insurance Corporation.

2. Savings and loans (or S&Ls). These banks offer the same kind of services that commercial banks do, but they specialize in mortgages and personal loans. S&Ls are government-chartered and insured in the same manner as commercial banks.

3. Credit unions. Membership is required as an employee, or you must be in a trade union or an association. Federal regulations do not limit the interest that credit unions may pay on savings accounts. Credit unions offer checking and savings accounts as well as personal loans and mortgages and often provide better rates than banks since they are nonprofit organizations. Their rates on savings and CDs are also higher than what a commercial bank will offer. Services are limited in some credit unions, but others, like the Pentagon Federal Credit Union in Alexandria, Virginia (800-248-5626), with over 450,000 members, offer low-rate credit cards, auto loans, and home improvement loans; and some have moved into offering mortgages with assistance from

FNMA (Fannie Mae), the Federal National Mortgage Association. The Navy Federal Credit Union in Vienna, Virginia (800-656-7676), is the world's largest credit union, with 1.5 million members including any nonmilitary family members of service personnel who live at the same address as the member. The Artists Federal Credit Union in New York City (212-366-5669) welcomes artists of any kind living anywhere in the United States. The American Baptist Credit Union (800-347-2228) offers accounts to anyone who is a Baptist church member anywhere in the Unites States, except Rhode Island and Massachusetts. In the African-American community, many churches have developed large credit unions for their members and neighbors, although banking services are limited. If you want to find a credit union that you may qualify for, call the Credit Union National Association (800-358-5710).

|||≣||| *Friday, the eagle flies.* |||≣|||

TRADITIONAL SAYING

CHECK-CASHING SERVICES

Avoid the check-cashing facilities that are found in many urban neighborhoods if at all possible. The fees they charge are exorbitant. It can cost you as much as 3 to 5 percent of your check. The additional charge of $1 to $2 to purchase money orders to pay your bills will cost you as much as 10 percent of your check. If you do this each month, you need to get a bank account.

BANK ACCOUNT SHOPPING LIST

Finding a bank means more than just going to the nearest corner to see if the bank has a large array of ATM machines. The most important questions can make the account-opening process very complex, and much of what you need to know may never be discussed as you fill out the forms and sign the signature cards. Consider setting up a relationship with a financial institution that is supportive of your financial goals.

Here are some basic questions to ask yourself before you choose a bank. The most important issue today is the cost of having a checking account. Banks are finding incredible new ways to charge fees to maintain an account. Some of them now charge for seeing a teller, for not using your preprinted deposit slips, and for making calls to the voice mail service to check your balance; the latest innovation is a $20 charge to close your account if it has been open for less than 3 months. Questions about fees are the most important question to start with.

1. What type of checking account best suits your needs? A basic, regular, or NOW account?

- A basic account offers bare-bones services at discount rates. It's a good one to choose if you plan to write only five to six checks per month and not use the cash machine.

- A regular checking account offers typical services at moderate prices. The fees for checking accounts can be as low as zero if you have a checking account that is linked to a savings account in which you keep at least a $500 to $1000 balance, or the fees can be as expensive as $15 a month for an account where you write 15 to 20 checks a month.

- A NOW account pays interest on your checking account and offers free checking and no monthly fees, but you must maintain a large minimum cash balance (usually $2000 to $5000). If your balance falls below the required minimum cash balance for even a day, you could get socked with a hefty $25 to $30 usage fee.

2. Are combined balances from checking and savings considered in determining fees?

3. What is the cost per check? 15 cents? 25 cents? 50 cents?

4. Does the account carry an automatic monthly service charge? $5? $10?

5. What hours are available for banking? Evenings? Weekends?

6. Are 24-hour cash machines available? Is there a charge per ATM transaction regardless of your balance?

7. How many branches does the bank have?

8. What are the bank's fees for the following:

- *Stop payment orders.* Fees can be as high as $15.

- *Returned checks.* The careless habit of writing checks that are returned, because you don't have enough money in your account to pay them, can cost up to $25 per check.

- *Money orders.* The post office is cheaper than the bank!

- *Certified checks.* This guaranteed way of making a payment means that the money is held outside of your account by the bank to cover this check, which you draw for a particular purpose. The cost can be from $5 to $15.

- *Traveler's checks.* The average cost is $1 per $100. If you are a member of the American Automobile Association, one of the perks of membership is that you can obtain traveler's checks at no charge.

9. How long will it take for a check to clear after it is deposited? Find out what the rules are in your state and what the bank's policy is on the "float." This is the time period between the day you deposit a check and the day you may draw money from that check out of the account. The amount of time that it takes for a check to clear depends upon the city in which it's drawn and that city's proximity to your bank. If the bank is a local one, the check can clear overnight, or it may take up to 3 days. If the check is from an out-of-town bank, the bank may put a hold on the funds for 6 to 10 business days.

10. How long will it take for a large deposit to clear? Large deposits can take five business days even if it is within the same bank if the amount is over $10,000. U.S. banking policy also requires that if you make a deposit of more than $10,000, it has to be reported to the Treasury Department in Washington. Some banks have a policy to hold large deposits and not allow them

to clear for your use for at least 5 to 9 business days. Keep in mind that if you open a savings account that has a checking privilege, for the first 30 days the bank can hold each deposit for at least 10 days.

11. Is someone available to show you how to balance your checkbook? Some banks offer this service for a fee. If balancing the checkbook is a problem for you, you will want to make an appointment with one of the platform officers, who will sit with you and go through the numbers, your outstanding checks, and the fees you may have forgotten to enter, and show you how the procedure is done. It will be worth doing this at least once, to get you on track.

12. Does the bank offer computer banking? Computer banking is the wave of the future, and if you own a PC with a modem, you will quickly discover how much time this service can save you. The bank provides the software; you pay for the phone line. Fees for this service can vary from zero to $10 a month. You can check your balances and see if a check has cleared by phone if you have a touch-tone phone, but the phone call can cost 75 cents per inquiry.

13. Does the bank offer bill-paying services? At what cost? Bill-paying services provided by banks can keep you from missing a due date on a mortgage or a loan, but this service can also cost you $1 per transaction plus as much as $17.95 a month for managing your account. If you write more than 20 checks a month, the fee is higher. Write your own checks and put the extra dollars into a savings account.

Once you have selected a bank, consider asking your employer to deposit your paycheck automatically into your bank account. This is to your advantage since it eliminates the possibility of losing the paycheck, cuts down on the time necessary for clearance of funds, and makes the cash available to you immediately.

Jessie Binga (1865–1950), a real estate broker who had made a fortune after many blacks migrated north to Chicago and Detroit where he owned property, founded the Binga State Bank in 1908 in Chicago. It was the first black-owned financial institution in the North. The bank flourished during the 1920s, building up a deposit base of nearly $2 million. The bank lasted through the stock market crash of 1929 and the worst years of the Depression because Binga refused to foreclose on many of the black homeowners whose mortgages were held by the bank. Binga was charged by Illinois state bank authorities with mismanagement of funds in 1932 and was forced to close the bank when he went to prison. He was eventually pardoned by President Roosevelt but was never able to regain his previous wealth and social status.

BORROWING MONEY

When it comes to borrowing money, there are two kinds of debt: dumb debt and intelligent debt. Dumb debt is the easy credit terms of finance companies and credit cards at inflated interest rates that are used to purchase items that go down in value the minute you take them out of the store or the showroom. Or the vacations, dinners out, evenings at the theater, and items that are long gone and forgotten when you are still paying for them 2 years later.

Intelligent debt is the loans that will give you some item or service that will eventually increase your net worth. A mortgage for a house that provides shelter and increases in value over a long period of time is an intelligent loan, particularly since the interest on a mortgage is tax deductible. A student loan to increase your earning capacity over the years is intelligent debt. When you're thinking about borrowing money, think about whether the debt you are incurring falls into the dumb or intelligent category.

Sometime in your life it will be necessary to borrow money, so it is advisable to begin building a relationship with a bank. Whether it's your first mortgage or a loan to pay for your education, to start a business, to buy a car, or to improve your home, you need to be aware of how banks rate their prospective loan customers. Look at the typical bank loans that you will apply for in your lifetime.

1. *Student loans.* Borrowing for college is often the second largest debt that you will incur in your life—the first one is a mortgage. Banks give student loans, but the banks go to government agencies to guarantee them. Once you complete school and begin working, payment is expected to begin 6 months later. Don't even think about not paying. If you default on these loans, your tax refund will be attached and used to secure repayment of your student loan. Your bank account and/or paycheck may also be levied, plus you are deemed ineligible for government-backed mortgages until the loan is paid.

2. *Secured loans.* A secured loan depends upon your presenting some form of collateral, such as a boat, car, etc., which can be repossessed if more than two payments are missed. When John Johnson started *Ebony* magazine in 1944, he had a good idea, lots of energy and enthusiasm, and a good track record with *Negro Digest* magazine, but he had to use his mother's furniture as a pledge to borrow the $500 he needed to get started.

3. *Unsecured loans.* An unsecured loan is based upon your character, reputation, and ability to pay back the debt. The loan may be a cash reserve emergency overdraft line, attached to your checking account, so you won't bounce a check. This privilege, based on your credit history, can also be expensive—up to 19 percent worth of interest.

4. *Mortgages.* This is probably the biggest debt you will ever take on in your lifetime. Shopping for a house is exciting, but before you set your heart on a little three-bedroom colonial with den, laundry room, and fireplace, sit down with a financial professional

or a mortgage broker and find out how much of a house you can afford. A good analysis will reveal the amount of cash you have available for a down payment, current interest rates, the type of mortgage that will best suit your needs, and the amount of mortgage payment you can handle every month. Then you will know the price range that you can look for when buying. If you have never looked around for a mortgage, you're in for a real education. The two basic choices are fixed-rate mortgages and adjustable-rate mortgages. Read the chapter on buying a house (Chapter 7) for a broader explanation of types of mortgages.

5. *Home-equity loans.* Essentially second mortgages, home-equity loans have become popular in the last few years in response to recent tax reform when the only tax-deductible interest that was allowed was on real estate financing. This kind of loan has to be used carefully or else you could find yourself turning your house into a Visa card and overspending.

||| ≡ |||| ≡ |||| ≡ |||| ≡ |||| ≡ |||| ≡ ||||≡|||| ≡ |||| ≡ |||| ≡ |||| ≡ |||| ≡ |||| ≡ ||||≡

The National Negro Finance Corporation was created in 1924 with $1 million as an investment and business expansion fund. Unfortunately, most of this money was lost in the banking failures that followed the stock market crash of 1929.

||| ≡ |||| ≡ |||| ≡ |||| ≡ |||| ≡ |||| ≡ ||||≡|||| ≡ |||| ≡ |||| ≡ |||| ≡ |||| ≡ |||| ≡ ||||≡

EASY CREDIT—A FABLE FOR OUR TIME

|||≡||| *One cannot feast and become rich.* |||≡|||

ASHANTI SAYING

Malik W. is a 20-year-old junior at Texas Southern University where 70 percent of his fees and tuition are paid for by financial aid or government-guaranteed student loans. He is studying prelaw and plans to take a summer job as a clerk at a law firm in Los Angeles. Just before he leaves the campus for his summer job, Malik is stopped on the street by a credit card hawker offering a

LUTHER GATLING, CEO

Budget and Credit Counseling Service
New York, New York

The reception area outside his office has a large, clear Lucite container filled with the chopped-up remnants of hundreds of credit cards—evidence of the thousands of people he has helped to get out from under the crushing burden of consumer debt since he started the Budget and Credit Counseling Service (BUCCS) in 1974. For 20 years, Luther Gatling has worked diligently to educate and assist people of all colors from all walks of life and all income groups to turn their lives around when they have gotten too deep into debt and can no longer manage their loans and credit cards.

BUCCS began as a division of the Community Service Society, a nonprofit organization, to help the many single mothers, widows, and young working couples in the community who were paralyzed with debt. Many of them had signed consumer debt contracts for furniture-financing deals, meat-purchasing plans, television rentals, and easy loans at exorbitant rates from finance companies. Debt fed by the added annual ritual of excessive Christmas shopping and high-interest credit cards slowly built up over time, and most people had no idea how to pay off the bills. The agency set up a storefront office on 125th Street in Harlem and offered credit counseling and debt management advice and assistance free of charge.

Gatling found that the hardest job was to get some of his clients to file for bankruptcy. Black people's bad experiences and distrust of the court system have engendered a disbelief that they can use the system for a benefit, so most of them don't take advantage of the bankruptcy system even when they are entitled to it. African-Americans are also plagued with a strong sense of shame at having to admit that they have failed and that they can't handle their bills, but it's a constitutionally guaranteed right in America to get out from under the debt when you can't cope any more. Gatling's weekly radio show, *The Credit Doctor*, is one of the few that brings useful credit advice to a community desperately in need of this knowledge.

BUCCS has made a strong commitment to providing financial education and to being a consumer advocate for fairer interpretation of the credit system and the bankruptcy laws. The organization works with clients to help them to begin to use credit wisely and to save for a goal, and it assists many of them with purchasing homes even when they thought it would never be possible.

*"*Black people don't understand the credit system because we've never been taught about it and how it works. Our school systems have failed us that way and the lenders have the advantage and the profit margins that come from not explaining the contracts as clearly as they should. Add to that the racist attitudes that are an inherent part of the financial business and you come up with a nightmare for people who don't understand what the game really is. The key is education, having a goal and some discipline.*"*

free baseball cap, key chain, and water bottle if he will fill out an application for some credit cards. He gives his summer job as an employment reference and is told by the credit card recruiter/salesman that he can include his financial aid stipend as part of his annual income. This will give him the minimum $200 a month income that the credit card companies want to see as income.

Malik applies for three different cards that day. Within a few weeks he receives cards from American Express, Visa, and MasterCard. Visa and Master-Card each give Malik a credit limit of $750 since he has signed a statement saying that he is over 18, has a social security number, and has enough income to pay the $20 monthly minimum that he will be billed until he graduates. American Express, a charge card, does not specify what limit he has on his charging privilege. The credit card bills are to be sent to Malik's home in Houston, Texas, even though he is going to be working in California for the summer.

Malik uses the credit cards to buy clothes for his work wardrobe, to eat out several evenings a week with new friends he meets at work, to buy a plane ticket to visit San Francisco and Berkeley for the Fourth of July 3-day weekend, and to take a cash advance to pay for a final weekend vacation in Santa Barbara before returning to Texas for his senior year.

By the end of the summer, Malik has maxed out on both the Visa and MasterCard accounts. When the billing statement finally reaches him, Malik owes nearly $3000 to American Express. After a 10-week summer job earning nearly $700 a week, Malik expected to have at least $3000 to pay a portion of his tuition and school fees. He figured he could work something out with the credit card companies after he returned to school. In September, Malik discovers that his savings account, where he had been sending half of his paycheck during the summer, has been attached by creditors. Malik has to take an extra student loan and find a second job to pay his share of school expenses for the year, and the judgments for nonpayment will stay on his credit record for more than 10 years.

Easy credit has become a financial nightmare for too many young African-Americans who have fallen into the "a-dollar-down-and-a-dollar-a-week" trap. Finance company contracts available through furniture stores, appliance dealers, and used car dealers encourage quick sales and offer easy credit terms, but no one explains what's in the contract's fine print to let you know what kind of deal you've gotten into.

Falling into these credit hustles is like volunteering for a new form of slavery; the shackles of debt can keep you entrapped in a lifestyle of extended payments, where you avoid the phone so you don't have to talk to bill collectors, have little or nothing to show for the debt, and are forever employed in a job you may hate just to keep up the payments. Blacks were denied even the most marginal credit for many generations or were forced to borrow from loan companies at exorbitant rates or from loan sharks at even more exorbitant rates, which made it impossible to ever recover from the debt. This all changed in the sixties, to our consumer peril, when access to credit became much easier. African-Americans are readily contributing their unfair share of the run-up in the $781 billion in consumer debt that Americans now carry.

‖≡‖ *The appearance of wealth prevents the accumulation of real wealth.* ‖≡‖
DR. NATHAN HARE
Howard University, 1968

ESTABLISHING CREDIT

Unless you plan to save for everything the way your grandparents did, you must establish a credit record. Like it or not, credit is a major part of your financial life and a critical key to building wealth if it is used wisely. One of your first financial responsibilities after finding a job is to establish credit. Even if you want to make all your purchases with cash or use a check, you will need a credit card—to rent a car, get an apartment, or reserve a hotel room. Insurance companies now check credit records before they will cover your car. Many employers check credit references before they hire you to see if you pay your bills on time to know if you will be tempted to pilfer from the company coffers. Landlords want to know if you will be reliable with the rent, so they check your credit report. In other words, you cannot escape this aspect of life in America. The federal government may be able to keep giving itself unlimited spending privileges and raising the debt ceiling, but you can't.

To establish credit, start by saving. Choose a bank that has a credit card that is offered with a savings account. Accumulate at least $1000 in savings and then apply for a personal installment loan. Since you have no credit history, the bank will probably hold the money in your savings account as collateral. Pay the money back on schedule, and if possible, prepay the loan. If you make all your payments on time —or do even better by paying off the loan early—this will be your first credit reference. You will accomplish the three C's of credit: collateral, character, and capacity. You have built up collateral, you have proved your character by paying on time, and your income shows that you have the capacity to meet the payment schedule that you agreed upon. Now the bank will be likely to issue you a credit card since you have established a good credit history there.

A number of different cards are available.

1. Secured cards. Secured cards are perfect for new borrowers or for people who have had a problem with credit in the past and want to reestablish a good record. You submit an application and a deposit of $500 to $1000 in a CD or a savings account. You will be offered a MasterCard or Visa card with a credit line that is equal to the amount you deposited in the savings account. You earn interest on the CD or passbook account, and you will begin to establish a clean credit reference. The interest on secured cards is usually quite high—19 to 22 percent. Some have an application fee of $50 to $60 and may also have high annual fees—about $50—but this kind of card is a way to reconstruct a healthy financial life, assuming you have learned your lesson about credit management. Contact a card rating service called CardTrak (800-874-8999) which issues a *Secured Card Report* for $5, listing the various banks that offer secured credit cards. Or write to: Box 1700, Frederick, Maryland 21702.

Here's a list of secured credit cards for people who have a problem getting credit:

Bank	Toll-Free 800 Number	Minimum Deposit	Interest Rate	Application Fee
American Pacific Portland, OR	879-8745	$1000	16.9%	$35
Chase USA Wilmington, DE	482-4273	$500	18.1%	$45
First Consumers Portland, OR	876-3262	$1000	18.9%	$39
Household Bank Salina, CA	395-6080	$1000	19.1%	$40
Key Federal Savings Havre de Grace, MD	228-2230	$1000	19.5%	$45

Each of these banks will report your credit history to the three major credit bureaus each month but will also keep your secured card status confidential. After a year of regular payments, they will also increase your credit limit and decrease the interest rate charged on the card.

2. Gas company credit cards. These are relatively easy to obtain and are also a good starting point; however, like secured cards, they have high interest rates—approximately 21 to 22 percent. Gas cards are also an easy way to tempt you to get into trouble with too much spending since they can be used for much more than just gas, oil, and a lube job. You can charge repairs, tires, and even lunch at some of the service stations that have restaurants. Many gas companies also offer mail-order catalogs full of temptation items like VCRs, portable phones, cameras, and other consumer toys you didn't know you needed, so be careful.

3. Department store cards. If you are a new customer without a credit reference, you may be able to get a starting credit limit of about $250 to $500 if you can establish that you have had a job for at least 6 months. As you continue to make regular payments on time, however, or before they are due, your credit limit will be increased.

4. American Express/Diner's Club cards. These are "charge" cards, not credit cards. The full balance must be paid at the end of each month. AmEx offers a card to college seniors and many young professionals in law, accounting, medicine, etc., with jobs paying at least $15,000 per year.

5. Debit cards. These cards offer the safest way to stay out of debt. A debit card draws the cash out of your bank account and transfers it to the store owner's account on the spot while you're making your purchase. No grace period, no outrageous interest payments, but no sale if there's no money in your account. There are two drawbacks here: You aren't building a credit history with a debit card, and, unfortunately, if the card is lost or stolen, you have little or no protection until you can notify the bank to close or block your account.

6. Affinity cards. These are credit cards that are sponsored by a bank in participation with some nonprofit organization. The bank donates a portion of the interest earned on your spending to the charity. Rarely are these low-interest cards since the bank uses some of its profit for the donation, so it's bound to charge you more. Rather than giving to charity this way, think about making your own direct donation, then you can get the tax deduction. If you pay the full balance or don't mind paying the higher interest, look into using the Unity Visa Card from the Boston Bank of Commerce, an African-American bank (800-59-UNITY) that has an exceptional program. The bank charges no annual fee and has a low introductory rate of 9.95 percent, but the rate rises to 18 percent after 6 months. The bank apportions 1 percent of its earnings among seven African-American charities: the Urban League, the NAACP Legal Defense Fund, the United Negro College Fund, the Children's Defense Fund, the Thurgood Marshall Scholarship Fund, the Jackie Robinson Foundation, and its own local Unity foundation.

||≡|| *Let poverty be a stranger in my household. For if I have no wife, then I am* ||≡||
poor; if I lack possessions, then I am poor; if my cloth is torn, then I am poor
PROVERB FROM DAHOMEY

HOW TO SHOP FOR A CREDIT CARD

Once you begin to establish a credit history, you should shop for credit the same way you comparison-shop for a car or a bank account. All credit cards are not the same. Low-cost bank cards are available. It is possible to have a

Visa card with a 10 percent interest rate and no annual fee! The BankCard Holders of America offers a list of low-cost credit cards with the addresses and phone numbers of the various institutions and the terms and conditions of each bank. Write to the BankCard Holders of America at 524 Branch Drive, Salem, Virginia 24153; or call 540-389-5445. The $4 it charges for the list is worth the time, money, and aggravation it will save you. On your search, consider these basic questions:

1. What is the interest rate? Is the rate fixed, or does it go up or down every 6 months in accordance with a market interest rate index, such as the prime rate or Treasury bills?

2. Is there an annual fee? How much is it? The average national fee is about $18. Although 42 percent of all banks have eliminated the annual fee, they have imposed other rates such as a $15 late charge for payments that are not received on time. Another fee is a ½ percent penalty or $25 for charging over your credit limit.

3. Is there a 25 to 30-day "grace period" on interest, or is interest charged from the first day that a purchase is made? Many banks are eliminating the grace period to improve their profits.

4. Is there a different interest rate for cash advances than for purchases? Cash advances usually have an 18 to 21 percent interest rate even though purchases may have only a 9 to 12 percent interest rate.

5. Is there an additional transaction charge for cash advances? Cash advances usually have a $2 to $3 transaction fee in addition to the higher interest charged.

6. Will the interest rate increase after a few months if you pay your balance on a regular basis or you begin using a competing credit card?

The Ram Research Group (800-344-7714) publishes a monthly list of the best deals available in credit card rates. For $5 you can get the latest available list. Here's a recent list:

No-annual-fee cards		
AFBA Industrial Bank	8.50%	800-776-2265
Wachovia Prime No-fee	8.75%	800-842-3262
USAA Federal Savings Bank	12.50%	800-922-9092
Security Savings Bank	12.52%	800-573-6089
Horizon Bank & Trust	12.90%	512-419-3462
Low-annual-fee cards		
Wachovia First Year Prime	8.75%	800-842-3262
Oak Brook Bank	8.75%	800-536-3200
Wachovia Prime for Life	8.75%	800-842-3262
Pulaski Bank & Trust	9.45%	800-980-2265
Federal Savings Bank	9.94%	800-374-5600

Many of these banks are small, out-of-the-way savings and loan lenders with very conservative guidelines for approving accounts, so be aware that if your credit is not up to snuff, you will be rejected. You may also be turned down if you are not a state resident.

Many young African-Americans have problems with credit, but the problems of credit mistakes are not exclusively ours alone; it is just more obvious in our community. The hidden information, unexplained credit terms, not reading the fine print and the psychological set-up of being too eager too soon to use the credit card as a status symbol of success. The United States is a nation living through the golden age of debt, but this also impacts our ability to build wealth.

‖☰‖ *Wealth will never come to those who fail to appreciate it.* ‖☰‖
FATHER DIVINE

CREDIT CARD CAVEATS

When it comes to credit, what you don't know can hurt you financially and legally, and credit card companies don't bother to make several facts clear in the fine print of the contract you sign. Here are a few of the hidden facts and fees they either don't make as clear as they should or tell you about.

1. Purchases of goods and services may carry an interest rate of 12.9 percent, but cash advances are usually charged at a higher rate, like 19 to 21 percent.

2. Low teaser rates with no annual fee may entice you to sign up, but they can go up. An interest rate of 6.9 percent may look good on the initial application, but after 6 months or a year it can become 19.5 percent.

3. The bank can sell your credit card contract to another institution without your permission and that new bank does not have to offer the same terms, rates, and privileges as the old bank.

4. If you have a complaint against the credit card company, it has the right to decide where and how any legal dispute will be handled and settled. If the company is located in Delaware, Nebraska, or South Dakota and you're in Texas, Georgia, or Maryland, are you going to show up in small claims court in another state and submit to binding arbitration at your expense to dispute a $200 mistake?

5. Credit cards are issued to make money from the interest rates charged on purchases and advances, and it costs the average bank $65 per year to issue the plastic and send out the monthly statements. If you regularly carry a balance of $200, the bank is breaking even on the cost of giving you an account. If you use the card a lot but pay your balance in full each month, the bank makes money on the 2 to 3 percent it charges the merchants who accept the card. But if you don't use the card enough for the bank to make money on your account, then it may close your account after a year and tell you to reapply later when you really need its services.

YOUR CREDIT REPORT

This report from one of the "big three" credit reporting agencies historically tracks your experience with credit. (See Figure 5-1 for a typical report.) You may be shocked when you see how much information appears on file. Your credit report documents the last three jobs you've worked at; every loan you've taken; every nickel you've charged for the last 7 years, including school loans, auto loans, gas cards, and department stores. Credit agencies don't create the information. They collect the data from all the various stores, banks, and companies that extend credit; then the credit agencies assemble this information for sale to subscribers, such as any lending institution, direct-marketing agencies, even landlords and potential employers who pay them for the service.

If you have never had a problem with credit or never had a reason to check your credit report, then you are one of the lucky few. If you have never seen your file, it may be a good idea to check on it to correct any errors that may be there—and there may be many. You are legally entitled to receive one free copy per year from one of the credit reporting agencies, so take advantage of this offer and see what the agency has on file about you. Errors in social security numbers and similar names and addresses can create mistakes—and credit rejections. It's up to you to challenge the information and correct it. Ask your bank which of the major credit reporting agencies it uses.

If you have ever applied for credit and received a letter of denial, the letter will tell the reason for rejection and which agency provided the information. You have 30 days to request a free copy of your credit report; otherwise you will have to pay $8 to $15 for it. If there is any incorrect information in the file, you have the right to challenge it. The agency will request proof of the accuracy of the challenged information from the reporting creditor; if the reporting creditor cannot prove the statement, the error is removed from your record. Even if the reporting creditor provides proof that the challenged information is correct, you have the right to insert a 100-word statement explaining your side of the story—perhaps you defaulted on a loan or were late paying your bills because you were laid off or there was a family illness. Write or call one of the three major credit agencies to get a copy of your report.

Please address all future correspondence to the address shown on the right. ••••••••••••••••••••••••► CREDIT REPORTING OFFICE
BUSINESS ADDRESS
CITY, STATE 00000
PHONE NUMBER

JANE BROWN
123 HOME ADDRESS
ANYWHERE, USA 00000

DATE 05/05/95
SOCIAL SECURITY NUMBER 123-45-6789
DATE OF BIRTH 04/10/58
SPOUSE JOHN

SAMPLE CREDIT REPORT

The first item identifies the business that is reporting the information.

This is your account number with the company reporting.

Number of months account payment history has been reported.

This is the month and year you opened the account with the credit grantor.

See explanation below.

This is the date of last activity on the account and may be the date of last payment or the date of last change.

The highest amount charged on the credit limit.

Represents number of installments (M = Months) or monthly payments.

The amount owed on the account at the time it was reported.

This figure indicates any amount past due at the time the information was reported.

See explanation below.

Date of last account update.

Credit Account	Account Number	Whose Acct.	Date Opened	Months Re-viewed	Date of Last Activity	High Credit	Terms	Balance	Past Due	Status	Date Reported
MACY'S	54229778	J	05/86	66	10/91	3500		0		R1	12/92
BANK OF AMERICA	355611251511	I	11/86	48	11/90	9388	48M	0		I1	11/92
J C PENNY'S	2953900000100673	A	06/87	24	10/91	500		0		01	12/92
VISA	11251514	I	05/85	48	10/91	5000	340	3000	580	R3	12/92

PAYMENT HISTORY – 30(03)   60(04)   90+(01)   08/90-R2,   02/89-R3,   10/88-R6<<<

Number of times account was either 30/60/90 days past due.

Date two most recent delinquencies occurred plus date of most severe delinquency.

COLLECTION REPORTS 05/92; ASSIGNED 09/92 TO MICRO COLLECTORS (800) 555-1234
CLIENT – COUNTY HOSPITAL; AMOUNT – $1100.25; STAT UNPAID 05/92; BALANCE – $1100.25
DATE OF LAST ACTIVITY 05/92; INDIVIDUAL; ACCOUNT NUMBER 787652JC

—•—•—•—•—•— COLLECTION AGENCY TELEPHONE NUMBER(S)—•—•—•—•—
MICRO COLLECTORS (800) 555-1234
—•—•—•—•—•—•— COURTHOUSE RECORDS —•—•—•—•—•—
LIEN FILED 04/91; BRONX; CASE NUMBER – 32114; AMOUNT – $26667; CLASS – CITY/
COUNTY; RELEASED 07/88; VERIFIED 09/90

BANKRUPTCY FILED 11/93; N.Y. SOUTHERN DIST ; CASE NUMBER – 673HC12; LIABILITIES –
$26,412; PERSONAL; INDIVIDUAL; DISCHARGED; ASSETS – $1,522

JUDGMENT FILED 07/87; NEW YORK; CASE NUMBER – 898872; DEFENDANT – JANE BROWN
AMOUNT – $734; PLAINTIFF – DEPARTMENT OF MOTOR VEHICLES, PARKING VIOLATIONS;
SATISFIED 03/89; VERIFIED 05/90

—•—•—•—•—•—•— ADDITIONAL INFORMATION —•—•—•—•—•—

FORMER ADDRESS 321 BEAVER ST, CHARLESTON, S.C. 42131

FORMER ADDRESS 427 BRYANT RD. BRONX, NEW YORK 10267

CURRENT EMPLOYMENT SALES MANAGER, WILSON'S DEPARTMENT STORE

—•—•—•—•—•—•— CREDIT INQUIRIES —•—•—•—•—•—

05/03/93 ALLSTATE INSURANCE
12/16/92 BLOOMINGDALE'S

02/12/93 STERN'S
08/01/92 CHEMICAL BANK

Figure 5-1. Sample credit report.

TRW Credit Information Service—free report once a year
Credit Report Request
P.O. Box 8030
Layton, Utah 84041
(800) 682-7654

Trans-Union Credit Information—first report free; $8 fee for
additional reports
P.O. Box 390
Springfield, Pennsylvania 19064
(610) 690-4904

CBI/Equifax—$15 fee
Credit Information Services, Inc.
P.O. Box 105873
Atlanta, Georgia 30348
(800) 685-1111

Note: Look for local credit reporting agencies in your local telephone directory.

Before you challenge information in your report, though, be honest with yourself. You may want to say it's the fault of the bank because it delayed posting your check, or the fault of the credit agency, or the fault of the post office because it was late delivering your check, but how much of that is really true? Still, all the information is reported by computer, and computers do make mistakes because they are run by human beings. The computer may be programmed to acknowledge that all payments are due on the first of the month, but your payment due date is the fifth of the month—so even though your payment was on time, the computer recorded it as being late.

|||≣||| *Wealth is really what you own and control, not how much you have in your* |||≣|||
pockets.

JOHN H. JOHNSON
Publisher of Ebony

THE COST OF CREDIT

Credit terms and interest rates are not sexy topics that make exciting dinner conversation with your friends, but it is critical to understand what the privilege of having a credit card will cost you. The average $2000 balance on a credit card at 18.1 percent interest has a minimum payment of $50 a month. If that is all you pay each month, then it will take 63.87 months to pay off that debt. That's a total of $3193.50. At a minimum monthly payment of $40 you will lay out $3994 over the 99.85 months it will take to satisfy that debt. All in all, the best way not to incur that debt is to use your credit cards judiciously.

HOW TO STAY OUT OF TROUBLE WITH CREDIT CARDS

Here are some tactics to help stem a problem that could quickly get out of control and leave you with a miserable lifestyle for several years as you try to work your way out of debt.

1. Don't carry all your credit cards with you, so you won't be tempted to use them. Leave them at home in the freezer, put them in the toy chest, stick them behind the bathroom mirror, seal them in an envelope in the safe deposit box—do whatever you have to, but get them out of sight. And don't order replacement cards when you get antsy for the sound of the charge plate and the feeling of power in the card.

2. Do some plastic surgery. Cut up the ones you really don't need—like the department store cards with the 21 percent interest rates. Those are the last places you need to go when you're depressed, need a lift, and want to treat yourself.

3. Don't accept all the credit cards that are offered to you. If you receive "preapproved" credit card offers, that doesn't mean you are obligated to take them. They just encourage you to spend more. The issuing banks are only doing themselves a favor. If you read the fine print, you'll see that many of these cards have high interest rates and very high fees. When a bank is paying

out 6 to 7 percent interest and charging 18 percent, who's getting the better deal?

4. Don't collect credit cards like baseball cards. Limit yourself to three credit cards: (1) a gas card for a record of travel expenses if you use the car for work, (2) a Visa, MasterCard, or Discover card for shopping purposes since most department stores accept these cards now rather than use their own credit card, and (3) an American Express card for travel purposes like hotels and car rentals. These should be more than enough.

5. Cancel all those shopping catalogs so you won't be tempted to get on the phone and let your fingers do the walking back into the world of debt. Keep those catalogs out of your mailbox by taking your name off the various junk mailing lists. You can do this by writing to the Direct Marketing Association, Mail Preference Service, 1101 17th Street, N.W., Suite 900, Washington, D.C. 10036-4704.

6. Put a limit on your charging and spending, depending upon your budget. Take a look at your monthly budget and canceled checks. If you are paying more than 20 percent of your take-home pay for debt payments, you're in trouble. This includes car loans, credit cards, and school loans. Stick to Grandma's old adage: If you don't have the money in your pocket, you can't afford it.

7. Try to save for important events or major purchases. If you plan to go to Nassau for vacation next year, save for it. Don't simply plan to use your credit card. You will feel a lot better when you return, knowing that you won't spend the next 9 months paying for a one-week trip.

8. Use your credit wisely. If you have a savings account or money-market fund earning 6 to 7 percent with a $3000 balance, why continue to keep a credit card with a balance of $1200 at an

18 percent interest rate? As of 1991, the tax law no longer honors such interest as deductible.

9. Start using a debit card, which looks like a charge card but takes the cash out of your bank account immediately. If you don't have the cash in the bank, you can't spend it.

10. Ask the bank to lower your credit limit. Every year when the bank renews your card, if you do a good job of paying your bills, the bank makes you feel like you're getting a special privilege by giving you more credit. Wrong! It wants you to spend more so it can make more when you run the debt higher. Call the bank up and say no. Bring your limit down to a level you can live with and stay out of trouble.

One of the richest African-Americans at the beginning of the twentieth century was not an oil-boom baron, but a watermelon farmer. Robert Chatham (1859–1929) started life as a slave and attended Prairie View University as a young man, but never gave up farming. His 1000-acre farm in Sealy, Texas, was advertised in 1916 as "the largest melon farm in the world." His second farm, 435 acres in McDowell County, had its own private railroad track built to reach his warehouse to accommodate the many shipments he made each season to places as far away as Canada and California. The Black Diamond watermelons he grew were a sweet Texas variety that were so popular that he sold as much as 600 carloads per year.

Chatham's wealth attracted the attention of the local press whenever he made large deposits—once as large as $20,000 in one day in 1920. Bank managers were available to him wherever he did business in any of the East Texas towns of Hempstead, Chesterville, Brookshire, Taiton, and El Campo where he owned and leased land. He never had to borrow money for his business, and unfortunately he kept all his cash in one bank, the Farmers National Bank, which went bankrupt in 1924. Chatham started over and became a broker for the crops of the other black farmers in the counties of Waller, Austin, and McDowell. After his death, his sons carried on the family business, which is now headed by a grandson, who still farms watermelons and vegetables.

BORROWING AND CREDIT

DO YOU HAVE TOO MUCH CREDIT?

If you collect credit cards like souvenirs or status symbols, you're on the wrong track, and this hobby can backfire in the wealth-building process. Even if they all have zero balances, and you never use them, and you have a perfectly clean credit history, the bank will probably ask you to close some of those accounts when you apply for a mortgage or a car loan. Consider how the bank may see your accumulated pile of plastic cards.

Let's assume you want to apply for a mortgage and you have 17 credit cards, each with a $2500 credit limit. From the bank's point of view, if you decided to go on a spending spree to furnish the new house and take a luxury cruise and then you lost your job, the bank would be concerned about how you could afford to pay the monthly minimum balance on all those accounts if you charged up to your available credit limit. As noted earlier, all you really need are two or three cards—a gas card, a Visa or MasterCard, and an American Express Card.

The National Negro Bankers Association was organized in 1906 as an offshoot of Booker T. Washington's National Negro Business League, which was founded in 1900. The association was created to establish a separate central depository bank particularly geared toward supporting and financing black businesses. At the initial conference, 51 black banks from 10 states were represented.

CREDIT SCORING

Though little known to most consumers, banks use a rating technique called *credit scoring* to evaluate your creditworthiness. Whether you want to get a mortgage or an auto loan, you will be put through the scoring system. This technique is based on your background and a point system that evaluates your risk potential. Lenders calculate your score based on your credit report plus additional information such as how long you've lived at your current address, how many years you've worked for your present employer, how old your car is, and whether you rent or own your own home. Credit scoring also reviews how much credit you have now, how much you have used it in the past, and what your potential is as a borrower based on your past payment history. Depending upon your accumulation of points, your loan is either approved or rejected.

Some credit reporting agencies are now beginning to supply the banks with a computer-generated credit scoring system that evaluates the information on file with a point system. A conservative system like the one shown in Figure 5-2 requires a total of 300 points for approval. Take the test and see how you qualify for a loan. You can improve your credit score by following a few of these guidelines:

1. Order a copy of your credit report and challenge any inaccuracies. About 42 percent of all credit reports have some errors, but it is your responsibility to get the information right. It can take 3 to 4 months to correct the data.

2. Get rid of the high-interest cards and pay more than the minimum monthly required payment.

3. Pay your bills on time. Credit scoring reviews your credit behavior over the last 6 months.

4. Cut up some of the cards you have and close the accounts in writing—to the bank and the credit reporting agency.

5. Don't make several loan applications at once. Too much borrowing in a short period of time appears risky and compulsive and can make your credit score drop like a rock.

6. Start creating a credit history if you don't have one by taking a passbook savings loan and paying it back early.

7. Stay in the same job for at least 3 years to give yourself a record of employment stability. Job hopping looks unreliable on a credit report.

MAIN STREET BANK

Date: _____ Account #: _____

Applicant: _____ Scored by: _____

BASE SCORE APPLICATION						SCORE
YEARS AT HOME ADDRESS	Less than 6 mos. 15	6 mos. to 2 yrs. 5 mos. 25	2.5 yrs. to 6 yrs. 5 mos. 34	6.5 yrs. to 10 yrs. 5 mos. 40	10.5 yrs. & over 50	
OWN/RENT	Own/Buy 56	Rent 38	Relative (Living w/ Parents) 30	Other (Trailer, Motel) 10		
BANK REFERENCE	No Account 20	Savings 38	Checking 38	Both 63		
YEARS ON JOB	Less than 6 mos. 10	6 mos. to 1 yr. 5 mos. 28	1.5 yrs. to 2 yrs. 5 mos. 32	2.5 yrs. to 5 yrs. 5 mos. 38	5.5 yrs. to 12 yrs. 5 mos. 42	12.5 yrs. & over 45
DEPT. STORE CHARGE/ CREDIT CARDS	None 0	Dept. Store 22	Major Credit/ Charge Card 35	Both 56		
AGE OF AUTO	No Auto 20	1-2 yrs. 42	3 yrs. 38	4-5 yrs. 33	5 yrs. & over 28	
HOME TELEPHONE	No Phone 0	One 25	Two 36	Three 42		
					SUBTOTAL	

IN-HOUSE RECORDS				
MOST RECENT RATING	Satisfactory 12	No Record 7	New Customer 7	Major/Minor Derog. -20
			SUBTOTAL	

CREDIT BUREAU				
MAJOR/MINOR DEROG.	None 18	No Record 7	One -2	Two -10	Three -30
# INQUIRIES OR TOO NEW TO RATE	No Record 12	No Inquiries 12	One 3	Two -6	Three -22
			TOTAL	

OVERRIDE AUTHORIZED BY _____

Figure 5-2. Sample score sheet for bank credit.

8. If you're rejected on a loan application, ask for an explanation before applying elsewhere. Some banks have more relaxed loan requirements than others. If the amount you are requesting is low, your loan officer may have the authority to override the computer's recommendation for rejection.

Richard Burton Fitzgerald (1843–1918), the son of freed slaves who were farmers, grew up in Chester County, Pennsylvania, where he and his brother Robert were educated at the Ashmun Academy in Chester before joining the Union Army during the Civil War. Robert became a teacher in one of the Freedmen's Bureau schools in the South, but Richard opened a brickyard, which promptly lost money and left him broke. He joined his brother in Durham, North Carolina; opened another brickyard; and married Sallie Williams, a missionary from Philadelphia. A 4 million brick order from the state nearly destroyed them when weather and damaged supplies made them renegotiate the deal, but they proved to the locals that they could make bricks.

In 1884, Richard landed a lucrative contract with the Duke family, owners of American Tobacco Company, and with their support his business grew eightfold over the next decade. He purchased many pieces of real estate around Durham and went into partnership with William Coleman, another black entrepreneur, to open a black-owned textile mill. The venture with Coleman did not succeed, although most of Fitzgerald's other enterprises did. The most significant remaining institution that Fitzgerald participated in founding was the Mechanics and Farmers Bank. It was a partnership that included John Merrick and A. M. Moore, both of the North Carolina Mutual Life Insurance Company; Dr. M.T. Pope; James E. Shepard; and William Gaston Pearson, the bank's first cashier. The bank was incorporated in 1907 with $10,000 of capital stock, and Richard Fitzgerald was its first president. It is still in operation under the direction of Julia Wheeler Taylor, daughter of John Wheeler, the second president of the bank.

STUDENT LOANS

More than half the African-American college graduates who have completed their education in the last few years have financed their way through school with student loans, which means that you are already graduating with a creditor waiting for your attention. The rules are that whether you complete your degree or not, within 6 months of leaving school with or without the sheepskin your favorite uncle will send you a little coupon book for payments.

The Direct Loan Consolidation Center, (800) 848-0982, a federal government agency, has been created to help you manage to pay down this debt with four different programs available to new graduates.

- *Income Contingent Repayment Plan.* Your monthly payment is based upon your income. As your income goes up or down, so do your payments. You have 25 years to repay the debt. If there is still a balance after 25 years, then the balance is forgiven, but you pay taxes on the forgiven debt as if it were a gift from the government.

- *Standard Repayment Plan.* Under this plan, you have 10 years to pay off the loans and must send in at least $50 a month. Actual monthly payments depend on your income and the amount of your debt.

- *Extended Repayment Plan.* This arrangement gives you from 12 to 30 years to pay off your loans, depending upon your loan amount, and requires a minimum monthly payment of $50. The total amount of payments over 30 years can be quite high.

- *Graduated Repayment Plan.* Under this plan, your payments start out quite low—$50 a month—and increase every 2 years as your income increases. The time period of the loan is from 12 to 30 years.

The Direct Loan Consolidation Center will roll all your separate loans into a single payment. It makes it easier to manage the monthly payments, and if you allow the agency to automatically deduct the payments every month from your bank account, the agency will reduce the interest by ¼ of 1 percent. The interest rate varies between 8½ percent and 9 percent.

Since the Equal Credit Opportunity Act passed, a lender cannot deny you credit under any circumstances if you qualify for it. Your race, sex, or marital status should not be an issue. Even if you are receiving public assistance, you cannot be turned down if you meet the guidelines. Women are also protected from discrimination. For instance, a married woman is allowed to establish credit in her own name based on her husband's credit. This is an especially good idea in the case of impending divorce.

II≡II   *Being well dressed does not prevent one from being poor.*   II≡II
PROVERB FROM ZAIRE

CREDIT PROBLEMS

Kenyatta and Danita M. have been married for 3 years and are both working at corporate jobs that they accepted after completing their graduate degrees. He is a regional sales manager for a computer company, and she runs the community affairs department of a local television station. They have a combined income of $132,000, and yet they can't seem to save any money. Most of the debt comes from the five credit cards they constantly use, the two car notes for Kenyatta's BMW and Danita's Jaguar, and the four student loans they are paying off for their educations. With their busy two-career lifestyles they have a regular housekeeper, order take-out dinners each night when they aren't out for some business event, attend an expensive health club to stay in shape, and entertain regularly at home for business and social networking. They both spend at least one weekend a month shopping for new clothes since they know that dressing for success is important in their high-profile jobs.

Danita wants to buy a house one day, but she doesn't know how they will do it. She doesn't want to give up the two-week Caribbean vacation they take each winter that costs them $3000 or the $2000 a month summer cottage they rent each year in Martha's Vineyard. They have gotten into the habit of skipping credit card payments one month and doubling up on payments the next month. They want to consider bankruptcy, but she knows it will look silly for two young "buppies" with their sizable paychecks to admit that they are in over their heads.

Being in debt can be the most emotionally devastating experience outside of death or divorce. Not being able to pay your bills does not reflect on your moral integrity or your worth as a human being, although some of the bill collectors would have you believe that. Getting help is the only way to deal with the situation.

Many couples get into debt very easily, can't figure out how to get ahead, and get lost in the issue of who is to blame for what when they try to face up to the problem. Fighting about who spent too much is hiding the issue and leads to more anger, frustration, and misery. Professional credit counseling agencies can help you work out what you owe and what you can afford to pay, and will save you the time and effort of negotiating with each creditor individually. Working with a counselor can save a marriage and turn around the financial problem, but it takes a commitment to correct what has started out as a comfortable dream and has slowly become a nightmare.

You can find such a local agency through the national hot-line number of the Consumer Credit Counseling Service listed in Appendix B of this book. You have to be careful about the advice you get from credit counselors and know whom the agency represents besides you. Some agencies are funded by the various creditors that you are trying to pay off, so even when you should file bankruptcy, they may not recommend it to you.

|||≣||| *Only poor men put on a show.* |||≣|||

CHARLES JOHNSON
Middle Passage, 1990

If you think you have credit problems but are not sure, take the following test and see how you do.

WARNING SIGNALS OF CREDIT PROBLEMS

(Yes or No)

1. Do you often pay bills after their due date?   _____

2. Do you find yourself dipping into savings or checking overdrafts to pay monthly bills?   _____

3. Can you afford to pay only the minimum amount due on your monthly credit card bills? _____

4. Are you skipping monthly payments on some bills altogether? _____

5. Have you ever misrepresented your income to obtain credit? _____

6. Are you using credit cards to make purchases that you used to make with cash? _____

7. Is the total amount you owe growing larger? _____

8. Are you reluctant to answer the phone or open mail because you fear it may be about overdue bills? _____

9. Are you losing sleep at night, fighting about money, or lying to your spouse, relatives, and friends about why bills aren't being paid? _____

10. Are you spending when you know you can't afford it just to "keep up appearances"? _____

If you answered yes to even one question, it's time to step back and ponder a solution. If you're getting collection letters in the mail and nasty phone calls for past-due bills, then you've definitely overextended your credit and need help paying off your debt. Don't consider bankruptcy immediately. If you declare bankruptcy, it will take 10 years to get your good credit back. Instead consult a credit counselor. You can find such an agency through the Consumer Credit Counseling Service listed in Appendix B.

THE CREDIT REPAIR HUSTLE

You have maxed out on all the plastic, may get downsized from your job, have trouble reading the mail each night, and are praying for a solution. You read a small ad offering to repair your credit. It sounds like it's too good to be true—and it is. These scams, found in small ads in the backs of magazines and in handbills passed out on the street, offer to clean up your credit—for a hefty fee (usually from $300 to $1000). Unfortunately, there is no such thing as credit repair, regardless of how much you may want to believe the false promise held out to you.

The "service" these con artists provide consists of writing letters to your creditors, which you could do yourself. They challenge everything that is in your credit report. Your creditors are required to respond to each challenge, in writing within a reasonable period of time. The "credit repairers" do this so many times that some of the creditors may get tired of responding and miss a month, which will give you a clean credit report for about 30 days. But that miracle doesn't last since all credit reporting agencies update their files each month.

At the worst, some of these fly-by-night con artists may also offer to "rebuild" your credit report by using a dishonest scheme like "borrowing" the name, address, and social security number of someone who is similar to you. They then create an altered version of your name or a phony social security number. Being in debt may feel like being in prison, but this deliberate fraud could land you in the real clinker.

COLLECTING WHAT YOU OWE:
HARASSMENT AND GARNISHMENT

A collection agency does have a right to call you if you do not make regular payments as agreed and will do so, but you have a right not to be harassed. The Fair Credit Reporting Act is regulated by the Federal Trade Commission. If you feel that a credit card company or a collection agency is harassing you unnecessarily, you have a right to complain to your state attorney general's office or to the Federal Trade Commission at the Bureau of Consumer Protection, (202) 326-3650.

Garnishments are wage attachments to your paycheck. Garnishing your wages is a legal process that any creditor can resort to if you do not come forward and respond to legal action taken to collect on a debt that you owe. A court will contact your employer and monitor the payments, taking at least 10 percent of your take-home pay as repayment of the loan. The record of such legal action will stay on your credit report for 10 years.

DEBTORS ANONYMOUS

If you have found yourself drowning in debt, yet can't stop yourself from the constant compulsion to shop and spend, then you have a serious problem with compulsive shopping. Look into getting professional help to turn your life around and start over. If you can't afford some sessions with a therapist, look for a local chapter of Debtors Anonymous. This is a national organization that offers the same kind of help to compulsive spenders that Alcoholics Anonymous does to its members. It is managed like most of the 12-step programs and works with individuals to develop some new habits and attitudes about how they are using their money.

Remember to use your credit privileges properly. Although the days of debtor's prison are over, you shouldn't take these obligations lightly. Trouble starts when you forget about saving and start spending without discipline. If you're tempted at a super sale to buy the dress, shoes, lamp, or couch that you just "have to have," think about two things:

1. How many hours must you work to pay for it?

2. What is the true price of the item once you add the rate of credit card interest?

It makes sense to borrow money for items that grow in value or for emergency situations that arise, but little else is worth the extra expense or the anxiety. Credit can help you achieve a greater financial prosperity, or it can become your worst nightmare. It's up to you.

FILING BANKRUPTCY—
THE LAST STRAW

When you can't take the pressure anymore for the phone calls, past-due notices, and collection letters in the mail, when your bills add up to twice your annual salary, and when your credit counselor can't help you, then you may have to consider bankruptcy. It's a drastic step and stays on your credit history for 10 years. The United States was founded on the principle of debt relief, but even though it is a constitutionally guaranteed right, debt relief through bankruptcy is absolutely the last resort, and there can be hidden consequences. It can interfere with getting a job, renting an apartment, as well as obtaining any further credit privileges. Even so, the high rate of consumer debt that many Americans have fallen into triggered 886,000 bankruptcies in 1995, the highest level in history—so far.

Even bankruptcy doesn't wipe out all debts. Debts that cannot be written off are student loans, back taxes, any debt to a government agency, parking tickets, alimony, and child support. The rules differ in each state about keeping your house, depending upon how much equity you have in the property. The fees for filing bankruptcy can be hefty—from $500 to $1000. And since you're already in financial trouble, any attorney who will represent you wants to be paid up front—in cash. If you want to take the risk of doing it yourself, you can, but the filing fees are still expensive.

Two Classes of Bankruptcy

There are two types of bankruptcy: Chapter Seven and Chapter Thirteen.

- *Chapter Seven.* This allows you to wipe out all that you owe (with the exceptions noted above) and start over again with a clean slate. Credit cards, medical bills, past-due rent, car loans, personal loans, and utility bills are debts that can be eliminated. If you forget to list a debt, such as a credit card or a personal loan, the creditor can still hound you for collection after you file.

- *Chapter Thirteen.* This is a workout plan where the court puts you on a repayment schedule for 3 years. The paperwork is overwhelming, and every penny that you receive has to be monitored by the U.S. District Bankruptcy Court. If your rich uncle dies and leaves you a healthy hunk of change, the court gets it first and pays off your creditors before you see a dime of it.

Chapter Thirteen is advisable when you do have the assets and/or future income (like an annuity) and need to work out a 3- to 5-year payment plan. Chapter Seven is best when you have no income, no assets, and no future hopes of ever paying off an overwhelming debt.

Figure 5-3, "What I Owe," offers you a simple worksheet for recording your debt. It is hoped that nine entries will cover your creditors. If not, use the worksheet in the figure as a model to create your own worksheet. A budget is still the most valuable tool for predicting what is going to happen, what is coming due, and when and what should be changed and renegotiated in changing your pattern of behavior and correcting the mistakes of the past.

WHAT I OWE

Creditor	Total Amount Owed	Monthly Payment	Due Date of Payments	Total Number of Payments	Date of Final Payment
	$	$			

Figure 5-3. Use this worksheet to record your debt.

SAVING MONEY IS HEALTHY AND HABIT-FORMING, AND IT'S THE FOUNDATION FOR BUILDING WEALTH

"Accumulating money is so easy, I'm surprised more people aren't rich. That's the way money works. The important thing is not how much money a person makes, it is what he does with it that matters."

A. G. Gaston
African-American millionaire in Birmingham, Alabama

Anyone who watched him growing up in Demopolis, Alabama, would have known that Arthur George Gaston was going to be a rich man one day. In 1901, at age 8, when the other kids in the neighborhood came over to play on the swing in his grandparents' backyard, Arthur charged them for the privilege—a button, a bottle cap, a pin, or a penny—but they had to pay something. When he reached junior high school, his classmates teased him about being a cheapskate, but when they wanted to take a girl out for a soda after a school dance, they came to him to borrow a dollar and Gaston would loan it to them—at 25-cents-a-week interest.

At 16, he had to drop out of tenth grade and go to work in the steel mills of Birmingham for 31 cents an hour to support his ill mother, but that didn't last long. Growing up within a stone's throw of Tuskegee Institute, Gaston was a great admirer of Booker T. Washington and deeply believed in Washington's principles of thrift, hard work, and self-reliance. Gaston lived at home with his mother and worked in the mill, but he carefully observed his friends and neighbors with the intention of starting a business one day. He religiously read all of Washington's writings and firmly believed in Washington's motto of "Don't do it just for the money. Find a need and fill it." Gaston began to search for a way to do just that.

It took him 15 years to save the money, but in 1923, after observing a few con artists collecting cash for funerals for people who were very much alive, Gaston started his first company, the Booker T. Washington Industrial Insurance Burial Company, collecting a dime a week from his policyholders. The new company nearly went out of business. Less than 6 months after taking an application, one of his first policyholders died and the cost of the funeral was $100. Gaston had only collected $3 from the deceased, and his capital in the company only amounted to $50.

After surviving this crisis, Gaston quickly decided that it would be a good idea to be in the business of owning the funeral home and formed a partnership with A. L. Smith, his father-in-law. Within a few months they opened the Smith & Gaston Funeral Home. The Smith & Gaston Funeral Home became legendary for its style of service—large limousines and uniformed chauffeurs—and the insurance company was quite successful for several years as the "cash cow" to support his other business goals. A few years later, Gaston purchased 30 acres of land outside the city, landscaped the property, named it the New Grace Hill Cemetery, and began selling burial plots.

Gaston realized that many of his friends and neighbors also wanted to be business owners but did not have the appropriate education about business or the required training in shorthand, typing, bookkeeping, accounting and office management skills. None of the white business schools in the South would admit Negro students, so Gaston found another need to fill. He created the Booker T. Washington Business College in 1939 to offer business education and management training classes for blacks. The college also provided its own tuition loan program for those students who could not afford the fees for the various classes.

Another important need Gaston observed was the need for lodging for blacks who traveled through the South to visit friends and family but had no place to stay because of the segregated motel chains along the highways. Visiting politicians and preachers who came to Birmingham for conferences and conventions did not have any public lodging or large local meeting rooms outside of a church basement. In 1954, he built the A. G. Gaston Motel in Birmingham, again using his own money and his own construction company. The motel, with its restaurant and nightclub, was a major attraction even for the locals since it included the unheard of luxury of air-conditioning.

Following the Korean war, black veterans who took advantage of the GI bill benefits and attended college wanted to develop businesses, but they could not get loans to start their operations. Black home buyers could not find lenders to finance mortgages to build homes, so Gaston filled another need for his community. In 1957 he raised $350,000 from local investors and founded the Citizens Federal Savings Bank in downtown Birmingham. In its 1995 annual report, the bank stated that it had assets of $81 million, and it is listed in *Black Enterprise* magazine as the twenty-first largest black-owned financial institution in the nation.

Gaston was also the financial savior of the early civil rights movement. When Martin Luther King was arrested during the Montgomery bus boycott, Gaston paid his legal fees and his bail. As civil rights demonstrators were attacked and jailed during the early sixties, Gaston posted over $160,000 of bonds for them. When the Ku Klux Klan bombed his motel and threatened him for his support of the civil rights workers, Gaston came back stronger and made a lifelong commitment to serving the community that had made him wealthy.

His proudest accomplishment in his later years was the A. G. Gaston Boys' Club. He donated $50,000 to establish a Boys' Club of America affiliate in the community. He spent much of his time there in his last years, before he retired from managing his business empire. Before his death, Gaston donated $300,000 to the club for renovations.

By 1987, his vast empire of businesses was valued at over $34 million. White investors who began to realize the profit potential for doing business in the black community made generous offers to buy his companies. But Gaston had strong faith in the skills and talent of the people he had groomed and developed as business leaders. That faith was exhibited in his final gesture of philanthropy and good business sense. To assure that Gaston Enterprises would remain in the hands of the African-American staff that he had trained to manage and develop these businesses, Gaston established an employee stock ownership plan that allowed the employees to buy the company for $4 million. It was his final executive decision. Gaston died in 1996.

In his autobiography, *Green Power,* which he wrote in 1966, Gaston shared many of the secrets of how he became wealthy. "No matter how little I made, I always kept a little bit for myself. It might have only been a dime or a quarter, but I kept that little bit for myself. And I always paid cash for everything. If I didn't have the cash, I didn't buy it. I never wanted to owe anybody for anything."

|||≣||| *A wealthy man will always have followers.* |||≣|||
NIGERIAN PROVERB

YOU HAVE TO SAVE MONEY

Too many African-Americans go overboard with an "I deserve only the best" approach to prove to ourselves and the rest of the world that we have now arrived at a level of income and comfort by the tangible treats that we own. Trying to play "catch-up" with conspicuous consumption is not the answer to building wealth and gaining the financial respect we seek. These spending statistics are confirmed in the data collected by marketing and advertising agencies that track the $400 million that flow through the African-American community. And less than 4 percent of those dollars is spent within the African-American community.

U.S. Census statistics for 1993–1994 confirms and compares incomes and savings for all racial and ethnic groups. The national average savings rate for all Americans is 3.9 percent, but African-Americans save less than half the national average, or 1.8 percent of their income. Although Americans as a whole seem to be afflicted with the "spendaholic disease," many African-Americans have developed an acute case of "mall-itis" with a "gotta-have-it-now" urgency that propels us into the stores each weekend. This "shop 'til you drop" attitude seems to come from a distorted belief that after so many years of being deprived and not being allowed to enjoy even the simplest of material comforts we have to make up for lost time. We cannot buy back the past by mortgaging our future with excessive credit card debt.

In 1838, Frankie Rollins, a free young black woman in Boston, was severely criticized for a statement she made to the Abolitionist Society following her first year of teaching literacy classes which the society provided for runaway slaves who had managed to reach Boston. "It is extremely difficult to teach the newly freed slaves to save money. Every penny they receive for any labor is quickly spent on flashy new clothes or useless trinkets before the day is over. They do not seem to understand that the money must be saved to feed and clothe them." If Rollins were alive today, she would still be disappointed and dismayed to learn that after so many years of earning money and with the increasing income being experienced by so many African-Americans, there is still a serious problem in our community with holding on to the gelt that flows through our fingers.

Although we may not be able to control our income, which is 12 percent below the average white family's income, in the comparative black-white wealth gap, we do have control over the spending side of the equation. Each of us can look back at parents or grandparents or other relatives who managed to accumulate far more in assets on much less income. And they did it by saving. They were extremely careful and thrifty with each dime that came to them. They never lost sight of how hard they had to work to get the simplest of basic comforts that we now take for granted. These ancestors would not be impressed with the desire to buy social status and esteem with just a quick flash of the plastic. The major social issue now is what kind of descendants have we become in the area of finance and investing.

Although we have not been welcome in most financial institutions, African-Americans have always managed to find a way to save. *Susus* are a communal saving practice that can be traced back to West Africa as early as the twelfth century. This cultural custom can still be found among many West Indians who relocated to the United States but did not have the minimum cash needed to open a bank account though they wanted to start saving money. A *susu* network is a commitment between friends and family members—usually people who all know each other and come from the same village on one of the Caribbean islands—to put in a fixed amount of dollars each week for a fixed period of time. Some *susus* have been known to grow as large as 25 to 30 people and have lasted as long as one year. Each person gives $5 to $25 a week to the pot. One person each week is designated from a predetermined list of names to take the money and keep it for his or her own personal use. This gives that person a sizable portion of cash which can be saved for an emergency or deposited in a bank. Every week, a new "pot of cash" is given to a different member of the group until each person has had a turn. This works well for new immigrants until they can accumulate enough cash to participate in the more established banking institutions.

|||≡||| *The best thing you can do for poor folks is not be one.* |||≡|||
REVEREND IKE

SAVING NEEDS THE RIGHT ATTITUDE

Saving money is not hard to do; you just have to want to do it. This isn't brain surgery, rocket science, or nuclear physics, and you don't need an M.B.A. from Harvard or Wharton to figure out how to do it. You just have to want to try and do what you can. And first dispense with the excuses that get in the way of doing it.

POPULAR EXCUSES TO NOT SAVE

When your grandmother told you that "A penny saved is a penny earned," she was wrong! A penny saved is worth two pennies earned—after taxes and inflation and with interest in the right bank account. She probably also told you, "He who is good at excuses is seldom good at anything else." These time-honored sayings rank right up there with "The dog ate my homework," or "The check is in the mail" or "I never got the bill." We have all heard them and used them when we were in a tight spot, but sooner or later they don't work and you have to get past them. Here are some excuses to definitely get past.

1. "I don't have time to think about it now." When are you going to get around to it? The cost of procrastination makes you another year older and deeper in credit card debt. You work hard and find time to pay the landlord, the bank, the phone bill, the insurance company, the druggist, the dentist, the gas company, and so on. When do you get around to paying yourself? The sooner you put yourself on your own payroll, the sooner you will feel more in control of where your life is going.

2. "My spouse will just spend it all anyway." Then put the money into a separate account with only your name on it. Let your employer deduct a fixed amount and put it into the company credit union. Open a money-market mutual fund and have $100 a month deducted from your paycheck. Next year when you can buy the new refrigerator for cash or take that summer vacation to Nassau without using the plastic, you will both be happy that you did it.

3. "My kids will drive me crazy if I tried this." Kids do what they are taught to do if you present it to them the right way. Let them get creative with ways to save money. Make it a challenge for them to be frugal. Tell them that whatever they manage to save from household expenses can be added to their allowance—if they put it into a savings account. Start cultivating these habits in them early and maybe one of them will become the next A. G. Gaston.

4. "I work hard so I deserve a few creature comforts." You also deserve to get more for your money since you work so hard for it. And you deserve to be debt-free and to build a comfortable retirement for yourself. None of this will happen unless you make a consistent effort and put some discipline into it. Who is more important in your life than you are?

5. "A couple of dollars won't make a difference." If you believe this, then you would have been paying lots of interest to A. G. Gaston each week. Two dollars a day adds up to the $60 a month you need to make an extra payment to clear up a hefty credit card balance, purchase a savings bond, or open a mutual fund investment account.

At the September 1995 annual Black Congressional Caucus dinner, the guest of honor was Osceola McCarthy, a quiet, unassuming woman from Hattiesburg, Mississippi. As celebrities and politicians made many speeches about her generosity, Ms. McCarthy sat humbly listening and seemed somewhat perplexed when she was given a standing ovation as the one person who deserved the most recognition that evening. At 85, she had just created a $250,000 scholarship trust at the University of Mississippi. She designated that the funds be used for the education of poor students, not necessarily black, who could not afford a college education. Ms. McCarthy was not a wealthy businesswoman creating an endowment from inherited wealth—she was a laundry woman who had dropped out of school after completing sixth grade. For the 75 years that she worked, McCarthy never had a credit card, did not own a car, had no air-conditioning in her small house, didn't drink sodas or possess a television or a VCR. She followed the basic, simple principle of disciplined savings and consistent deposits into her account and held a sacred belief in the concept of compound interest.

GET REAL ABOUT YOUR MONEY HABITS

The little daily habits we fall into cannot be denied if we are going to change them. Count the number of times you order take-out or a pizza for dinner. How many times a week do you take a cab when you could walk those 12 blocks to the meeting. Thrift has to become a conscious and consistent daily effort. Develop a "tightwad" attitude. Use reverse psychology on yourself and do some creative thinking. You aren't depriving yourself; you're working on becoming wealthy. Think about how A. G. Gaston started out.

1. *Try mind control.* Put a sign on the bathroom mirror and rehearse this each morning as you brush your teeth, "I can't afford!" Before you buy anything, ask yourself twice if this is a basic necessity, do you really need it, and can you find something cheaper? Give yourself this positive affirmation each day: "I am becoming a thrifty and prosperous person each day with each new dollar that I save."

2. *Practice saying NO.* Say it to your friends, your children, your spouse, your colleagues, yourself. Let them know that you have a goal more important than an afternoon at the mall. Arrange to spend time with them that does not cost money—a walk in the park, a visit to a museum or library.

3. *Don't fall for the "it's only ..." trap.* Raffle tickets at work, the street vendor with the books and calendars, an extra $2 here, $5 there. Do this four or five times a week and you can easily go through $25 or $30 a month without thinking about it.

||≡|| *A race which cannot save its earnings can never rise in the scale of civilization.* ||≡||
FREDERICK DOUGLASS
in North American Review, 1884

WHY AND HOW TO SAVE
YOUR MONEY

You don't have to assume a Scroogelike behavior, or develop a "bah-humbug" attitude toward spending money, but saving is vital. Developing a sense of financial discipline is the simplest and most successful way to begin a life of financial independence.

WHY SAVE?

Family emergencies always occur unexpectedly (that's why they are called emergencies!), and you can rely on them having a price tag attached. Make your own list, but here are a few that are typical:

- A sudden death in the family; you have to fly home and pay funeral expenses.

- Some hit-and-run driver smashes into your car in a parking lot, demolishing a headlight, and you have a $500 deductible on your insurance to save money. The repair bill comes to $497.

- Your company may relocate and merge with another one. You just bought a house and you don't want to move, so you may get laid off.

- A long-term illness occurs, your disability insurance payments won't start for another 45 days, and you have no more sick leave or vacation days.

- You need expensive dental work, and your bill is not covered by your insurance.

Hoping for a miracle won't solve these problems and if you don't have the cash, you will resort to borrowing, which puts you deeper in debt, or begging from you friends, which can eventually hurt a good relationship.

In addition to emergencies, you need to save for special situations like vacations and education.

SET UP A FUND FOR EMERGENCIES AND SPECIAL SITUATIONS

Getting through tough times are a little less aggravating if you have put away some cash for the unexpected. A minimum of 3 months living expenses should be your goal. Look at your budget to see how much that is. You will sleep better at night if you don't have to worry about getting nasty calls from the bank about your mortgage payment while you're looking for another job. If you work freelance, sell on commission, or have some form of uncertain income, you need to save as much as 6 months of living expenses for emergencies. And don't count on that big check for a $20,000 commission/royalty/settlement to see you through. It can be as unreliable as the lottery. Windfalls have a way of not quite showing up when you need them. And although creditors like the phone company or your landlord may be sympathetic enough to listen, they need their income, too; and after a few weeks, they don't want to hear the excuse. Set a goal so you can avoid the habit of making excuses. Typical goals for saving include these:

- You want to attend a family reunion in Atlanta next year, and it will cost $1200 for you and your family to go.

- Your apartment building may be going co-op next year, and you want to be able to buy it when the chance arises.

- You want to return to school for a job certification training that will help you get a better job.

- That old clunker you've been driving has 120,000 miles on it, and your mechanic refuses to take your money for another repair job. You need $6000 for a decent used car, and your insurance payments will double.

- Your brother plans to run for city council, and you want to contribute $1000 to his campaign.

Review the goals you wrote down for your life situation in Chapter 3 in the section "What Do You Want to Do by When?" If you have some new ideas to add to that list, redo it. You don't have to be locked into a goal that doesn't work for you, and you can adjust your goals as you need to as emergencies or special situations arise.

|||≣||| *Anyone who has struggled with poverty knows how expensive it is to be poor.* |||≣|||
JAMES BALDWIN

MAKE THE EFFORT AND DO
WHAT YOU CAN

An ideal goal would be to save 10 percent of your paycheck; do 15 percent if you don't have any debts. If that's too much of a cash crunch for you, then do what you can. If you can start with only a dollar a day, get started. That's as simple as giving up a bag of potato chips and a soda that you don't really need. Pass up the candy bar at the newsstand. Walk the 10 blocks to the movies instead of taking the bus. Your heart and liver will thank you for it one day, and you won't have to buy new clothes, just a new pair of sneakers.

Once you're comfortable with the idea of doing $1, then make it $2 a day, then $5 a day, then $10 a day, until you finally reach a point where you look forward to seeing how much you can put away and feel good about it instead of feeling deprived. If saving these amounts on a per-day basis is too difficult, try doing it on a per-week basis.

Take all the extra change out of your pockets at night and leave it out on the dresser. Put it in a jar for a few weeks and then let the kids roll the coins in money wrappers. When you take the rolls to the bank, you will be surprised at how much has accumulated—and all without effort! So be sure you put that money into a savings account.

THIRTY FAST WAYS TO FIND AN EXTRA $50 A MONTH

Walk to the movie instead of taking a cab, make long-distance calls only on weekends, turn off all the extra lights in the house, and lower the thermostat—you know the tried-and-true ways to save. In addition, here are 30 other ways to start saving immediately and stretch your dollars farther than you ever thought possible.

Shopping

1. Carry only the exact amount of cash you will need for the day: bus fare, tokens, lunch.

2. Shop with a list of what you need to buy. Going into the supermarket without a list guarantees that you spend more than you planned and that you buy stuff you don't need.

3. Use coupons only if they make the brand-name products cheaper than the store brand. Otherwise, buy only generic products. Many of them are produced by the brand-name companies on a special contract for the chain stores. Why

MARK GRIFFITH, COFOUNDER

Central Brooklyn Federal Credit Union

"There was a lot of talk about economic development in the community but you still had to go 20 blocks to find a bank, and many branches of the major white banks were closing down. When they did let you open an account, they wouldn't make a loan to you. We thought somebody should do something about the problem. That somebody turned out to be us." That was during the summer of 1989. Mark Griffith, a graduate of Brown University (1985), and Errol Louis, a graduate of Harvard University (1984), two young African-American brothers, born and bred in Brooklyn, started the Central Brooklyn Partnership and founded the Central Brooklyn Federal Credit Union. The credit union opened its doors in April 1993, in a former bank branch that had closed after one of the many bank mergers, leaving the neighborhood with one less financial institution and limited banking services.

"We make it as easy as possible for neighborhood residents to open an account. Twenty dollars and the proper form of I.D. is all you need. Ten dollars buys you a lifetime membership; the other $10 is a deposit to your account. All you have to do is want to start saving and we will support you in your effort." The response to their offer has brought nearly 5000 members into their branch in the heart of Bedford-Stuyvesant.

Regulated by the National Credit Union Association, a federal government agency, accounts are insured for up to $100,000 as are regular commercial bank accounts. The credit union offers loans up to $10,000 at competitive rates for members and nonmembers of the Brooklyn neighborhood, including loans for small businesses, loans for home-based businesses, car loans, debt consolidation loans—anything except mortgages.

Saturday is the busiest day at the credit union, especially with the special program of youth services for kids who want to open accounts. Much of Saturday's traffic is at the separate window for youth members which is open only on Saturday mornings and is managed by other youth members. These members must be between 6 and 17, have a social security number, and have a parent accompany them and cosign for them when they open the account. The membership fee for kids is $7.50, and it costs $10 to open the account. Being a youth member means having access to regular financial literacy workshops, internships with adult members of the credit union, and the opportunity to work part-time in the banking area.

Mark Griffith and Errol Louis are regularly featured in the media for their achievement and have both been praised as successful young men to watch who are making a difference in the financial lives of the people in their community.

"When we talk about financial institution building we have to look at the political power that can come out of that institution. Here we're trying to bring together the nationalists and the capitalists and make them realize that they need each other in the struggle for economic justice."

should you pay the brand-name companies' advertising expenses when you don't have to?

4. Purchase staples in bulk at a warehouse outlet market. Items like rice, flour, sugar, toilet paper, napkins, detergent, and garbage bags are one-third less there, and they never spoil.

Food

5. The average take-out lunch is $5, so brown-bag it a few days a week. Lunch from home is healthier than take-out meals, and you won't waste the leftovers from last night's dinner.

6. Become a vegetarian and eat creative bean casseroles two or three times a week. Red meat is too expensive. And the vegetable dinners you make are much healthier for you than most of the take-out meals you have delivered.

7. Eat in for one month. Share potluck supper with your neighbors and friends. Socializing over a meal does not have to be expensive if you do it at home.

Personal Care and Grooming

8. Wash your sweaters in Woolite and save the $3 that a dry cleaners will charge.

9. Find a hairstyle that doesn't cost you $35 to $40 a week to care for. African-American women have created more than six black millionaires over the last century paying for special hair care. Now its your turn to build some wealth for yourself. Get your hair done for special occasions or as a special treat after you have gotten out of debt and saved $1000.

10. Purchase generic or store-brand shampoo and save a dollar or two on the price. Your hair will get just as clean without a famous brand name.

11. Do your nails yourself. You can give yourself the $10 manicure while you watch a movie on Sunday night. Those false nails can run as high as $30 a week and eventually ruin your own nails in the long run.

12. Make your own cosmetics from items in your refrigerator and your cupboard. There are excellent books in the health food store and the library that tell you how do it. Plain fresh yogurt makes a great moisturizer; rosewater and witch hazel combined make a good astringent; egg whites are a good facial mask.

13. Do your dry-cleaning in bulk in one of the machines that looks like a dryer and cut the cost by half.

Entertainment

14. Get your best-sellers at the library. You have already paid your taxes for this privilege, so use this public service. If the latest Terry McMillan isn't available, spend 50 cents and sign up for the reserve list and wait. Meanwhile, pick up a book on financial planning and expand your financial awareness.

15. If possible, get your videos at the library too. Videos are available at most libraries, and there is no rental fee if you return them on the date they are due. That's another $2 to $6 you can save each weekend.

16. Remember that the library also has magazines. Many libraries allow you to check out copies of popular magazines for up to one week. Cancel subscriptions for those magazines you are too busy to read.

17. Economize on movie tickets. Do you really need to be the first on your block or in your office to see the first-run movies? If the kids just have to see the latest mind-numbing thriller before it gets to the discount movie houses for $1, take them to

the Saturday matinee. It is usually half price or less. The theater managers offer this discount since the place would normally be empty at that hour of the day—and you will probably be able to hear the actors on the screen.

18. Instead of buying a newspaper, get your morning news on the radio and take a library book with you to read on the way to work. Somebody else will probably leave a paper on the train or the bus which you can pick up.

19. Take advantage of free concerts in local parks, museums, library exhibits. Your tax dollars have already paid for them, so go out and enjoy them.

20. Use discount cards and two-for-one specials to go to the theater. You can cut the price of a show by 50 percent.

Clothing

21. Buy pantyhose, socks, and underwear at 60 percent off retail direct from manufacturers through their discount catalogs. Call their customer service 800 numbers to order catalogs.

22. Rent a fabulous formal gown for that once-in-a-lifetime occasion. For $40 to $75 you can look like you just stepped out of a designer showroom without spending next month's rent for one evening.

23. Shop special sales. End-of-the-year clearances at boutiques that have seasonal specials often have unadvertised two-for-one sales on good classic clothing. Get on their mailing lists to know when these sales will be held.

24. Shop in consignment shops. Many department stores and wealthy people often donate designer clothing and end-of-the-season clothing to thrift shops for special sales for charity and for the tax deduction they receive. A brand new Pauline Trigere coat selling for $3000 in Bergdorf's might be found here for $300.

Miscellaneous

25. Buy next year's Christmas cards, gift wrapping paper, and decorations on December 26 and store them in the back of the closet.

26. Write a letter to a friend rather than call. The cost of a stamp, 32 cents, is cheaper than most calls, even at weekend rates, and the letter will last longer than the phone call.

27. Stop smoking! Does it really make sense to put a match to $2 a day?

28. Join a travel club and save 25 to 30 percent on vacation trips.

29. Check out garage and yard sales for housewares, toys, books, lamps, etc. When you find one of those $20 Tupperware sets for $2 you'll get hooked on this habit.

30. Barter your time or a special skill with a friend. Baby-sit for her when she wants a special night out. In exchange, she will do your hair if she is a beautician or your taxes if she is an accountant.

Follow just half these steps for one month, and you will easily find the extra $50 to $100 a month to put into a savings account or a money-market fund. Trust me, it works!

A MUTUAL AID SAVINGS SOCIETY

Mutual savings societies were the financial backbone of most black communities after Reconstruction. The Saint Luke's Penny Thrift Savers Society came into being in 1888 as a mutual aid society for the domestic workers, day laborers, and small black businesses in Richmond, Virginia. Members opened an account with $1 and deposited 5 or 10 cents a week to build up savings, with the goal of building a home one day or saving for old age since social security did not exist at that time and most workers did not have jobs that provided pensions. Some also hoped to start a business one day.

Maggie Lena Walker, born black, female, and poor in 1867, joined the society at age 14 when she experienced the benefit of its aid following the brutal murder of her father. She was deeply committed to the society's principles of racial solidarity and thrift. She rose through the ranks until she was elected as grand secretary in 1899. Then she discovered that the treasury had only $31.61 and the unpaid bills were over $400. She immediately launched a campaign to generate new memberships and renew old ones. Within 2 years she had doubled the membership, expanded the thrift program, paid off the debts, started a weekly newspaper, called the *St. Luke's Herald,* and began a printing business. A department store was founded to provide consumer goods to black customers at reasonable prices. The children of members were given cardboard boxes to save their pennies in; when the pennies became a dollar, the children were allowed to open their own accounts. Youth members were supported in their efforts to be industrious by being given jobs in the society's businesses. They handled the paper route, ran errands, did cleaning chores, and worked in the store.

By 1903, Walker took the monumental step that credits her with being the first woman—not just the first black woman, but the first woman—to start a bank in the United States. After seeing how black customers were treated by white banks when they wanted to get mortgages, she used $9000 of deposits from the members to start the St. Luke's Penny Thrift Savings Bank, with the slogan "Bring It All Back Home." A dollar was all that was required to open an account. Within 15 years the deposit base had grown to $376,000 and the bank had financed 645 black homeowners in Richmond.

At the beginning of the Depression when 8812 white banks failed, Walker arranged the merger of St. Luke's with two other black lending institutions and formed the Consolidated Bank and Trust Company of Richmond. The bank was strong enough to survive the Depression and was able to loan $150,000 to the city of Richmond to cover the payroll for all of the city's schoolteachers for the winter of 1931. Walker was active in the bank's management, being referred to as St. Luke's grandmother, until she finally retired due to ill health in 1933 and died the following year. Maggie Walker's legacy of thrift and financial planning has survived her and continues to support African-American homeowners and businesses. The Consolidated Bank and Trust is still in existence today in downtown Richmond and is the oldest black bank in America.

|||≡||| *The haves and the have nots can often be traced to the dids and didn'ts.* |||≡|||

WILLIAM RASPBERRY
Washington Post *columnist*

WHERE TO PUT YOUR SAVINGS

CREDIT UNIONS

Credit unions provide many of the same services as a bank, but the rates can be lower by 2 to 3 percent on loans when you do have to borrow money. Because they are also nonprofit institutions that give dividends to members from the profits they earn on the loans they make, the dividends received on a savings account will be higher than the interest paid by a commercial bank. Large corporations, government agencies, and several membership organizations make these special services available to members to help build savings. Many churches in the African-American community have established credit unions to provide a service for church members who may not have such a good credit rating or want to support the lending programs of the church.

PASSBOOK SAVINGS

If you are starting small, this old standby is still the easiest way to open an account at your bank. The minimum deposit is typically about $250 and pays 2¼ to 3½ percent in interest. If you don't want your money tied up in a long-term commitment and don't want higher interest, than this is for you. You can put your money in today and take it out tomorrow. This is called a liquid account.

CERTIFICATES OF DEPOSITS

CDs are not as liquid as a passbook savings account, but the interest rates they pay are higher. CDs, also called time deposits, are loans that you make to the bank. They can be purchased for as little as $500 at most banks. You can buy a CD for a period of 90 days or for as long as 5 years. The interest rate is guaranteed for a specified length of time. The longer the time, usually, the higher the interest rate but that isn't always the case. It is a good idea to shop around for higher interest rates on CDs. Sometimes a stockbroker will have access to out-of-town banks that pay higher interest rates.

Each Wednesday, the Federal Reserve Bank posts its discount rate to banks; that is the rate at which the "Fed" will accept loans as collateral from the bank and gives the bank credit for those loans at a discounted rate. The bank, in turn, adjusts its CD rates accordingly.

Remember, however, when you buy a CD for a fixed period, your money is locked in. If you need your cash back before the time period has expired, you may lose the interest and also pay a penalty for breaking the time deposit contract. This is in effect a loan you grant to the bank; it is therefore insured for up to $100,000 by the Federal Deposit Insurance Corporation.

SAVINGS BONDS (U.S. SERIES EE)

Savings bonds can be purchased at any bank for as little as $25. They will double in value in 7 to 12 years. Interest rates may adjust twice a year or quarterly to compete with CDs and money-market rates. Beginning in January 1990, if your joint-filing income is less than $60,000, then you may buy U.S. bonds for a child's college education and the bonds will be nontaxable. However, if you cash savings bonds in before they mature, you will lose money, and if the cash is not spent on tuition, you will lose the tax deduction.

INSURED MONEY-MARKET ACCOUNTS

These are simply glorified money-market funds that have only U.S. Treasury bills and short-term government notes in them; the rates are usually a bit higher than that paid on a passbook savings account, and the money-market account is just as liquid. In addition, the account is insured, plus you can write checks against your money-market account if you need to.

MONEY-MARKET MUTUAL FUNDS

These differ in two ways from the insured money-market account: they pay a higher interest rate, and they are not insured. Money-market mutual funds include forms of short term-debt in their portfolio which carry slightly more risk than government notes; this higher risk is why you get a higher rate on these accounts. Portfolios usually include short-term bond notes and corporate commercial paper (corporations can legally write a postdated discounted check to keep cash available for day-to-day operating expenses), banker's acceptances (short-term trade notes on imported shipped goods), and Treasury bills. Check-writing privileges are available for emergencies, but checks must usually be written for a minimum amount of $500 each.

GET SOMEONE TO HELP YOU

If you have no self-discipline and need an outside influence to help you help yourself, enroll at work in a payroll savings plan. Your employer automatically deducts a specified amount from your paycheck and deposits it directly into a credit union account or a bank savings account or uses it to buy a savings bond for you. A payroll savings plan is a good bet for those with holes in their pockets or slippery fingers. After the first few paychecks you will adjust to having a few less dollars and won't notice the difference. Within a few months you will get excited when you see what is growing for you.

BEFORE DEPOSITING YOUR SAVINGS

Before you open your savings account, ask the banker to explain how the interest is compounded at that bank. Daily? Quarterly? Semi-annually? This can make a difference in your interest income. Note the following:

Compounding Period	1 Year	5 Years	10 Years
Daily	1054.67	1304.90	1702.76
Quarterly	1053.54	1297.90	1684.70
Semiannually	1053.19	1295.78	1679.05

Note: If you decide to withdraw any money from your account the day before the end of the compounding period, then you will not earn any interest during that time.

Compare the figures above, which show you the various rates of return on $1000 in savings at 5¼ percent, but compounded at different periods. (Also see Table 6-1, which shows how $100, compounded monthly, grows over a period of years.)

Table 6-1

Savings over the Years

This table shows what a monthly deposit of $100 grows to over a period of years.
Compounding is monthly, and deposits are made at the beginning of the period.

Interest Rate	5 Years	10 Years	15 Years	20 Years	25 Years	30 Years	35 Years	40 Years
1.5%	6,234	12,954	20,197	28,003	36,418	45,487	55,261	65,797
2	6,315	13,294	21,006	29,529	38,947	49,355	60,856	73,566
2.5	6,397	13,646	21,858	31,162	41,704	53,648	67,181	82,513
3	6,481	14,009	22,754	32,912	44,712	58,419	74,342	92,837
3.5	6,566	14,385	23,698	34,788	47,996	63,727	82,460	104,771
4	6,652	14,774	24,691	36,800	51,584	69,636	91,678	118,590
4.5	6,740	15,177	25,738	38,958	55,507	76,223	102,156	134,618
5	6,829	15,593	26,840	41,275	59,799	83,573	114,083	153,238
5.5	6,920	16,024	28,002	43,762	64,498	91,780	127,675	174,902
6	7,012	16,470	29,227	46,435	69,646	100,954	143,183	200,145
6.5	7,106	16,932	30,519	49,308	75,289	111,217	160,898	229,599
7	7,201	17,409	31,881	52,397	81,480	122,709	181,156	264,012
7.5	7,298	17,904	33,318	55,719	88,274	135,587	204,345	304,272
8	7,397	18,417	34,835	59,295	95,737	150,030	230,918	351,428
8.5	7,497	18,947	36,435	63,144	103,937	166,240	261,395	406,726
9	7,599	19,497	38,124	67,290	112,953	184,447	296,385	471,643
9.5	7,703	20,066	39,908	71,756	122,872	204,913	336,590	547,933
10	7,808	20,655	41,792	76,570	133,789	227,933	382,828	637,678

In 1991, Congress passed the Truth in Savings Act (TISA), which requires that banks give accurate and clear answers about what the true interest rate is that you will earn on your savings. Banks used to lure depositors with toasters, blenders, and flashlights but left them in the dark about what they were really earning. Before TISA, banks would pay interest on only 88 percent of the amount you deposited into your account since the bank is allowed to lend out only 88 percent of its dollars—the Federal Reserve Bank restricts 12 percent of a bank's assets for a cash reserve cushion. Under TISA, the commercial banks, credit unions, and savings and loan associations are required to compute the savings rates in annual percentage yield figures to give an accurate estimate, which clears up the hidden deductions.

A. G. Gaston's 10 Tips for Building Wealth

1. Save a part of all you earn. Take it off the top and bank it. Money does not spoil. It keeps.

2. Establish a reputation at a bank or a savings and loan association. Save at an established institution and borrow there. Stay away from loan sharks.

3. Take no chances with your money. Play the safe number, the good one. A person who can't afford to lose has no business gambling.

4. Never borrow anything that, if forced to, you can't pay back.

5. Don't get "big-headed" with the "little fellows." That's where the money is. If you stick with the "little fellows," give them your devotion; they'll make you big.

6. Don't have too much pride. Wear the same suit for a year or two. It doesn't make any difference what kind of suit the pocket is in if there is money in the pocket.

7. Find a need and fill it. Successful businesses are founded on the needs of people. Once in business, keep good books. Also hire the best people you can find.

8. Stay in your own class. Never run around with people you can't compete with.

9. Once you get money or a reputation for having money, people will give you money.

10. Once you reach a certain bracket, it is very difficult not to make more money.

7

||||≡ ||||≡ ||||≡ ||||≡ ||||≡ ||||≡ ||||≡||||≡ ||||≡ ||||≡ ||||≡||||≡

BUYING A HOUSE

"To be landless is a crime."

Nelson Mandela

In an 1857 business credit report written by R. G. Dun (the precursor of the Dun and Bradstreet business credit reporting firm), Stephen Smith of Philadelphia was described as "the king of the Darkies with $100m." The report referred to the annual income of Stephen Smith, a former slave who had built a large business in Philadelphia. Smith, who later became an AME minister, had formed a partnership with William Whipper, another freed slave, to create and operate one of the largest coal yards and lumber businesses on the East Coast beginning in 1849. When Smith died in 1873, he had an estate that comprised "several thousand bushels of coal, over 2,250,000 feet of lumber and 22 railroad cars which he used to transport his goods." The value of Smith's estate was over $500,000, which included an interest in a local bank and 52 pieces of property in downtown Philadelphia, his residence at 921 Lombard Street, and the original coal and lumber yard which was located at Broad and Willow Streets. Several more properties were located in Columbia, Pennsylvania, where Smith and Whipper also sold coal and lumber.

Land has been a major measure of wealth in almost all cultures, since there is no substitute for it. Whoever owned the land had significant control over what happened in the community even if they weren't around to manage and maintain it. African-Americans were brought to this country to do the development part of the job. Most slaves were from agrarian cultures and were skilled at cultivating the land—they just weren't allowed to own any of it. As Americans moved west in the 1830s, even free blacks who tried to become pioneers and join the expansion into the new states beyond the Mississippi River were prohibited from participating in the land-rush races for free homesteading property. Black townships managed to spring up in isolated prairie locations across the country—New Philadelphia, Illinois; Nicodemus, Kansas; Langston, Oklahoma, to name a few—but many were wiped out in the Depression and the drought of the 1930s. Many of the early entrepreneurs cited in this book had land as the basis for their wealth, but not without considerable sacrifice.

If African-Americans had received the 40 acres and a mule, the set of tools, and the $50 that was promised by Abraham Lincoln, we would be a lot further along in the wealth-building process. However, Andrew Johnson, Lincoln's vice president, quickly canceled that commitment, and it has been a nightmare experience ever since for African-Americans who want to buy a decent place to live. The arguments for reparations for slavery have become a moot point of contention among liberals, historians, and wishful thinkers, while the majority of African-Americans still struggle to find affordable housing in neighborhoods where they will not be greeted by burning crosses on their lawns and broken windows and fire bombs in the middle of the night.

|||≡||| *The ache for home lives in all of us, the safe place where we can go as we* |||≡|||
are and not be questioned.

MAYA ANGELOU
All God's Children Need Traveling Shoes, 1986

The ugliest experiences of American bigotry have come out of race riots that started around issues of housing in large urban areas as well as in quiet, well-maintained suburbs even when blacks could afford to pay the "black tax," the deliberately inflated price often charged to blacks moving into the suburbs in the sixties and seventies. Although laws have been passed and legislation has been put in place to create fair housing, African-Americans still find it hard to purchase a home. In 1991, the Federal Reserve Bank acknowledged that black and Hispanic mortgage applicants were rejected two and three times more than white applicants. The Community Reinvestment Act (CRA), passed by Congress in 1973, has put pressure on major banks to lend to the depositors in the community, but many institutions still manage to find various ways around the expected compliance with the law by making in-kind donations of property and services to the community rather than loans. *The Wall Street Journal* recently reported that mortgage approvals for African-Americans and Hispanics have increased by 38 percent in the last 2 years, but home ownership among these groups still runs 40 percent lower than among their white counterparts.

Owning the roof over your head and the land under your feet is a piece of the Great American Dream that African-Americans subscribe to like any other ethnic group, but none of the other groups have found it as difficult to take that first step. Some African-Americans are reluctant and apprehensive about even making the effort to buy a home. They are fearful of being rejected by buyers, ripped off and cheated by white real estate brokers who continue the discriminatory practice of steering minorities to undesirable neighborhoods, or losing money on appraisal costs and mortgage application fees paid to lending institutions that don't explain what all the requirements are to qualify for a mortgage.

Perseverance, planning, and preparation are the only solution to achieving the goal of owning a house, and it is worth every minute of sacrifice and struggle that goes into it. Owning your own four walls will give you a stronger sense of financial well-being and a greater feeling of self-esteem as well as a good tax shelter.

James Wormley (1819–1884) started as a hack driver working out of his father's livery stable on West 15th Street, 10 blocks from the White House. After a futile trip to California during the gold rush, he returned to D.C. and became a chef in one of the private clubs for the political pundits of Washington. This led to a stint as the chef for the U.S. ambassador to the Court of St. James in London. When he returned to Washington in 1870, many of the local politicians financed his venture to open Wormley's Hotel

*in 1871 at the southwest corner of 15th and H Streets. It included a
banquet hall and catering facility serving the elite of Washington, D.C., and
Wormley operated it until his death. His son took over the management of
the hotel and sold it in 1893.*

THE WRONG WAY TO BUY A HOUSE

Fred and Martha D. have been saving for a house for more than 3 years. Each Saturday night they get the Sunday papers and plan to make the Sunday trip to various neighborhoods, going to model homes, looking at open house listings, and checking out "For Sale" signs in front of properties they like. Martha has decided that she must have a four-bedroom colonial, two-and-half baths, a spacious kitchen, a separate dining room, a two-car garage, and a laundry room. Fred wants a house with a basement so he can have space to start a small business on the side repairing computers, to earn a few extra dollars to help cover the mortgage. Their two kids want separate bedrooms, a TV room, a big backyard, and a place near a playground.

To find the property first and then to try to find the money to buy it, regardless of the price, is the road to heartbreak and financial ruin. Too many first-time home buyers make the mistake of falling in love with a property they can't really afford and draining themselves of all financial resources to try to buy it. Looking at classified ads, reading real estate brochures, gazing at photo layouts, dreaming about new kitchens, and counting closets will set you up for heartbreak if you start there. Save that part for last.

The second mistake first-time buyers make is to not do enough homework and learn to avoid some of the easy pitfalls of the real estate business. Lawyers, brokers, bankers, inspectors, and home sellers are trying to do a deal and make a buck. If you don't take the time to understand that these professionals owe you more than a smile and a handshake, you can be seriously burned and spend the next few decades paying for their mistakes.

||≡||| *Dirt is much more valuable than diamonds.* |||≡||

Eartha Kitt
1985

BUYING A HOUSE THE RIGHT WAY

Buying a house also takes time. This is not a nickel-and-dime deal you can walk away from if you change your mind after 6 months, like selling a car if it doesn't suit your needs any longer. Be prepared to commit at least one year to learning about mortgages, dealing with brokers, searching for the right property, and talking with lawyers before you even make an offer, come to contract, and set a date for the closing. First things first. Get out your calculator, lay out the facts, and determine how much house you can afford, without getting emotional about the process.

This is the largest investment and the most serious financial decision most people will ever have to make in their lives. And often the most complicated. Like everything else in the wealth-building process, buying a house has to be a long-term goal with carefully planned steps. The only way to make it a reality is to put a pencil to it and do your homework. The first step is to get out of debt and clean up your credit and save for that down payment. Lenders want to see 2 to 3 years of clean credit, and you must have the down payment in your name in a savings account for at least 90 days before applying for your mortgage.

How Much House Can You Afford?

The average house in most urban areas where African-Americans live today costs $120,000. You will have to clear up most of your debts on credit cards, car notes, and student loans and keep those expenses down to less than $300 a month. The monthly payment for principal, interest, taxes, and insurance (referred to as the PITI—the major part of the loan) will be approximately $1000 a month. Depending upon your interest rate and local property taxes, this will give you about $840 of monthly deductions for the interest and taxes, which will save you a bundle on your federal 1040 form each spring.

Different lenders have different guidelines for how large a mortgage you can borrow. Some will limit you to three times your salary; others will limit you to a monthly payment of only one-third of your monthly gross income. The ratio will vary according to the lender and the interest rate.

Put down as much as you can afford as your down payment. This is your immediate equity in the house. If your down payment is less than 20 percent of the purchase price, or $24,000 on our hypothetical house in the city, then you may be asked to pay for private mortgage insurance, which can jack up the monthly payments by another $100 a month.

How Much Mortgage Can You Afford

Interest Rates	Annual Income											
	$15,000	$20,000	$25,000	$30,000	$35,000	$40,000	$45,000	$50,000	$55,000	$60,000	$65,000	$70,000
6.5%	$49,000	$65,900	$82,400	$98,800	$115,300	$131,800	$148,300	$164,800	$181,300	$197,700	$214,200	$230,700
7.0%	47,000	62,600	78,300	93,900	109,600	125,300	140,900	156,600	172,300	187,900	203,600	219,200
7.5%	44,600	59,600	74,500	89,400	104,300	119,200	134,100	149,000	163,900	178,800	193,700	208,600
8.0%	45,000	56,700	70,900	85,100	99,300	113,500	127,700	141,900	156,100	170,300	184,500	198,700
8.5%	40,600	54,100	67,700	81,200	94,800	108,300	121,900	135,400	149,000	162,500	17,100	189,600
9.0%	38,800	51,700	64,700	77,700	90,600	103,500	116,500	129,400	142,400	155,300	168,200	181,200
9.5%	37,200	49,500	61,900	74,300	86,700	99,100	111,400	123,800	136,200	148,600	161,000	173,400
10.0%	35,600	47,400	59,300	71,200	83,000	94,900	106,800	118,600	130,500	142,400	154,300	166,100
10.5%	34,200	45,500	56,900	68,300	79,700	91,100	102,400	113,800	25,200	136,600	148,000	159,400

■ *Interest Rate*   □ Annual Income   □ Mortgage Amount

1. PREQUALIFY YOURSELF

Start with your current income, your budget, and your credit report. What are you spending on rent, utilities, living expenses? Look at your income, your budget, your credit report—examining these realities will determine how much house you can afford. A down payment requires between 5 percent and 20 percent of the price of the house, depending on the real estate market at the time that you are looking. It is safe to assume a 10 percent down payment, although there are various state and federal government mortgage programs like Fannie Mae that allow you to buy a home with as little as a 3 percent down payment and a less-than-perfect credit report.

2. PUT TOGETHER A TEAM TO HELP YOU

You want to put together a team of people who have basic knowledge that you will need to guide you through the maze of buying a home. They will help you sidestep some of the usual pitfalls and be successful without losing your patience, your money, and your nerve. Your team should include a real estate broker, a lawyer, and a house inspector.

A Real Estate Broker.   This is probably the first real estate professional person you will encounter, but, remember, the real estate broker does not work for you. Unless you sign a contract and pay a fee to a broker to assist you in finding a property, keep in mind that he or she is being paid by the seller and represents the seller's interest, not yours. Any information that you provide on your application regarding your employment, savings, income, and credit history will be used to evaluate you and could be used to pressure you into a contract. Don't give in to some of the pressure tactics you'll hear like, "This is the best time to buy." "Mortgage rates will never be this low again." "You'll never find a deal this good on a house like this." A broker is as anxious as you are to close the deal—but not for the same reasons.

There are some real estate brokers who have become "buyer's brokers." They will work for you for a fee—usually an hourly rate or a percentage of the sale price—to guide you through the process and explain the intricacies of the contracts and the lending arrangements.

Find out how long a real estate broker has been in business. Is he or she full-time or part-time? Is this person a schoolteacher moonlighting on the weekend to make a few extra dollars to finance a new car, or is this person a seasoned professional with several years of experience? Does he or she have professional contacts with attorneys and mortgage lenders who can save you hours of time and aggravation in getting a contract and resolving the financing issue? Does he or she return calls in a timely manner and offer you courteous and straightforward answers to all your questions about the property? Make sure you get everything in writing from the broker and do not allow him or her to tell you something will be done or taken care of without getting it in writing.

Does the broker have an exclusive listing, or is the broker part of a multiple-listing service that allows several brokers around the region to show the same houses. You may be looking at a property and paying for an inspection report on a house that is already in contract through another office and your broker will not be aware of it for several days.

Sallie Wyatt Stewart (1881–1951) taught elementary school in Evansville, Indiana, for 32 years until her husband's death in 1929. She was forced to decide if she should sell his lucrative real estate business or become a licensed broker and manage it herself. She took the state licensing exam and became the first black woman to own and manage a real estate firm in 1930.

The Lawyer.   You want an attorney who has considerable experience with lending institutions and financing arrangements and can explain what the pros and cons are of each mortgage clause if you don't understand it. Ask for a detailed list of what you can expect as his or her duties in the contract and closing process. Ask the attorney for a written outline of the fees that will be charged and what will be included for those fees. What exceptions will there be in the fee process? What will you be charged if there are several meetings and conference calls and the contract falls apart and you must start the process all over again? You don't want any surprises at the last minute and an unexpected bill for phone calls, faxes, and meetings that you are not aware of. Some attorneys calculate contract and closing fees as a percentage of the cost of the house, say 1 percent of the purchase price as a rough guideline for their total services. You should also choose an attorney who is familiar with the Fair Housing Law and any issues of housing discrimination that may occur in the brokerage relationship and with the lending institution.

An Inspector.   Inspectors are independent building professionals with experience as contractors, engineers, architects, and building inspectors who know how to look at the roof, the wiring, the plumbing, the grounds, and the windows and find flaws and problems that you may not be able to see. They may charge $150 and up to visit a property and walk through it for you. They should examine it, give you a written report of any problems with the building, and advise you of what work may or may not need to be done. They can spot any termite damage, foundation problems, and housing code violations, which could cost you thousands of dollars to fix. This can help you decide to walk away from a potential problem or to negotiate a reduced price before you go to contract.

Table 7-1

Summary of Real Estate Financing Techniques

Technique	Description	Considerations
Fixed-rate mortgage (FRM)	• Fixed interest rate, usually five years or more. • Equal monthly payments of principal and interest until debt is paid in full or until loan matures, if earlier. (See balloon mortgage.)	• Offers stability of debt service. • Limited availability when interest rates are rising. • Interest rates may be higher than other types of financing. • Fixed-rate loans are rarely assumable.
Variable-rate mortgage (VRM) and adjustable-rate mortgage (ARM)	• Interest rate changes based on a financial index, resulting in possible changes in monthly payments, loan term, and/or principal. • May have rate or payment caps.	• Readily available. • Starting interest rate is slightly below market, but payments can increase sharply and frequently if index increases. • Payment caps prevent wide fluctuations in payments but may cause negative amortization (i.e., interest accruals).
Balloon mortgage	• Monthly payments based on fixed or variable interest rate. • Usually short-term. • Payments may cover interest only, with principal due in full at term end.	• Offers low monthly payments but limited or no equity buildup. • When due, loan must be paid off or refinanced. • Refinancing poses high risk if rates climb.
Assumable mortgage	• Buyer takes over seller's original (often below-market rate) mortgage.	• Lowers monthly payments. • May be prohibited if there is a "due on sale" clause in original mortgage. • Not permitted on most new fixed-rate mortgages.
Seller take-back (purchase-money) mortgage	• Seller provides all or part of financing with a first or second mortgage.	• May offer below-market interest rate. • May have a balloon payment requiring full payment in a few years or refinancing at market rates, which could sharply increase debt.
Wraparound mortgage	• Seller keeps original low-rate mortgage and extends additional financing; buyer makes payments to seller, who forwards a portion to the lender holding original mortgage, and keeps balance. • Offers lower effective interest rate on total transaction.	• Lender may call in old mortgage and require higher rate. • If buyer defaults, seller must take legal action to collect debt.

Technique	Description	Considerations
Growing-equity mortgage (GEM)	• Fixed interest rate, but monthly payments may vary according to agreed-on schedule or index.	• Permits rapid payoff of debt because payment increases reduce principal. • Buyer's income must be able to keep up with payment increases.
Zero-rate and low-rate mortgage	• Appears to be completely or almost interest-free because interest is built into loan principal. • Large down payment and one-time finance charge; then loan is repaid in fixed monthly payments over short term.	• Permits quick ownership. • May not lower total cost (because of possibly increased sales price).
Reverse-annuity mortgage (RAM)	• Borrower, who owns mortgage-free property and needs income, receives monthly payments from lender, using property as collateral.	• Can provide homeowners with needed cash. • At end of term, borrower must have money available to avoid selling property or refinancing.
Shared-appreciation mortgage (SAM)	• Below-market interest rate and lower monthly payments in exchange for a share of profits when home is sold or on a specified date. • Many variations.	• If home appreciates greatly, total cost of loan jumps. • If little or no appreciation, lender receives below-market return. • If loan matures before home is sold, refinancing at higher rates may be necessary.
Renegotiable-rate mortgage (rollover)	• Interest rate and monthly payments are constant for several years; changes possible thereafter. • Long-term.	• Original form of adjustable-rate mortgage.
Buy-down	• Developer (or third party) provides an interest subsidy that lowers monthly payments during the first few years of the loan. • Can have fixed or variable interest rate.	• Offers a break from higher payments during early years. • Enables buyer with lower income to qualify. • With variable-rate mortgage, payments may jump substantially at end of subsidy. • Developer may increase selling price to offset buy-down.
Rent with option to buy	• Renter pays option fee for right to purchase property at specified time and agreed-on price. • Rent may or may not be applied to sales price.	• Gives renter time to obtain down payment and decide whether to purchase. • Locks in price during inflationary times. • Failure to take option means loss of option fee and rental payments.

Table 7-1

Summary of Real Estate Financing Techniques (cont.)

Technique	Description	Considerations
Land contract	• No transfer of title by seller until loan is fully paid. • Equal monthly payments based on below-market interest rate with unpaid principal due at loan end.	• May offer no equity until loan is fully paid. • Buyer has few protections if conflict arises during loan.
Graduated-payment mortgage (GPM)	• Lower monthly payments rise gradually (usually over 5 to 10 years), then level off for duration of term. • With variable interest rate, additional payment changes possible if index changes.	• Easier to qualify for. • Buyer's income must be able to keep pace with scheduled payment increases. • With a variable rate, payment increases beyond the graduated payments can result in negative amortization.

3. SHOP AROUND FOR A LENDER

Look in the Sunday real estate section of your local newspapers and you will see several ads from banks and mortgage companies. Call about half a dozen of them and request the brochures and application packages that they are quite willing to send out. Make an appointment to discuss the application process and the types of mortgages you may be able to apply for. These guys are going to make a lot of money off you in the next few years and will try to snow you under with intimidating language about points, rates, commitments, and fees which will come out of your pocket, so sit down and insist that they cut through the jargon and explain it all to you in fourth-grade terms, if necessary, so you will understand what you're paying for.

‖≣ ‖‖‖≣ ‖‖‖≣ ‖‖‖≣ ‖‖‖≣ ‖‖‖≣ ‖‖‖≣‖‖‖≣ ‖‖‖≣ ‖‖‖≣ ‖‖‖≣ ‖‖‖≣ ‖‖‖≣ ‖‖‖≣

Myrtle Foster Cook (1870–1951), a black Canadian by birth, moved to St. Louis from Oklahoma when she married her second husband, Hugh Oliver Cook, in 1910. As a schoolteacher, she saw the problems faced by her colleagues in opening bank accounts and trying to get mortgages to buy or build homes. After she retired, she devoted all her time, using her church contacts and club connections, to establishing the Home Seeker's Loan Association of Kansas City in 1926 as a credit and lending source for blacks to get mortgages. She later became the director of the People's Finance Corporation in Kansas City and was the largest stockholder in the company.

‖≣ ‖‖‖≣ ‖‖‖≣ ‖‖‖≣ ‖‖‖≣ ‖‖‖≣ ‖‖‖≣‖‖‖≣ ‖‖‖≣ ‖‖‖≣ ‖‖‖≣ ‖‖‖≣ ‖‖‖≣ ‖‖‖≣

LEARN THE LOAN APPROVAL PROCESS

Find out what the procedure is for processing the mortgage application, what papers you are responsible for providing, and how long the process will take. Ask what fees you will have to pay besides the application fee. You'll be surprised at the expenses that will be charged to you. The application fee is just the beginning. You may or may not pay points, which is another way of getting extra interest out of you. You'll pay for the bank's appraisal, the bank's attorney, the bank's inspection report, a commitment fee if you want to lock in the interest rate for 90 days, an extension fee if you can't get your closing details worked out within the 90-day commitment period—the list goes on, and you should be prepared.

THE MORTGAGE MAZE

Mortgages are still the last of the tax shelters for the poor working person as well as the rich, but mortgages can be a nightmare to understand. Mortgages have changed in the last decade as lenders have become more innovative in getting you to sign on the dotted line. Nowadays you have several options. Some are explained here. Also see Table 7-1.

Fixed 30-year mortgage. This is the traditional standby that most people opt for, with the same payment for the next 360 months. Suppose you get a $120,000 mortgage, keep it for 30 years, and make all your monthly payments, including commitment fees to lock in a low rate (from $200 to $500), title insurance (1 percent of purchase price), homeowner's insurance (from $400 to $800 a year), and closing costs (from 3 to 8 percent of the purchase price). In all, you will spend over $360,000 in that time, and $240,000 will be interest! You can reduce that cost by paying an extra $100 a month. An extra $100 a month can reduce a 30-year mortgage to 21 years and 7 months.

Fixed 15-year mortgage. Like the fixed 30-year mortgage, the rate is locked in. But because the time over which you pay is halved, the monthly payment is much higher. However, this will allow you to own your home much sooner and pay less interest over the life of the loan. You will also build up your equity much faster with a 15 year mortgage. Play with the numbers and see if you can afford it.

Adjustable-rate mortgage (ARM). The advantage here is that the beginning interest rate is usually 2 or 3 percentage points lower than that for the fixed-rate mortgages, but since the rate can fluctuate, the gamble you're taking is which way it will go over the next few years. The floating interest rate will change your monthly payments every 6 months. It may go up $100 or $200 or go down by the same amount. If you get a mortgage at a low rate, and you don't plan to be in your house for more than a few years, and you have some kind of flexibility in your budget, then you can choose this option. This is not for those with uncertain incomes and tight budgets. As interest rates float up and down, after 5 years you may be writing a larger check on this note than you would on a fixed-rate mortgage. See Table 7-2.

Graduated-rate mortgage (or two-step mortgage rate). This isn't a Texas innovation but a way for low-income, first-time home buyers to get a mortgage. After 5 to 7 years, as your income increases, your mortgage payments will be adjusted upward to give the bank a higher interest rate payment. At that time, you have the option of refinancing or paying the higher rate. You're in trouble if you get downsized and have to take a lower-paying job.

Table 7-2
Adjustable Rates Versus Fixed Rates
On a $100,000 mortgage, the ARM starts at 6.75 percent and goes up to 12.75 percent over 4 years. A fixed-rate mortgage at 9 percent offers no surprises.

	ARM	Fixed Rate
First year	$ 6,717	$ 8,972
Second year	$ 8,626	$ 8,908
Third year	$10,523	$ 8,838
Fourth year	$12,407	$ 8,761
Total	$38,273	$35,480

MORGAGE RATES CHANGE EACH YEAR						
Type of Mortgage	1990	1991	1992	1993	1994	1995
6-month ARM	8.26%	7.5%	5.59%	4.65%	6.25%	6.85%
15-year fixed rate	9.75%	8.90%	7.87%	6.75%	8.85%	8.75%
30-year fixed rate	9.95%	9.15%	8.35%	7.25%	9.18%	9.21%

HOW AND WHERE TO LOOK FOR A MORTGAGE

The Federal National Mortgage Association (FNMA), also referred to as Fannie Mae, was created by Congress in 1938 to raise money from shareholders and make the funds available for mortgages to moderate and low-income home buyers. Because of Fannie Mae, many banks, savings and loan companies, and some credit unions have become a source of affordable mortgage money. Income and employment guidelines are much more flexible in these programs. Scholarship grants, child support, boarder income from relatives, and newly hired workers moving from public assistance to a job or from school to a first job are given broader consideration than a large commercial bank would offer. To assist you with the basic information to start the home-buying process, FNMA has developed a brochure called "Are You Ready to Buy a Home?" Call (800) 688-HOME to obtain a free copy.

FNMAs MORTGAGE PROGRAMS

Beginning in 1995, Congress has set aside over $80 million for FNMA to use for low- and middle-income, first-time home buyers in several major cities where the required down payment is only 3 percent of the purchase price of the house or condominium being purchased. This effort offers considerable support and flexibility to first-time purchasers and eases the way through the mortgage maze. Applicants must participate in a loan counseling program, a

Current monthly gross income $_____

Current housing expenses

   Rent $_____

   Utilities $_____

   Renter's insurance $_____

Relevant housing expenses $_____

(How does this compare with the monthly mortgage payment chart below?)

Other debts

   Credit card payments $_____

   Student loans $_____

Estimated homeowner's expenses

   Monthly mortgage $_____

   Homeowner's insurance $_____

   Property taxes $_____

   Utilities $_____

   Condo/co-op fees $_____

   Improvements costs $_____

30-Year Fixed-Rate Mortgage Monthly Payments (Interest and Principal)

Mortgage Amount	8.5%	9.0%	9.5%	10%	10.5%	11%	11.5%	12%	12.5%
$ 50,000	$ 384	$ 402	$ 420	$ 439	$ 457	$ 476	$ 495	$ 514	$ 534
55,000	423	443	462	483	503	524	545	566	587
60,000	461	483	505	527	549	571	594	617	640
65,000	500	523	547	570	595	619	644	669	694
70,000	538	563	589	614	640	667	693	720	747
75,000	577	603	631	658	686	714	743	771	800
80,000	615	644	673	702	732	762	792	823	854
85,000	654	684	715	746	778	809	842	874	907
90,000	692	724	757	790	823	857	891	926	961
95,000	730	764	799	834	869	905	941	977	1,014
100,000	769	805	841	878	915	952	990	1,029	1,067

Figure 7-1. Home-buying worksheet.

credit analysis workshop, consumer education seminars, and mortgage application training classes. Individual counseling is provided for applicants after they have completed a series of workshops. Income requirements are lower than the average income usually required to buy a house.

FNMA has designed two experimental programs to encourage home ownership for people with lower incomes and poor credit ratings.

- The Community Home Buyer's Program is for families with incomes between $25,000 and $40,000 and requires a 5 percent minimum down payment. Condos, two-family homes, and single-family homes are included in some cities.

- The Acorn Pilot Program accepts applications from families with incomes in the $15,000-to-$30,000 range. For more information, call (800) 7FANNIE, Monday to Friday, 9 to 5.

GETTING READY TO BUY

Review Figure 4-3 in Chapter 4. Then complete the worksheet in Figure 7-1.

SHOPPING FOR A HOUSE

Now you can go look at houses. The three major requirements to remember when buying property are *location, location,* and *location!* Cost, convenience, and transportation come next, but location is *the* most important factor, when you buy and when you sell.

Here are some basic tips to remember when you begin to look for a house.

1. Talk to brokers, mortgage bankers, attorneys, and neighbors. Let people know you're in the market to buy, and they will share leads with you. This is a good way to discover unadvertised properties that are not yet listed with a broker. The people you talk to may refer you to tax sales, estate sales, and tax foreclosures. Tax foreclosures and estate sales are rarely

advertised and are only available through brokers who are tagged by HUD and the bank to handle these sales. Ask around and find out who they are.

2. Look at a neighborhood that's being renovated and improved, where house prices are going to increase. If the real estate values are going up, then your price will go up in the next few years if you want to sell. Is the house in a neighborhood that is convenient to your job? How long will it take you to get to work? How far away are the schools? The grocery store and the dry cleaners? What about public transportation when you won't have the car? Are there other benefits and amenities in the neighborhood like churches, public parks, good lighting, on the street parking, garbage collection?

3. Look for houses that are underpriced because the house needs work, not because the location is bad. You can always fix up the house, but you can't change the location. Don't put too much money into a house that you're planning to resell in a few years. A basic facelift and some repairs can raise the value of a property considerably. Let the next buyer add all the luxuries.

4. Check the tax assessment. Compare it with that of other houses in the area. If it is low for the neighborhood, you may be able to reduce the tax bill before you buy the house, but you must also find out if that assessment will change after the sale. Many cities raise property taxes on homes as newer and higher values are established after the title changes hands. It may put you in a higher property tax bracket and increase the monthly expenses for escrow.

||≣|| *Black people are land people, they jived us into the city.* ||≣||

JOHN WILLIAMS
Author, 1976

APARTMENT RENTERS

Some city dwellers in apartments, particularly condo and townhouse complexes, may have a rent-to-buy option. This allows you to decide if you want to own a property and have the tax advantages that go with being a homeowner. Your management may have a lease arrangement that will allow you to pay an extra $100 a month, which will be used as a down payment. After one or two years of renting, you must decide if you are interested in purchasing the space. You need a good real estate lawyer to explain the pros and cons of this contract and be clear about how definite your options are for buying.

KNOW WHAT YOU'RE BUYING

CO-OPERATIVE APARTMENTS

Co-op conversions were a big thing in the late seventies and early eighties when landlords wanted to get out of the headache of building ownership and pass the problem on to the tenants. When you get a co-op apartment, you are *not* buying real estate. You're investing in the corporation that owns the building and purchasing shares with the other tenants who reside there. You share management responsibility with a co-operative board of residents who review your application to become a fellow resident and co-owner. The apartment that you move into is secured by the shares. You get a special class of mortgage and also have to pay a separate maintenance fee with other residents for the upkeep of the building.

Questions to ask when you buy a co-op. What is the maintenance fee? How often does it change? Are there any balloon payments on the building's mortgage? Is there a special tax abatement on the property which is about to expire? When was the building mortgage last refinanced? Are there any major capital improvements, like a new boiler, a new intercom system, or a new roof, that are anticipated soon? How much of the building is owner-occupied? How much of the building is rented out to tenants, who don't care as much about the property as you do as an owner? Is the co-op board insured for any liabilities in the general area of the halls, sidewalks, and street outside the building?

DEMPSEY TRAVIS, CEO

Sivart Mortgage Company, Inc.
Chicago

When Dempsey Travis graduated from DuSable High School on the South Side of Chicago in 1939, he wanted to do more than work in the stockyards like his father, Louis. He tried to go to college, but he couldn't pass any college entrance exams, including the one for Roosevelt, the black university. The Army rescued him from a series of dead-end jobs in 1942, but after he was shot in a race riot, he was more determined than ever to achieve some of his dreams.

Travis returned home to work in the stockyards and studied at Wilson Junior College at night until he was accepted at Roosevelt, graduating in 1949. He went on to Kent School of Law, where he discovered real estate and the brokerage business. His mother had to loan him the $50 needed to take the real estate licensing exam. When he opened his real estate "office," it was an orange crate and an upturned trash can for a desk in the corner of an office that belonged to a lawyer, who wanted a share of his commissions. His wife, Moselynne, worked for another business during the day and typed letters and forms for him each night as he worked to find properties and clients for his business.

Travis's first major problem in the early 1950s was to find homes for thousands of blacks crammed into the South Side of Chicago. These clients were hard-working people with good jobs, savings, and a desire to buy a home. Up to now, blacks wanting to buy a home were forced to take "land contracts" that stipulated that with one missed payment the buyer lost all equity in the property. Regardless of how many years a family had been making steady payments, illness or job loss could devastate a family's interest in a house. Evictions were carried out without notice and were quite legal.

Urban renewal programs, which were developing around the city, were displacing black families all over the South Side, with no arrangements made for relocation. One by one, Travis began to find whites in the Douglas Park area and the West Side who were willing to sell to blacks. Then came the next problem. White banks did not want to finance most of these mortgages, fearing the race riots and panic selling that would destroy homes or lower property values.

In 1953, Travis put together the capital and the political connections necessary to open the first black mortgage banking firm, and by 1961 his company, Sivart Mortgage Company in Chicago, was the first black company approved by the Federal Housing Administration and the Veterans Administration to receive public funds and provide mortgages for black homeowners.

"I think every black entrepreneur has to have a whole lot of social worker in him. Yet I've found that you can deal fairly with people and make a lot of money at the same time. There's just a different set of rules for black people, if there are any rules. But you can't let that rule your life. You can't let the jaws of that trap close down on you. You just have to know how to avoid them."

|||≡||| *If it is true that land does not belong to anyone until they have buried a body* |||≡|||
on it, then the land of my birthplace belongs to me, dozens of times over.

ALICE WALKER
In Search of My Mother's Garden, 1983

CONDOMINIUMS

With condos you're buying real estate. You own the four walls and get a mortgage on that space with a deed and a title. You also have to pay a monthly maintenance fee to the management of the building for upkeep, but it is usually a lot lower than the fee on a co-op.

|||≡ ||||≡ ||||≡ ||||≡ ||||≡ ||||≡ ||||≡||||≡ ||||≡ ||||≡ ||||≡ ||||≡ ||||≡ ||||≡

Thomy Lafon (1810–1893)—a "gens de couleur libres," a free person of color—opened a small store in New Orleans in 1843 and, in addition to his retailing ventures, was a real estate speculator and money lender. Some accounts report that he owned property worth more that $500,000. The 1880 census shows his property valued at $413,000. Lafon was widely known for his philanthropy, and at his death he funded an endowment that helped to create Xavier University. In addition, he offered two lots (real estate) as a site for the first orphanage of the Louisiana Association for the Benefit of Colored Orphans. The balance of his estate, worth $600,000, was willed to a charity run by nuns who had cared for him in his youth.

|||≡ ||||≡ ||||≡ ||||≡ ||||≡ ||||≡ ||||≡||||≡ ||||≡ ||||≡ ||||≡ ||||≡ ||||≡ ||||≡

8

BUYING INSURANCE

"I was making money so she had a beautiful funeral. Thank God for that. Didn't have to put the saucer on her. I've seen that happen to many of 'em, didn't have no insurance or belong to no club. While you was laying out, there was the wake, they put a saucer on your chest and everybody who comes in, drops a nickel or dime or a quarter to try to make up for the undertaker."

Louis Armstrong
Autobiography, 1979

The Free African Society was founded in 1787 by Richard Allen and Absalom Jones in Philadelphia as the first black mutual aid organization in America. It was created to provide political, religious, educational, and social services for the growing population of freed blacks who had settled in Philadelphia after the Revolutionary War. The group had a mission statement which was "to look after the poor, bury their dead, care for the widows and educate the orphaned black children" of its members. Another edict in the charter specified that any member who was found guilty of public drunkenness or disorderly conduct or was delinquent with his or her dues was dismissed from membership.

By 1810, several members of the society decided that it was time to form a separate insurance company. The African Insurance Company was established at 529 Lombard Street, with a capital base of $5000, by three free blacks, Joseph Randolph, Carey Porter, and William Coleman, who were also members in good standing of the African Methodist Episcopal church. A portion of each member's dues was put into an insurance fund to guarantee the kind of benefit we expect today from an insurance settlement: to pay for the funeral of the deceased member and to provide income and shelter for the surviving family members of the deceased. The African Insurance Company continued as a separate business until 1840.

172

In the days of slavery, burial in the African-American community was a degrading experience. Slaves were never given the respect of a Christian funeral by a white minister, slave owners frequently resented and refused the cost of a decent coffin for burial, and bodies were rarely embalmed.

III≣ IIIII≣ IIIII≣ IIIII≣ IIIII≣ IIIII≣ IIIII≣IIIII≣ IIIII≣ IIIII≣ IIIII≣ IIIII≣ IIIII≣ IIIII≣

"Burying people was the only business the white folks would let us get into back in those days because none of the white undertakers would touch a black body," says J. Mason Davis, of Birmingham, Alabama, relating the story of how his family started in the insurance business. Protective Industrial Insurance Company of America (PIICA) in Birmingham, Alabama, dates back to September 1899 when Charles Morgan Harris and his sister, Hattie Davenport, established the Davenport and Harris Funeral Home. After a few years in business, they saw the need for a burial association for blacks in Alabama. Although the black population, in general, was poor, consisting mostly of small farmers, sharecroppers, miners, and steel-mill workers, poverty did not inhibit the desire for a decent and respectful funeral. Domestic workers and day laborers, schoolteachers and doctors were all buyers of these policies. The state insurance commission gave permission to found the Protective Burial Society. PIICA was the first company in the state to market a family group policy that insured an entire family of up to seven persons for a weekly premium of 35 cents. The company is the oldest continuing business owned and managed by blacks in Alabama.

III≣ IIIII≣ IIIII≣ IIIII≣ IIIII≣ IIIII≣ IIIII≣IIIII≣ IIIII≣ IIIII≣ IIIII≣ IIIII≣ IIIII≣ IIIII≣

After Emancipation, the poverty that controlled the lives of most ex-slaves made it necessary to "pass the hat" to pay for the funeral of the departed relative. It became a symbol of family pride in the African-American community to give an elaborate funeral for the deceased relative, no matter how impoverished and deprived a life he or she had lived. Ending up in potter's field was considered a shameful failure for the entire family. A majestic funeral also represented the beginning of the journey to a better life in the next world. Expensive funerals may also be the continuation of an African tradition that is still practiced today. In many of the coastal countries of West Africa, particularly Ghana and Nigeria, it is a social custom for the family of the deceased to provide an elaborate handmade casket symbolizing the wealth and status of the loved one who has passed on.

Most black insurance companies were begun during the Reconstruction period; they were started as a secondary business by the funeral director. Prepaid savings policies were created to guarantee that the insured could afford to have the proper Christian burial he or she desired. Some elderly African-Americans still own special policies that are earmarked to pass to the funeral director at the time of their death.

Selling burial insurance and being a mortician were jobs that made up the first line of business for most blacks who didn't want to be day laborers or domestic servants. Unfortunately, without an organized industry and little or no government regulations to control how they did business, a small cadre of black con artists and hustlers took advantage of the working poor and began collecting money for companies that did not really exist.

Based on how they have been treated over the years, African-Americans have good reason to be skeptical about trusting insurance companies—especially those in the mainstream marketplace. White insurance companies that normally refused to sell life insurance to Negroes made out like bandits in selling burial insurance in the black community. During the Depression of the 1930s (and even as late as 1960), it was not unusual to see a white insurance salesman going door-to-door on Saturday mornings collecting the nickel or dime a week in a lifetime of endless payments on policies that were never "fully paid up." Many African-Americans felt a distorted sense of pride at "being accepted" and having a policy with a white insurance company, believing that policies with a white company were more secure and reliable than the Negro burial policies. However, in time many blacks were disappointed to discover that their insurance company had gone out of business, or that the premiums they had been paying had not been delivered to the insurance company's home office and therefore their policies had been canceled without their knowledge. These negative experiences have created a strong resistance among African-Americans to buying life insurance. Even today, some spouses express resentment about buying life insurance, stating that they don't want to leave behind a rich mate who will live a better life after they are gone.

||≣ ||||≣ ||||≣ ||||≣ ||||≣ ||||≣ ||||≣ ||||≣||||≣ ||||≣ ||||≣ ||||≣ ||||≣ ||||≣ ||||≣

The National Insurance Association (NIA), originally named the National Negro Insurance Association, was formed in 1921 by a group of black insurance men in Durham, North Carolina, who wanted to create a standard of ethics among the many black insurance companies that had been formed. So many Negroes had been swindled by small groups of con men that there was a clear need for a set of guidelines and professional ethics to give credibility to those companies that were interested in doing legitimate business. Sixty men representing thirteen black insurance companies came together to found the trade association, which is still in existence today. Charles Clinton Spaulding, president of North Carolina Mutual Life Insurance Company, was elected as the first president of the organization.

||≣ ||||≣ ||||≣ ||||≣ ||||≣ ||||≣ ||||≣||||≣ ||||≣ ||||≣ ||||≣ ||||≣ ||||≣ ||||≣ ||||≣

Out of the original 78 black insurance companies that existed when the NIA was formed in 1921, only 13 are still operating. They are listed in Table 8-1.

Table 8-1
African-American Insurance Companies Still in Business

Atlanta Life Insurance Co. Atlanta Georgia	Security Life of the South Jackson, Mississippi
Booker T. Washington Insurance Birmingham, Alabama	Southern Aid Life Insurance Richmond, Virginia
Central Life of Florida Tampa, Florida	United Mutual Life Insurance New York, New York
Golden State Mutual Life Los Angeles, California	Universal Life Insurance Memphis, Tennessee
Majestic Life Insurance New Orleans, Louisiana	Williams Progressive Life Opalousa, Louisiana
North Carolina Mutual Durham, North Carolina	Wright Mutual Life Detroit, Michigan
Protective Industrial Insurance Birmingham, Alabama	

‖≡‖‖‖≡‖‖‖≡‖‖‖≡‖‖‖≡‖‖‖≡‖‖‖≡‖‖‖≡‖‖‖≡‖‖‖≡‖‖‖≡‖‖‖≡‖‖‖≡‖‖‖≡

When John Merrick and Aaron Moore founded North Carolina Mutual Life Insurance Company in 1898 in Durham, North Carolina, they had no idea they were creating a black financial empire that would support homes and businesses for more than a century. They had to survive the payment of their first policyholder, who died within 6 weeks of buying a policy. The weekly premium of 5 cents did not cover the face amount of the policy, which was $50, to cover the cost of the deceased's funeral. Fortunately, Charles Clinton Spaulding, a trained actuary, was hired shortly thereafter as general manager of the company. Beginning in 1893, under Spaulding's guidance, the company's assets grew. By the time of his death in 1923, the company had assets of $100 million in real estate and investments. North Carolina Mutual is still the largest black-owned insurance company in America. The company has now diversified into the investment management business for pension funds and has created the New Africa Investment Fund under the guidance of Maceo Sloan.

‖≡‖‖‖≡‖‖‖≡‖‖‖≡‖‖‖≡‖‖‖≡‖‖‖≡‖‖‖≡‖‖‖≡‖‖‖≡‖‖‖≡‖‖‖≡‖‖‖≡‖‖‖≡

Life insurance still has a strong association with death and burial, particularly in the African-American community, which makes it a very unattractive financial product. No matter who you are, morbid issues like death and dying are totally foreign concepts when you're young and beginning to acquire a few assets. Insurance isn't sexy; you can't drive it, wear it, or eat it; and the big payoff doesn't come along until you're gone. Add to that the endless confusion and complexities of the costs and the various types of policies, and life insurance becomes the most misunderstood area of the financial planning process. A 1989 study by the Federal Trade Commission concluded that life insurance is so contradictory that the average consumer, not just the African-American buyer, is unable to get an accurate understanding of what he or she is really buying. Most people don't even try to learn the basics. If nothing else, the special clauses, exceptions, and tentative conditions that fill the policies make them seem like a carefully crafted swindle.

Keep in mind, though, that the primary purpose of life insurance is and has always been to take care of your dependents and any family members who rely upon you to have food, shelter, and clothing. It goes well beyond paying for the funeral and the cemetery plot. If African-Americans are going to build firm financial foundations for their families, a life insurance policy is the best way to prevent financial ruin for a succeeding generation. If you are responsible for the financial well-being of a spouse, children, and other family members, then you need life insurance. On the other hand, if you do not have anyone who will starve to death if you die and leave them without a basic means of survival, then you need to consider buying only enough life insurance to bury you.

In 1957, Cirillo McSween, a Panamanian-born graduate of the University of Illinois, was hired by the New York Life Insurance Company in Chicago. He was the first black insurance salesman to work for a major white insurance company. New York Life management was convinced that there was no market for its policies in the black community since the company did not sell burial policies. African-Americans, it was believed, could not afford anything more than the cheaper "dime-a-week" policies, and would not be interested in buying more expensive coverage. Within a year, McSween had sold a million dollars of insurance and had broken all sales goals that had been set for him. McSween became the first black member of the Million Dollar Roundtable, the insurance industry's hall of fame.

SELLING YOU INSURANCE

If you rely on the insurance agent to educate you correctly about what you should buy, you could be making a serious mistake. Keep in mind that insurance agents and financial planners who sell insurance are really salespeople, and they have a built-in conflict of interest because they are there to advise you, but they are also there to earn a commission. The higher the premiums for the life insurance that you purchase, the more money they make, which is why they prefer to sell whole-life insurance—the most expensive insurance you can buy. Insurance agents know that you aren't anxious to add this expense item to your monthly budget, so they are prepared to sell you on the idea.

The agents know your objections and excuses before you do and come well armed with very logical answers to dismiss them. They also know how to pressure you into making a decision right away for what may be the wrong policy, telling you that without that policy, if you die tomorrow you will leave your family on welfare. Fear tactics work for many people, particularly when the argument leads them to believe that all their financial concerns can be met with one insurance policy. Nothing could be further from the truth.

Insurance agents will also try to convince you to purchase a policy because it is "a forced savings plan," or a "tax-deferred" savings for college tuition, or an "additional source" of retirement income. These arguments sound good, but they are not. That's because there are much more profitable ways to invest your dollars to meet these other financial goals.

WHAT KIND OF INSURANCE DO YOU REALLY NEED?

Insurance is simply about buying protection—protection of your assets and, more importantly, protection for your family. It is purchased to replace the income stream that you provide to support and care for your loved ones. The death benefit of a policy is to protect your family from economic hardship and deprivation when you are no longer there to provide for them. Nothing more, nothing less.

If you're young, single, and childless, with no mortgage and no aging parents who depend upon you for support, then skip this section about life insurance and go on to the section on disability insurance. A life insurance agent will argue that you should buy it as an investment in your future while you're young and in good health and while the rates are low because of your age, but forget it. There are better ways to build investment assets for yourself. As long as you have group life coverage available as a benefit in a health insurance plan through your job, that is probably enough to pay your final debts and give you a decent burial.

If you are married and both of you are working, then any group life insurance that you have through your job is still sufficient, especially if you have no children, no mortgage, and no major expenses. But for a working couple with two or three children, school loans, future college bills, private school tuition, dental bills, summer camp fees, a mortgage, a car note, and lots of credit cards (your typical American family!), the story is different.

A young father with all these financial responsibilities needs more than $1 million of life insurance to meet all these obligations over a lifetime. A single parent should carry at least $250,000 of term life insurance made out to whoever is chosen as the guardian for the children, especially if the guardian is the child's grandparent. Many African-American grandparents, as senior citizens with limited financial resources, are finding themselves suddenly left with the unexpected financial responsibility of caring for small children.

HOW MUCH INSURANCE DO YOU REALLY NEED?

A recommended rule of thumb is 5 to 8 times your salary, but that's not carved in stone. It really depends on how many people you support financially and what other resources you have. If your assets are tied up in real estate or a family business that would have to be sold in order for your family to survive, you may need more than that. Your need is based on your personal savings profile, your family budget, and your present net worth. Before you buy, use the worksheet in Figure 8-1 and decide for yourself.

Once you know how much insurance you need, you must decide which is the best policy to buy. Term? Whole life? Universal life? No matter what names the insurance companies give them: flexible life, adjustable life, conservative life, new classic whole life, convertible premium life, modified life, there are still only two types of insurance policies: term life and cash value (whole life and universal life are types of cash-value insurance).

BUYING IN STAGES

When they were first married in 1964, Herb and Nora D. bought a $10,000 whole-life policy on Herb. Six years later when their daughter, Margaret, was born, they bought two more whole-life policies for $25,000 each. In 1975, when they bought their house and had another child, they borrowed the cash values out of all the policies (by then it was less than $4000) to add to their savings to

Immediate expenses:

    Funeral costs $_____

    Final medical costs $_____
    (Your health insurance
    may not cover everything.)

    Legal fees and court costs $_____
    Estate taxes
    (Total assets over $600,000 will owe
    federal estate taxes; ask your accountant
    for the state inheritance tax limit.)

Current debts:

    Mortgage balance $_____
    Car note/credit cards $_____
    Other loans $_____

Future expenses:

    Annual living expenses $_____

    (minus a decrease in the insured's living $_____

    expenses, allowing for at least 5 percent
    inflation times the number of years to
    replace your income)

    Total future living expense $_____

    Child-care costs $_____
    Family emergency fund $_____
    College tuition bills $_____

What assets do you have now?

    Savings accounts, CDs, etc. $_____
    IRA/Keogh accounts $_____
    Group life insurance $_____
    Employer's pension benefit $_____

    Mutual funds/securities $_____
    Current life insurance $_____
    Other assets $_____

Total assets available

    Social security survivor's $_____
       death benefit
    (Write to SSA for an estimate.
    Families with small children are

    entitled to social security death
    benefits until the youngest
    child reaches 18.)

Total assets minus total need $_____

Additional insurance needed $_____

Figure 8-1. Insurance worksheet.

make the down payment. Herb decided that they needed more life insurance to cover the mortgage and take care of the children in case he died suddenly, so they bought two more whole-life policies for $10,000 each and a $5000 policy on each of the children. Their insurance agent showed them cash-value projections that implied that they would have up to $37,000 in 20 years to send the children to college. The agent also indicated that if the money wasn't used for college, they could convert the policy to an annuity and draw on it for extra retirement income.

With all these policies, Herb and Nora are now spending $1658 a year on insurance premiums—and they still don't have enough insurance protection. What they really need is $500,000 of 20-year level term insurance on each of the adults in the family, but the insurance agent is not interested in selling them this kind of insurance because he would only earn $120 as a commission on the two term policies which is much less than he earns on the whole-life policies since his commission is a percentage of the policy's first-year premium. If Herb and Nora had spent the same dollars on a term policy, a retirement annuity, tax-deferred savings bonds, or zero-coupon bonds for their children, they would have a lot more in savings and investment assets today to show for their dollars.

TERM INSURANCE

If you took out $750,000 worth of life insurance, it could cost you as much as $8920 a year if you bought a whole-life policy or $400 a year if you bought a term policy. Both policies will pay your beneficiary $750,000 if you die. Term insurance costs much less than whole life because there is no cash value to it. If it expires and you don't renew it, you cannot cash it in and get money back. That's the biggest difference between term and whole life. (See Table 8-2.) As you get older, you are a greater risk, so the cost of term will increase every year unless you buy a kind of policy called a level-premium policy. When you purchase term life insurance without level-premium payments, you will renew the policy each year. When purchasing term life with level-premium payments, you make a commitment to the insurance company to keep the policy for a specified number of years, which allows the premiums to be averaged

Table 8-2
Comparison of Types of Life Insurance

Policy Type	Cost	Return in Cash Value	Control Over Investment Mix	Fees and Service Charges	Flexibility	Tax Treatment
Term	Low	None	None	Low	Very flexible: Amount can be changed at will	Premiums not deductible; proceeds not taxable
Whole life	High	Poor Avg. 5–7%	None	Not disclosed but very high	Poor: Money locked into cash value	Same as term; cash value tax deferred. Interest on loan only deductible as other interest under 1986 tax return
Variable life	High	Varies: Tied to stock and bond markets	Some: Client may choose from mutual funds managed by company	High commission and service fees	Average: Withdrawal of money is very complicated	Same as whole life
Universal life	Medium	Varies: Tied to selected financial indexes such as T-bills	None: Company sets interest rates	High in first years; decreases in later years	Good: Dividends can be withdrawn and premiums can be varied	Same as whole life

SOURCE: Chart courtesy of Warren, Gorham & Lamont, Inc., Boston, Massachusetts.

out over that period of time. This means that you will pay the same premium at age 45 as you did at age 25, even though you have become a greater risk. Realize though that opting for the level-payment premiums will cost you more annually in the early years, by comparison, in order to keep the premium unchanged as you age. The anticipated cost analysis of a $100,000 policy for a 35-year-old male nonsmoker would look like this:

	Term Life	Whole Life	Universal Life
Annual premium	$146	$862	$664
Cash value after 5 years	None	$5550	$7498*

*Assuming 8% dividends (which don't exist anymore!).

A 35-year-old woman can buy $250,000 of 15-year level term for $230 a year. The same policy for a 35-year-old man would cost $293 a year.

Buy as much term insurance as you can afford. Term policies are often overlooked and underrated, and most insurance agents will not tell you about them because the agents do not earn a large commission on these low-cost policies. The concept of "buy term and invest the difference [the difference between what you would pay for term and what you would pay for whole life]," popularized by the A. L. Williams Insurance Company during the eighties is still a feasible idea. (See Table 8-3.)

Table 8-3

Saving in a Whole-Life Policy Versus
the "Buy-Term-and-Invest-the-Difference" Concept

$100,000 Whole-Life Policy for a 35-Year-Old-Male Nonsmoker (based on after-tax values)

Age	Whole-Life Annual Premium	Term-Life Annual Premium	Cash Value in Whole-Life Policy*	Money-Market Fund Yielding 8%	Tax-Deferred Annuity Yielding 10% Annually
40	$1,968	$ 180	$ 7,770	$ 10,892	$ 11,545
45	$1,968	$ 249	$ 21,490	$ 26,132	$ 29,338
50	$1,968	$ 367	$ 39,420	$ 47,315	$ 56,726
55	$1,968	$ 574	$ 63,230	$ 76,469	$ 98,766
65	$1,968	$1,025	$134,590	$168,098	$262,736

*Dividends have been used to buy added insurance. Keep in mind that the cash values exceed the premiums paid and the policyholder must pay taxes on the difference when it is withdrawn and the policy is canceled.
SOURCE: Chart courtesy of Lifestyle Planners, Inc., Brooklyn, New York.

IIΞ IIIIΞ IIIIΞ IIIIΞ IIIIΞ IIIIΞ IIIIΞIIIIΞ IIIIΞ IIIIΞ IIIIΞ IIIIΞ IIIIΞIIIIΞ

Theodore Martin Alexander, Sr. (1909–), established the first black-owned insurance agency in Atlanta, Georgia, in 1931. It eventually grew to be the largest black-controlled general insurance brokerage firm specializing in risk management in the South.

IIΞ IIIIΞ IIIIΞ IIIIΞ IIIIΞ IIIIΞ IIIIΞIIIIΞ IIIIΞ IIIIΞ IIIIΞ IIIIΞ IIIIΞIIIIΞ

THE CASH-VALUE ARGUMENT

Many people buy cash-value insurance because they consider it an investment. Life insurance companies are the largest financial institutions in the world, with nearly $2 trillion, yes, trillion, in assets in government securities, long-term mortgages (usually for office buildings, shopping centers, apartment complexes), and some corporate bonds. Maybe even junk bonds. If you purchase a *participating policy,* you get a share of the income from these investments in the form of dividends. If you get a *nonparticipating policy,* you receive what is called *excess interest,* but there is no legal contract that says the company has to pass it on to you. The only "guaranteed" rate of return on your cash value in a nonparticipating policy is the 4 percent that is required by law, which is about equal to what you would earn from an account in most savings banks.

When you buy whole-life, or cash-value, insurance, you pay the highest premiums for coverage. Most of what you pay in the first year goes into the agent's pocket as a commission plus administrative charges and front-end expenses levied by the company. Whatever is left over, which is usually nothing until after the second year, is invested.

An agent will tell you that one reason to buy a cash-value policy is that you can borrow from your policy for retirement or for college tuition. The insurance company will allow you to do this once you have made enough payments, although it may take up to 6 weeks to receive the funds after you've requested them; also, the company will charge you interest on the money you borrow, which seems a bit outrageous since it's your money. If you do not pay back the loan, the company won't bill you or harass you to repay it, but your heirs will suffer the cost of this by the decreased death benefit. The total loan plus all accrued interest will be deducted from the final death payment. If you cancel the policy at any time, the loan, plus interest, will be deducted from the cash value that has built up within the policy. Borrowing on newer policies can cost you as much as 10 percent interest; if the company is paying dividends of only 8 percent, you're losing money when you take out the cash value. It would be more economical to buy the extra coverage with a low-cost term policy that you will keep for about 10 to 15 years. By then you won't need as much coverage.

Another favorite sales pitch that is used with young applicants is: "Purchase a low-cost 10-year-payment vanishing premium policy and get it over with. You can always borrow out the cash value later if you need it for retirement or college tuition." Agents are trained to come up with these and 50 other reasons to convince you to commit to a payment plan that goes on for 8 to 10 years, which completes policy payment. What they don't tell you is that this method usually doesn't buy enough coverage. The fine print in a vanishing premium policy also carries a warning that if future dividends are not enough to cover the true cost of the insurance, additional payments may be required.

If you must buy a cash-value policy, universal life is cheaper than whole life and builds cash values sooner. Whole life is the most expensive kind of coverage. Comparing premiums is not the best way to judge the true cost of a policy. The interest-adjusted index gives you a more accurate cost per $1000. Ask your agent to give you the formula and explain the indexed-adjusted net costs. Most of what you pay in during the first year goes to cover the commissions income for the agent, set-up fees for the insurance company, administrative expenses, and mortality charges. People also forget that the proposed illustration is just a projection of future earnings based on an interest rate that may or may not be realistic over the next ten years. Nothing is guaranteed about those future dividends.

A good compromise suggested by some industry experts is to buy two policies. One should be a low-cost universal life policy for $50,000 or $100,000 that will last for a lifetime. The second should be a term insurance policy for $500,000 or $600,000 that will expire in 15 to 20 years. The major concern is to get the coverage you need at a rate you can afford. Compare and shop for the best rates.

When you are looking for an insurance company, don't bypass smaller, lesser-known companies. Many of them have better dividend records and lower expense charges than the industry giants because they have lower overhead costs. The cash value of your policy depends on how well the company is managed, and the larger companies don't have perfect track records for being the best managed or for paying higher dividends because of their size. Actual dividends compared with the projected illustrations the agents show you, particularly for the large well-known companies, may well be lower than promised.

SWITCHING POLICIES

If you're thinking of switching policies, talk to several companies and ask for comparable illustrations using the same interest rates and payment schedule. But if you have had your current cash-value policy for more than 5 years, it probably isn't a good idea to switch to a cheaper policy with better cash-value projections because those projections aren't guaranteed. Changing cash-value policies is complicated. You've already paid for the front-end commissions and administrative expenses, and it isn't worth repeating the expense. If you have held a dividend-paying policy for more than 5 years, whether it is whole life or universal life with a limited-payment premium policy, then you will also trigger a tax bill if you switch. Uncle Sam wants his share of those tax-deferred dividends. In any event, don't switch or cancel any existing policy until the second replacement insurance company has accepted you and issued a new policy.

If you have a term policy, switching is no problem because there is no cash value to consider. If you pay annually, you may get some of your premiums back if you decide to change in midyear.

Keep in mind that switching policies may also require that you take additional medical exams. Since the beginning of the AIDS epidemic, many companies request physical exams and medical records for all policies, term or permanent, of $100,000 or more.

Every insurance company is legally allowed to cancel your policy or not pay the death benefit if you die under certain circumstances, such as suicide, within the first two years your policy is in effect. If that two-year contestability period has expired, it may not be feasible to switch policies to another company. Also, if you misstate your age on your original application, the company will adjust the death benefit based on what the premiums should have been using your correct date of birth.

REVIEW YOUR POLICIES EVERY 5 YEARS

As you get older and plan to retire, your insurance needs should decrease. By then, the mortgage is usually paid off, the children are gone, and you've accumulated a good pension, or you should have. You will probably only need about $50,000 or $100,000 of insurance, if any, to supplement a retirement income for your spouse and to pay off any estate taxes that may arise for your children.

OTHER ALTERNATIVES

If you choose to buy cash-value life insurance, buy your policy directly from the company. This can save you between $300 and $500 because your payments the first year will not go to paying an agent commission—since there is not agent. This means that you start building up cash value almost immediately. Several companies have begun offering no-load (no-commission) or low-load (low-commission) insurance policies by mail order. The front-end costs of these policies are less because no commission is charged and no agent will call you. To find out more about these policies contact the Council of Life Insurance Consultants, 600 W. Jackson Boulevard, Chicago, Illinois 60661; or call (312) 993-0355.

HOW DO YOU GET HONEST ANSWERS?

Talk to bank officers, accountants, tax attorneys, or a fee-only certified financial planner who isn't going to try to sell you a product. Do some homework. Go to the library and look for an A. M. Best rating book on insurance companies. Best, the most well-known independent insurance company rating service, offers free publications that tell you everything you need to know and more about insurance companies. Look in *Best's Review, Best's Insurance Reports,* and *Best's Flitcraft Compend* in the business section of any large public library and try to select a company that has been given an A rating. Insurance companies are also rated by three other independent research services that may assist you in getting information:

Duff & Phelps, (312) 368-3657

Moody's Investor's Services, (212) 553-0377

Standard & Poor's, (212) 208-1527

Or contact the following rate comparison firms:

First Ameritas, (800) 337-5433

TermQuote, (800) 444-8376

SelectQuote Insurance Services, (800) 343-1985

LifeRates of America, (800) 457-2837

Each of these firms gives rate comparisons for at least five nationally known companies, and no agent will call you to make a sale.

If you want an individual evaluation of your existing policy, here is an independent consulting firm that can help you with honest answers and no sales pressure:

Insurance Information, Inc.
23 Route 134
South Dennis, Massachusetts 02660
(800) 472-5800

This firm does not sell insurance, but for a $50 fee it will review your existing policy and compare it with the same type of policy from at least five other companies. Keep them in mind also for evaluating your auto and home-owner's insurance policies.

NICO is an independent consumer advocacy group that is the watchdog of the industry. It charges $25 to run a computer comparison of policies, including whole life, universal life, term life, and tax-deferred annuities. You supply the data. NICO also publishes two useful guides: *A Buyer's Guide to Insurance* ($3.50 with a self-addressed stamped business envelope) and *Taking the Bite Out of Insurance* ($11.95), which concentrates on life insurance. Send requests to:

National Insurance Consumer Organization (NICO)
121 N. Payne Street
Alexandria, Virginia 22314
(703) 549-8050

Make sure you put the truth about your health status on the application. The National Medical Information Bureau is a computer information system, much like the credit reporting agencies, shared by all insurance companies. It compiles all health-related data about your health insurance usage over the last 7 years. If you have ever paid for a doctor's visit or had medical treatment that was reimbursed by health insurance, that information goes into the National Medical Information Bureau's computer. When you apply for life insurance, this database is checked to see if you have given accurate information on your application. With the AIDS-related health crisis in America, life insurance companies are requiring a physical examination for anyone who applies for more than $100,000 of life insurance coverage. You can request a copy of your medical information report by contacting:

National Medical Information Bureau
P.O. Box 105, Essex Station
Boston, Massachusetts 02112
(617) 426-3660

HEALTH INSURANCE

IIIƎIII *Living longer is the best revenge.* IIIƎIII
KELVIN BOSTON

African-Americans have a unique cultural and historical experience with health care in America which has to be acknowledged. The African practice of self-treatment using the natural pharmacopeia of herbs and nutritional care has always been preferred over traditional physician-provided medical care, partly because of our cultural heritage and partly because of poor treatment—frequently an absence of treatment—by the medical community. Nurse and midwife care to produce more babies for the slave owner was usually the only medical attention blacks received during slavery. After slavery in the South, racism kept most African-Americans out of hospitals and away from getting medical care even in vital emergencies—the death of Bessie Smith, myth or fact, is quite well known to older African-Americans. The alleged story is that Smith's injuries from an automobile accident forced her friends to take her to the nearest hospital emergency room in Clarksdale, Mississippi, one night in 1937, and she bled to death because the white physicians refused to treat her since she was black.

The Tuskegee syphilis experiment and similar bizarre stories of medical maltreatment of African-Americans fostered a well-founded distrust of doctors and the medical system. White doctors who did treat black patients often kept them waiting until all white patients had been cared for. Medical treatments were not explained, and prescriptions were usually given without regard to the cost of medication and with no instructions about the proper use of drugs. This historical experience, along with the high cost of medical treatment and health insurance, has led to a practice among African-Americans of waiting until a health crisis arises and going to the emergency room for care. At that point, it is often too late for treatment that can reverse bodily damage.

The high cost of health insurance has become a national crisis that is still being debated in Congress by politicians, doctors, insurance companies, and citizens of all ages and ethnic groups. At one time, most of us could rely upon our employer to provide health coverage, but with increasing unemployment, corporate downsizing, and the escalating cost of health insurance, more Americans are going without coverage. Especially because of the high cost, many small businesses have cut back on coverage or eliminated it completely. As a result, more than 40 million Americans are without health insurance.

If your company does provide health insurance, then you are fortunate, but you may also be required to share a larger part of the price tag for this benefit because of the prohibitive costs. With the daily changes in the rules and guidelines for services that are available to you, it is imperative that you remain aware of what is paid for by the company and what you are responsible for yourself. If you are paying for it yourself, you must take advantage of all the possible options that are available to you, so you must find out exactly what they are.

The choices made available by your employer are typically either a traditional group plan or an HMO (health maintenance organization). Make an appointment and ask your benefits counselor to explain the details of your coverage. If the initial coverage excludes preexisting conditions or specifies treatment limitations, you need to know and be prepared by saving for an emergency until you are protected. In many cases, unfortunately, insurance companies are getting more involved in the day-to-day management of HMOs and are focusing on cutting costs rather than giving service.

Also ask if there are restrictions on experimental care. Some forms of experimental treatments that have not been thoroughly tested or approved by the Food and Drug Administration may or may not be reimbursed under your plan. Ask your insurance company for an explanation of what is not covered. Will it pay for transplants? Dialysis? Chemotherapy? Nutritional therapy? See Figure 8-2 for a list of things to check on.

If you and your spouse are both covered by health insurance, don't assume that you have duplicate coverage. You will never be paid twice for the same illness. Insurance companies communicate with each other and coordinate payments on family claims. The National Medical Information Bureau in Massachusetts (mentioned earlier) maintains records indicating all insurance coverage by all companies, much like your credit report.

Type of Policy: HMO_____ Group_____ Supplementary_____
            Reimbursement_____ Percent_____

Coverage: Major medical_____ Hospital_____ Comprehensive_____

Lifetime maximum limits: _____ $250,000? $500,000? $1,000,000?

Deductible amount: _____ Per family member _____ # per year _____

Services covered:
        Hospitalization_____
        Prescriptions_____
        Physical therapy_____
        Intensive care_____
        Surgery_____
        X rays and tests_____(Is there a per diem limit?)
        Second opinion_____
        Psychotherapy_____
        Experimental surgery_____
        Ambulance service_____
        Private nursing_____
        Home health care_____
        Office visits_____
        Chiropractic care_____
        Eye care_____
        Well-baby care_____

Can the policy be converted to an individual policy if you leave the job?

Does the policy cover experimental cancer treatments?

What is the age limit for dependent coverage? Does it cover students away at school?

Are you allowed an annual physical each year?

Does it provide a mammogram each year for women over 50?

Does it pay for prescription drugs?

Figure 8-2. Health insurance checklist.

If you don't have insurance, check into getting it. To not have health insurance is like going to Atlantic City without a round-trip ticket to get home: You're begging to go for broke and get stranded. Whether your company offers it or you must purchase it yourself, your health plan should provide two basic types of protection:

- *Hospital expense payment plan.* Usually this is Blue Cross/Blue Shield, which pays for hospital room and board for up to 120 days and includes general nursing care and surgical procedures.

- *Major medical plan.* This covers what the hospital plan does not: lab tests, X rays, and prescriptions. With an HMO you pay a flat monthly fee regardless of the treatment and the number of visits. You may not, however, choose anyone you wish for your family's primary-care physician. You must choose from among a group of doctors who are affiliated with the HMO. If you visit another physician you must pay for it yourself.

PREVENTION IS STILL THE BEST CURE

The five leading causes of death among African-Americans in 1995 were heart disease, diabetes, cancer, hypertension, and AIDS. African-American women have a higher rate of death from diabetes, hypertension, and breast cancer than any other group of women. Much of the problem is a result of the lack of regular checkups, and so the diseases are frequently detected too late.

All these diseases are behavior-related and can be mitigated by lifestyle choices and the control of stressful issues in one's health and well-being. The best way to protect your health is to eat properly, take off weight, and follow a moderate exercise program. The most important preventive measure you can take advantage of through your health insurance plan is to get a regular medical checkup each year.

DISABILITY INSURANCE

Patricia M. was laid off from her position as human resources coordinator with a major corporation in Atlanta in a company-downsizing move a few years ago. Patricia used her severance pay to start a temporary employment agency and career counseling service out of her apartment. Because of her many business connections, she got several lucrative contracts right away, opened a comfortable office in the Midwood section of town, and hired three employees. As a single professional with a teenage daughter, Patricia signed up for a group health insurance plan for herself and her employees, which included a small life insurance policy option. She also started a small 401(k) plan and was beginning to enjoy her growing business and a little prosperity.

After 3 years, Patricia finally achieved the dream she had always had of buying a luxury condominium in a high-rise building in downtown Atlanta, and her accountant agreed that it was a good tax deduction to have a mortgage. Six months after the closing, Patricia had an open-house party to celebrate the new look of her apartment. She had borrowed $18,000 and ordered custom-made furniture, a designer kitchen with marble countertops, and every state-of-the-art gadget she had ever dreamed of owning.

On the fifth anniversary of her business, Patricia gave a party at a restaurant to celebrate her success. As she was driving home later that evening, a taxi went out of control and slammed into the side of her Honda Accord. The collision killed the taxi driver and left Patricia with a broken leg, crushed ribs, and a back injury that kept her hospitalized for 3 months and 17 days. It took another 6 months for her to recuperate in a convalescent home. Her doctor's main concern was that she be able to walk again one day. Patricia's physical therapy bills, home attendant care, and living expenses came to more than $187,000 that year. Her 401(k) investments and savings were depleted after the first 5 months, but the bills kept coming. Without her direction, the employment agency faltered and was dissolved. The bank foreclosed on her apartment, and her daughter's car was repossessed. Although she had health insurance, many of her expenses for a home-health care aide, special medical transportation, and physical therapy were only partially covered by her insurance.

If she had purchased a disability insurance policy, she would have received up to 70 percent of the take-home pay she had before the accident and would have been able to keep many of the assets she had worked so hard to accumulate. In addition, the insurance policy would have paid the rent on her office and kept the place going for up to 18 months until she could return to work.

Patricia hired an attorney to sue the taxi company, but the case will take 5 years to get to court with all the meetings, medical hearings, depositions, and negotiations that are held before a settlement can be reached. After a year, Patricia's worker's compensation of $175 a week was depleted, and her social security disability payments provided only the limited amount of $680 a month. This successful businesswoman was forced to move into a public housing project and begin collecting public assistance for 2 years until she was able to reestablish herself professionally. When the lawsuit is finally settled, her attorney will take one-third of whatever cash settlement is offered, and she will be required to reimburse the department of social services for whatever income assistance she has received because her injury was considered temporary.

‖☰‖   *Health is a human right, not a privilege to be purchased.*   ‖☰‖
SHIRLEY CHISHOLM
Former congresswoman

Disability insurance is essentially paycheck protection. Forty-eight percent of all mortgage foreclosures occur because the homeowner did not have disability insurance coverage. Thirty-six percent of all small businesses fail for the same reason. If you're sick and can't work, it replaces 60 to 70 percent of your income. If you're under 35, there is a 65 percent chance that at some point in your life you'll experience a disability that will keep you out of work for at least 6 months and possibly as long as 2 years. And the bills will keep coming. Don't expect social security to take care of you. Less than 30 percent of all the applications for social security disability are approved for payment. The rules are so restrictive that it is nearly impossible to receive.

If you're young and single and have no dependents, or if you're divorced and a single parent, disability insurance should be your first insurance purchase after you buy health insurance. In most states, your employer must provide worker's compensation, but that may be only short-term disability coverage for up to 90 days at approximately half your current salary. Longer-term payments require lengthy applications and compensation board hearings, and it may take 6 to 9 months before a payment plan is approved.

Some employers offer a group disability insurance plan as part of your employee benefits, called a salary continuation plan. It is better than worker's compensation protection, but it has limits and provides coverage that only lasts for 5 years and may offer only half of your salary. These plans do not have cost-of-living increase options to protect against lifetime disability. Like your health insurance, this benefit disappears when you leave your job, and it cannot be converted to an individual plan.

Membership in various professional associations sometimes provides group disability coverage, but this also has its limits. If, for some reason, the insurance company for the association decides to challenge your claim, it may cancel your policy and reimburse you for all the premiums paid through your membership group rather than honor your claim.

IF YOU NEED A PRIVATE DISABILITY POLICY, HERE'S WHAT TO LOOK FOR

If you're self-employed or your employer's coverage is inadequate, here's what you need to know when investigating private disability policies. A disability policy can be costly, but it is available based on your business and professional status. Some companies specialize in lifetime disability protection only for white-collar executives; professionals such as doctors, lawyers, accountants, and engineers; bankers; and people in other technical and managerial jobs. Blue-collar workers will have to rely on personal savings or union benefits under worker's compensation. A limited disability policy can be purchased by people in these job classifications, but only for a period of 2 to 5 years. Certain employment classifications such as mechanics, truck drivers, police officers, salespeople, and writers normally cannot purchase disability insurance because of the danger of the job or the erratic pattern of income.

Find a policy that is guaranteed renewable and noncancellable by the insurance company. Once the company approves you as an acceptable risk, it can only drop you if you stop making your payments. Be sure you understand how the provider defines disability. Here are some other terms you need to be familiar with:

1. *Waiting period.* The cost of the policy depends upon the waiting period you choose. The longer you wait to begin collecting monthly disability checks, the less the policy costs you. You have a choice of a 30-, 60-, 90-, or 180-day waiting period. If you have sufficient sick time, vacation leave, and savings to cover a long illness, then a 90-day waiting period can save 30 percent on your premiums.

2. *Residual payments option.* If you have this option and you return to work part-time or at a reduced salary, the insurance company will replace the lost income as long as there was a drop in income of at least 20 percent. This helps if you have a heart attack or a stroke and cannot resume full duties.

3. *Monthly income benefit.* The amount of monthly income the policy pays is normally 60 percent of your monthly salary. For long-term policies, in certain occupational classes, up to 70 to 75 percent coverage is available. If you pay the premiums yourself, the disability income is not taxable. If your employer pays for the insurance, then the payments are taxable income.

4. *Cost of living adjustment.* If you have a long-term illness, this option allows you to have an annual percentage increase in the disability income that you receive. You specify the increase in percentage when you fill out the application. The higher the increase percentage chosen, the higher the cost to you.

5. *Length of coverage.* You can purchase disability coverage for as short a period as 2 years or as long as a lifetime. The longer the coverage period, the more the insurance costs.

Before deciding on a disability policy, analyze your assets and financial obligations to determine how much income you would realistically need if disabled. Figure 8-3 can help you do this. Shop around and compare companies. See Figure 8-4 for a comparison of disability policies.

INSURANCE YOU DON'T NEED!
Some kinds of insurance are just a bad buy:

Specific "dread disease" insurance. The special exceptions and narrow requirements are so prohibitive on this kind of policy that you may never be able to collect on it. And what if you never get cancer (or whatever dread disease it covers)?

Total monthly income required:_____

Available Resources (per month)

Social security benefits $_____

Employer disability benefits $_____

Spouse's earnings $_____

Other income $_____

Other disability benefits $_____

Reduction in expenses $_____

Earnings on savings and investments $_____

Earnings on IRAs, pensions, etc. $_____

    Total Disability Income Needed:_____

Figure 8-3. Income protection planning checklist.

Credit insurance. Dollar for dollar, this is the most expensive way to buy protection to pay off your debts in case of death or disability. Use the money to buy extra term coverage.

In-hospital insurance. These policies promise up to $100 a day, but don't waste your money; they don't cover any medical expenses. Spend the extra dollars on additional medical coverage.

Air travel insurance. The cost may seem to be a small amount, but this kind of insurance is very overpriced. For the peace of mind that you purchase, get more term insurance.

Life insurance on children. Unless you happen to be the parent of a child star in a sitcom, like one of the Cosby kids, or you

	Quality Individual Policy	Typical- Membership Policy	Typical Group Policy
Can the policy be canceled?	No	Yes	Yes
Can premiums be increased?	No, only decreased	Yes	Yes
What is the premium cost?	High	Medium	Low
What is the duration of payment for own occupation?	Age 65 (or less if desired)	5 years	Two years
Are benefits payable during a period of partial disability?	Yes, a portion of the total benefit may be paid	Yes, pays 50% of total benefit for 3 or 6 months	No
If you work part-time, will you collect any benefit?	Yes	Yes, but limited to 3 to 6 months	No
Can benefits be paid beyond age 65?	Yes	Yes, usually for accident only	No
What are elimination period options?	30, 60, 90, 180, 365 days	Varies, usually one or two choices ranging from 30 to 365 days	180 days
Can future benefits be hedged against inflation?	Yes	No	No
What is the maximum monthly benefit?	Up to $10,000+ based on percentage of earnings	$2,500	$1,500
Are basic benefits offset by Social Security or employer payments?	No	Yes	Yes
Can Social Security benefits be guaranteed by option?	Yes	No	No

Figure 8-4. Comparing disability policies.

	Quality Individual Policy	Typical-Membership Policy	Typical Group Policy
Does policy pay dividends?	Yes	No	No
Is policy portable?	Yes	No	No
Are you covered for pre-existing conditions? own the policy	Yes	No, for the first 12 months you	No
When does the policy terminate?	Nonpayment of premium; age 75	Nonpayment of premium; age 65; master policy terminated; membership terminates; retirement	Nonpayment of premium; age 65; group terminates employment within group terminates; retirement

Figure 8-4. *(Cont.)*

see your little Jelani as the next Michael Jackson, don't bother. Even if children are major income sources for the family coffers, it would be a devastating emotional loss, rather than a financial loss, if something happened to them. Some insurance agents encourage you to add a children's rider for $5000 to $10,000 to your policy for about $60 to $75 a year, telling you that you can use the payout for college costs. This kind of rider may not seem expensive, but those dollars could be put to better use in a growth mutual fund set aside for a college education. The total return on a mutual fund is much better, and you have more control over what happens to the money. If you want tax-deferred savings, then buy a zero-coupon Treasury bond or a U.S. savings bond in your child's name for each birthday.

ERNESTA PROCOPE, CEO AND FOUNDER

E. G. Bowman, Insurance Brokers
New York, New York

At 13, after her debut at Carnegie Recital Hall playing Rachmaninoff's "Prelude in C Sharp Minor," Ernesta Procope was convinced that she was well on her way to her chosen career as a concert pianist. After graduating from New York City's High School of Music and Art, she began studying music at Brooklyn College. A year later she dropped out of school when she married Albin Bowman, a Brooklyn real estate developer. Now, instead of having her name in lights on a theater marquee, she has been graced with title "First Lady of Wall Street."

Bowman's husband encouraged her to get an insurance license and manage his busy real estate office in the Bedford-Stuyvesant section of Brooklyn. She began selling auto $25-down insurance, life insurance, and property and casualty coverage to the Brooklyn residents who made up her client base. Some of the properties Bowman bought and developed were in areas that the white insurance companies would not cover because of the location. Rather than disappoint his neighbors, Bowman took the unbelievable risk of insuring them out of his own pocket. A few years later, the insurance companies trusted his judgment when they saw how little he had lost after taking this risk. Then Ernesta found herself a widow.

When she married John Procope, she kept the Bowman name for the business and continued to sell insurance to homeowners and small black businesses in her Brooklyn neighborhood. But the race riots of the 1960s nearly wiped her out. Procope received 90 cancellation notices in one day as white insurance companies redlined the area and refused to extend coverage again for hundreds of properties. Faced with the prospect of financial ruin, Procope called Governor Nelson Rockefeller and demanded that something be done to protect inner-city homeowners and small businesses. That phone call led to the creation of the New York "Fair Plan," a state-run program that guarantees property insurance for urban neighborhoods and has become a model program for urban insurance in 26 states.

In 1969, Procope began to focus on commercial accounts, beginning with the Bedford-Stuyvesant Restoration Corporation. By 1976, she decided to cross the Brooklyn Bridge and expand her horizons. Her clients now include the large commercial properties in the caverns of Wall Street and *Fortune* 500 companies such as PepsiCo, IBM, Avon Products, Philip Morris, and Tiffany, with gross commissions of over $30 million a year.

"We cannot wait for others to pave the way.... We know the resistance, we know the prejudices, but we must overwhelm prejudice with excellence and endurance. So we'd better be creative, be trained, be prepared, come up with some new angle, a new product that would attract a prospective client. You've got to be innovative if you're going to survive. And this is only the beginning."

SOME FINAL WORDS

Remember, the main purpose of insurance is to preserve and protect your assets so that you will have something to pass on to your heirs. The true meaning of financial planning is building a dynasty: creating a firm foundation for the next generation to move up the financial ladder and leaving behind economic support for the well-being of our children. That begins with a commitment to protect the assets and the lifestyle we have struggled to attain.

INVESTING TO BUILD WEALTH FOR A LIFETIME

"Dollars not only count, but they rule."

Charles T. Walker
An Appeal to Caesar, 1901

In 1987, the wizards of Wall Street were stunned by the leveraged buyout of the McCall Patterns company. Some of the largest and sharpest investment banking groups had offered proposals on the deal and inexplicably found themselves eliminated from the negotiations by an outsider—a maverick who was not a member of the select fraternity of money men who maintain quiet control of the world of corporate finance. Not only did the winning bid go to an outsider, but he was an individual investor none of them had ever heard of—an African-American attorney, Reginald Francis Lewis, who had never dreamed of being a Wall Street insider. For many years, he had thought that the only way to make a decent dollar would have been by playing football.

Reg Lewis made financial history with the purchase of McCall Patterns using only $1 million of equity ($500,000 from a MESBIC, a minority business development lender, and $500,000 of a personal loan from the J. P. Morgan Company) along with $30 million of debt to put the deal together. Within 3 years, Lewis had restructured the company, expanded the product line, and finally sold McCall Patterns to a British company for $64 million, which netted him and his investors a 90-to-1 profit on the initial dollars invested. A year later, he bought TLC Beatrice Foods, Inc., for $987 million in another leveraged buyout. No one was more surprised and ecstatic than Lewis himself to discover that he had again managed one of the biggest coups on Wall Street.

Born December 7, 1942, in East Baltimore, Maryland, Reg Lewis grew up as the average black kid on the block who preferred hanging out on the playground with his friends to studying for the SATs. His well-meaning parents, who divorced when he was still a child, were supportive of whatever efforts he aimed for and even assisted him with his paper route to have money. When Lewis finished high school, his facility with a football was better than his grades, so he got a sports scholarship to Virginia State. Lewis was on his way to that "pro-ball" career he had dreamed about—or so he thought. A shoulder injury in his sophomore year forced him to rethink everything, and so he enrolled in the university's pre-law courses. One of the program benefits was a trip to visit Harvard Law School—if you made decent grades. Lewis accepted the challenge that changed his life.

The following year, Lewis took the trip to Cambridge and was so captivated by the opportunities he saw there that he managed to talk his way into the school without ever taking the entrance exam. He graduated from Virginia State and went north. Upon graduating from Harvard with honors, Lewis headed for a small Wall Street law firm. It was in New York that he discovered the business of leveraged buyouts and corporate takeovers and met many of the movers and shakers of Wall Street. Within 3 years Lewis started his own law firm and focused on buying and selling small businesses using venture capital.

Reginald Lewis was the first African-American to be included on the *Forbes* 400 list of the wealthiest people in America and did not mind sharing the wealth. He made the largest single contribution of any donor to Harvard Law School and set up a foundation at Virginia State, his alma mater, to encourage other African-American students to study math, science, and business. Thousands of dollars were contributed to many other African-American foundations and causes. Reg Lewis and Buddy Fletcher, another African-American investment manager, made the largest individual contributions to the NAACP to sustain it through its financial crisis in 1991.

In 1993, at the peak of his financial power, Lewis died of a brain tumor at age 52. His financial empire, TLC Beatrice, is still growing under the direction of his wife, Loida Lewis, his half-brother Jean Fugat, and his daughter. Lewis knew the meaning of risk, recognized the high-stakes profits that were available to him, and was willing to put in the time, the hard work, and take on the risk of borrowed capital to make it happen.

‖☰‖‖ *Growth always involves the risk of failure.*   ‖☰‖‖
HOWARD THURMAN

Reg Lewis didn't become a wealthy man by fearing risks or by giving up if he failed after the first try. He had tried other ventures before the McCall Patterns deal. He had attempted to buy Park Sausage Company in Baltimore, but someone else got there first. He was outbid for a group of radio stations in Texas. The purchase of a leisure furniture company in California fell apart at the table at the time of the scheduled closing because the owner didn't like the idea of selling his family business to a black man. It took several years of doing his homework, studying the market, and learning the rules of the game before he finalized the deals that made him wealthy and successful.

It is amazing how many African-Americans think there is some secret formula to succeeding on Wall Street and building wealth. But there is no separate resource of secret financial information about the inner workings of Wall Street. There's no locked door marked "For Whites Only" when it comes to Wall Street and the wealth-building process. Everyone (except Ivan Bosky, and we all know what happened to him!) has access to this largest and most profitable financial market in the world. It is available to the small investor as well as the largest pension-fund manager—but you have to seek it out. And you have to overcome your fear of taking risks.

The fear of investing harbored by most African-Americans seems to come from years of believing that we are financial outsiders in the economy. Instead of thinking positively and anticipating profits, there is an extremely negative attitude among African-Americans that perpetuates limited insight about the stock market and any financial risk that may incur a loss. Even among middle-class African-Americans who have a comfortable buffer or savings in the bank, there is an attitude that investing is a white man's game. Nothing could be further from the truth. Most of that attitude can be cured with a serious infusion of information, but you have to make the effort to get that information. The emotional dynamics that dominate most of our lives has no place in the financial arena. Hard cold facts, clear data, and logic are the only way to arrive at realistic money-making decisions, and that is the trap for most African-Americans. In an all too human pattern of avoiding what we don't understand, we hang onto the emotional paranoia that there is more to the game than we are being told.

Even though *risk* is the key word that stops most African-Americans from investing, risk is a fact of life. The air we breathe, the cars we drive, the food we eat, the trains and buses we ride each day—all carry some amount of risk, but we keep functioning and growing despite the negative possibilities. The courage, fortitude, and determination that drove runaway slaves to seek a better life at the risk of death seems to crumble and disappear when confronted with the financial pages and a Wall Street ticker tape.

But too many African-Americans are plagued with a deep-seated distrust of anything having to do with financial risk. Because of this fear of risk, they automatically dismiss the stock market—and anything else outside the bank— as being beyond their capacity to understand or participate in. *Wrong!* African-Americans may lack the sophistication, the information, and the experience of being in the investment game, but so do most other Americans. In this case, what you don't know can leave you broke after a lifetime of working, with nothing to show for it.

‖☰‖ *When you understand investing, you understand American business.*   ‖☰‖

JOSHUA SMITH
Maxima Corporation

AFRICAN-AMERICANS' MISCONCEPTIONS ABOUT WALL STREET

The two most common misconceptions that many African-Americans— and many other Americans—have are these:

1. You need a lot of money to get started in the stock market. *Wrong!* You don't need a million dollars like Reg Lewis to get into the investment game. You don't even need $10,000 like so many investment ads tell you. If you have gotten out of debt and have built up an emergency savings fund, and have $1000 that you are willing to risk, you are ready to open an investment account. You can start with as little as $100 a month and build a comfortable nest egg for yourself.

Saving versus Investing. First you must understand the difference between saving and investing. Saving means safety, guaranteed income, predictable results, and the decreased value and diminished purchasing power of your dollar—in other words, little or no risk. Guaranteed interest rates are designed to favor only the bank—not you. U.S. government Treasury bills, notes, bonds, and certificates of deposit that are FDIC-insured may allow you to sleep easier at night, but they will not make you rich. Even the FDIC, the Federal Deposit Insurance Corporation that protects bank deposits, is shaky after the onslaught of bank failures that occurred in the early nineties.

Many African-Americans open passbook savings accounts and buy CDs in several banks around town, often going 20 blocks out of their way to get an extra half a percent of interest on a 6-month CD, not realizing that all this effort to earn a few dollars is futile. A combination of the fear of risk and the lack of experience with financial institutions outside of banks stops many African-Americans from ever considering investing in anything that isn't FDIC-insured.

2. The stock market crashed in 1929! Or 1933! Or 1987! The reactions of many African-Americans to the idea of investing in stocks seems to be focused on an event that occurred so long ago that most of us weren't even around to remember it, yet we cling to the bad news like it happened yesterday. Yes, the market dropped in 1929, but in the last 60+ years government controls have made it less disastrous to invest. And, yes again, the last devastating crash of 1987 saw the market drop over 1500 points in a 5-day period. But smart investors who knew quality stocks bought as many shares as they could afford and tripled their money by being calm and realistic about what good stocks can achieve for a balanced portfolio. Smart investors who have been through the ups and downs of the market did not sell, so they did not really experience any losses. (See Figure 9-1.)

The stock market is not like a trip to Atlantic City. In Atlantic City, you know that you're probably going to leave your money there. At least in the stock market you have a 50-50 chance to make some money. Those are better odds than what you get at a blackjack table. After that devastating drop in 1987, the market recovered within 15 months and set new heights when the Dow Jones Industrial Average, the most famous market index, went over 5000 in November 1995. Anyone who had made an investment in a comfortable mixture of stocks, bonds, and Treasury bills in 1929 or even in 1987 and has stayed fully invested has made much more money than keeping it all in CDs in the bank.

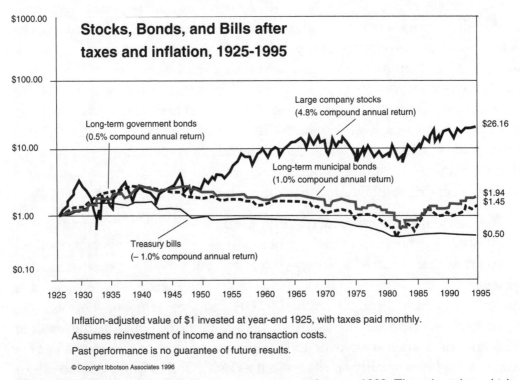

Inflation-adjusted value of $1 invested at year-end 1925, with taxes paid monthly.

Assumes reinvestment of income and no transaction costs.

Past performance is no guarantee of future results.

© Copyright Ibbotson Associates 1996

Figure 9-1. The stock market has gone up consistently since 1993. There have been highs and lows, but each low has never been as low as the previous drop and each high is higher than the previous high.

Remember, a loss really only occurs when the stock or the bond is sold. If the price goes up and down every day or every week, it does not matter to you if you ride out the ups and downs over a decade or two. Take a look at the numbers in Figure 9-2 comparing the long-term aspects of the market and the results after the two major crashes that everyone likes to talk about. Despite the crashes, the trend on both charts is upward—stocks are increasing in value.

The lesson here is, hold on for the long-term! It cannot be said often enough: Investing in the stock market is a long-term commitment. You must decide to hold onto an investment for at least 5 years. To change your mind after 6 months is almost a guarantee of losing money, particularly if you have opened your account at the beginning of a flat trading period or a down cycle. If you put your emotions on hold and look at the historical patterns of how

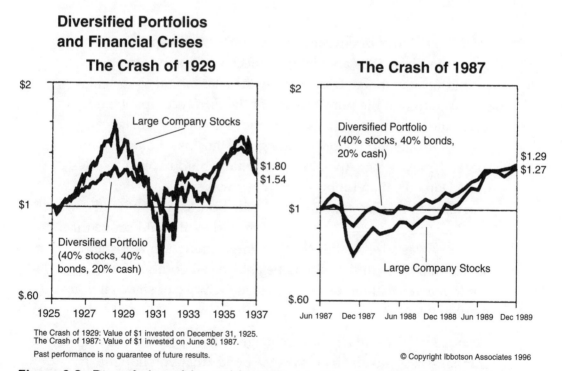

The Crash of 1929: Value of $1 invested on December 31, 1925.
The Crash of 1987: Value of $1 invested on June 30, 1987.

Past performance is no guarantee of future results.

© Copyright Ibbotson Associates 1996

Figure 9-2. Diversified portfolios and financial crises. If you can hang in for the long term, chances are that you'll come out with a profit.

stock prices perform over time, you will understand why it's important to invest on a long-term basis.

THE TYPES OF INVESTMENT RISK

If you want your money to grow, you have to take some risks. The saying "No risk, no reward" is true. And unless the growth of your money exceeds taxes and inflation, you are losing money. On the other hand, it's important to know the kinds of risk there are so you can know the best way to handle them. Anticipating risks is a part of the business of being a financial being.

There is no such thing as a risk-free investment so stop looking for that miracle. The collapse of the savings and loan banks taught us that in the early nineties. Even though they were federally regulated and insured, many stockholders in these companies lost a bundle and the federal government was left to bail out the depositors.

> *Market risk.* Stock prices move up and down in response to news events and how they are likely to affect a company's image, profits, or operations. For example, the Alaskan oil crisis had a serious effect on the public image of the Exxon company and made the stock price fall. Even though a company's balance sheet is strong and the profits are good, the "psychology of the market" may be negative. Imagine what would happen to sales at McDonald's if an unfounded rumor was suddenly started that all the beef was contaminated with botulism! Think of how much money the company would lose before it could prove that the story was false. Is the company large enough to withstand such a public assault? Will you be able to sell your shares to a willing buyer without taking a loss on the price of shares if you want to get out?

> *Financial risk.* Would a sudden change in the operations of a company affect its payments on the bonds that you bought? If the president of a company suddenly died in a plane crash, are

there other strong managers who could still operate the company profitably?

||||≡ ||||≡ ||||≡ ||||≡ ||||≡ ||||≡ ||||≡||||≡ ||||≡ ||||≡ ||||≡ ||||≡ ||||≡ ||||≡

BET Holdings (BET), the parent company of Black Entertainment Television, was the first African-American company to be listed on the Big Board, the New York Stock Exchange, in 1991. It was the dream of Robert L. Johnson, BET's founder and a former executive at National Cable Television, to start a black-oriented cable network. He took the risk with a personal loan of $15,000 in 1978 and launched the company in 1979. BET has expanded to include Emerge and YSB magazines and has $50 million in annual revenues and over 19 million outstanding shares that are publicly traded.

||||≡ ||||≡ ||||≡ ||||≡ ||||≡ ||||≡ ||||≡||||≡ ||||≡ ||||≡ ||||≡ ||||≡ ||||≡ ||||≡

Economic risk. What external factors can affect a company's profits? Certainly, events like the OPEC oil crisis of the seventies or a shipping strike can. The management has no control over these events, but it will have to cope with the crisis and find a way to work with it until it is resolved. Meanwhile the stock price may fall 10 or 12 points. That does not mean that the underlying value of the investment is not a good one. The decision you must make is, do you sell the stock or wait for it to recover?

Interest rate risk. If you had bought Treasury bonds 20 years ago at 14 percent interest, you could have sold them at a great profit 5 years later when rates dropped to 8 percent. However, if you bought bonds at 6 percent and the rates climbed to 8 percent 2 years later, you would have to take a loss if you wanted to sell them off before maturity.

INVESTING TO KEEP UP WITH INFLATION

Look at your own life if you want to understand inflation. What was bus fare when you were 10 years old? What is it now? What was the cost of a candy bar then? How much is a Hershey's today? Inflation is why you must invest in order to maintain the purchasing power of your dollar. The sum of $10,000 today will be worth $6139 after 10 years at a 5 percent inflation rate; that means that what you can purchase today for $6139 will cost you $10,000 to purchase just 10 years from now. After 20 years, $10,000 has the buying power of $3769 today. (See Figure 9-3.)

THE FINANCIAL PYRAMID OF RISK

Take a look at the investment pyramid in Figure 9-4. The "safe investments" are at the pyramid's base. The closer to the base, the safer the investment—that's where you'll find passbook savings, CDs, savings bonds, money-market funds, insured money-market accounts, cash-value life insurance, the equity in your home. Safe investments allow you to sleep at night, but they do not outpace inflation in their growth, nor do they give you a sufficient return on your dollar to maintain the strength of your dollar's purchasing power.

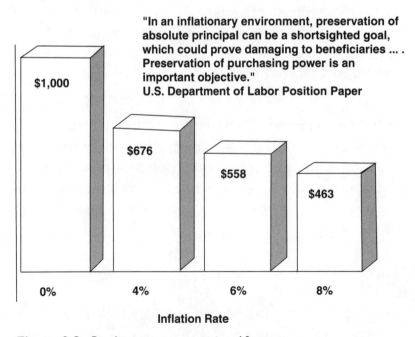

"In an inflationary environment, preservation of absolute principal can be a shortsighted goal, which could prove damaging to beneficiaries ... . Preservation of purchasing power is an important objective."
U.S. Department of Labor Position Paper

$1,000

$676

$558

$463

0%   4%   6%   8%

Inflation Rate

Figure 9-3. Purchasing-power erosion, 10 years.

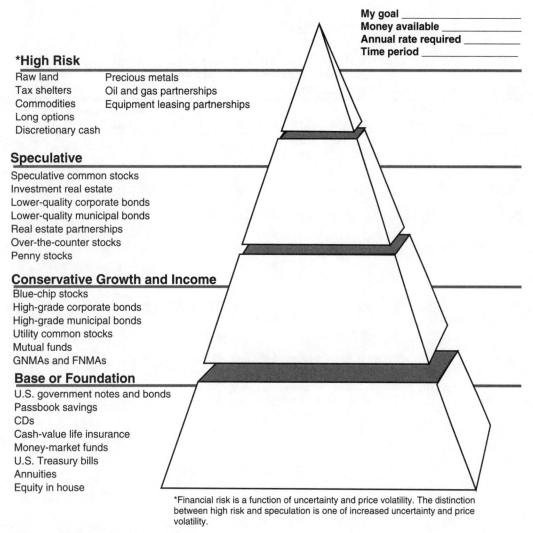

My goal _____
Money available _____
Annual rate required _____
Time period _____

*High Risk

Raw land   Precious metals
Tax shelters   Oil and gas partnerships
Commodities   Equipment leasing partnerships
Long options
Discretionary cash

Speculative

Speculative common stocks
Investment real estate
Lower-quality corporate bonds
Lower-quality municipal bonds
Real estate partnerships
Over-the-counter stocks
Penny stocks

Conservative Growth and Income

Blue-chip stocks
High-grade corporate bonds
High-grade municipal bonds
Utility common stocks
Mutual funds
GNMAs and FNMAs

Base or Foundation

U.S. government notes and bonds
Passbook savings
CDs
Cash-value life insurance
Money-market funds
U.S. Treasury bills
Annuities
Equity in house

*Financial risk is a function of uncertainty and price volatility. The distinction between high risk and speculation is one of increased uncertainty and price volatility.

Figure 9-4. Investment pyramid.

After taxes and inflation, you are technically losing money in any investment that is guaranteed and insured. That is the price you pay for safety and lack of risk. (See Table 9-1.)

Now go up to the middle of the pyramid. Here are moderate-risk investments: stock mutual funds, GNMAs, FNMAs, long-term-growth blue-chip stocks, utility stocks, real estate, tax-deferred annuities.

Table 9-1

Effects of Taxation and Inflation

(See why your 5.5 percent savings account is losing you money)

MARGINAL TAX BRACKET: 34.0 percent
(Combined federal, state, and local taxes)

ESTIMATED INFLATION RATE: 4.0 percent

Before-Tax Earnings (%)	After-Tax Earnings (%)	After-Tax Earnings and Inflation (%)
5.00	3.30	−1.30
5.50	3.63	−1.63
6.00	3.96	−1.96
6.50	4.29	0.29
7.00	4.62	0.62
7.50	4.95	0.95
8.00	5.28	1.28
8.50	5.61	1.61
9.00	5.94	1.94
9.50	6.27	2.27
10.00	6.60	2.60
10.50	6.93	2.93
11.00	7.26	3.26
11.50	7.59	3.59
12.00	7.92	3.92
12.50	8.25	4.25
13.00	8.58	4.58
13.50	8.91	4.91
14.00	9.25	5.24
14.50	9.57	5.57
15.00	9.90	5.90
15.50	10.23	6.23
16.00	10.56	6.56
16.50	10.89	6.89
17.00	11.22	7.22
17.50	11.55	7.55
18.00	11.88	7.88

This table demonstrates that you need to earn more than 13 percent on a taxable investment and 8 percent on a tax-free investment in order to have true 5 percent earnings after taxes and inflation.

At the top of the pyramid are the high-risk investments: commodities (like pork bellies, orange juice, and wheat futures), long options, aggressive growth stocks, penny stocks, speculative first issues of stocks that have never been sold before on an exchange, real estate partnerships, sector funds, specialty stocks, high-yield bonds (junk bonds), oil and gas partnerships, cable technology, heavy-equipment leasing partnerships, over-the-counter stocks. Don't even think about this stuff unless you're ready for a wild, fast ride very possibly to bankruptcy. You have to be willing to take a double-or-nothing sucker bet on being an instant millionaire in a day. Not for novice investors or nervous nellies.

Initial public offerings, known as IPOs, are introduced usually through penny stock brokers. Most prices are agreed upon before the listing is done on the exchange. The real money is made in a new hot stock like NETSCAPE by being the first owner in the first hour that it is issued and selling it quickly as it is bid up in price, which usually happens *very* quickly. Some of these new issues of hot stocks have jumped as high as $75 to $80 a share in the first day's trading. Don't get into this game if you're not a pro and don't have nerves of steel.

IIIᴇ IIIIᴇ IIIIᴇ IIIIᴇ IIIIᴇ IIIIᴇ IIIIᴇIIIIᴇ IIIIᴇ IIIIᴇ IIIIᴇ IIIIᴇ IIIIᴇ IIIIᴇ

Joseph Searles III, a former football player, left his position as an aide to New York City Mayor John V. Lindsay to become a partner in the brokerage firm of Newburger, Loeb and Company in 1970. Searles was the first African-American trader on the New York Stock Exchange floor.

IIIᴇ IIIIᴇ IIIIᴇ IIIIᴇ IIIIᴇ IIIIᴇ IIIIᴇIIIIᴇ IIIIᴇ IIIIᴇ IIIIᴇ IIIIᴇ IIIIᴇ IIIIᴇ

If you don't have the nerve to buy medium-risk blue-chip mutual funds and municipal bonds, don't even consider getting into a high-risk area like precious metals. Gold, silver, and platinum are not investments that you want to buy unless you can afford to play this game like a hard-as-nails trading pro with lots of big bucks behind you and unless the thought of losing about $25,000 doesn't make you break into a sweat.

As an average "middle-of-the-road" investor, stick to a basic portfolio of mutual funds which can be diversified into all classes of stocks, bonds, precious metals, real estate, and government securities. Keep your gold and silver purchases to a nice piece of jewelry or a wedding band.

A good way to handle risk is to diversify your portfolio. Diversification means spreading out the risk among several types of investments. In other words, don't put all your eggs in one basket. Many people think buying a CD, a money-market fund, and a municipal bond gives them a diversified portfolio—not true. They are all the same kind of fixed-income investment (loaned money for different time periods!), so there really isn't any great investment mix. Good diversification is like a balanced diet—not all one kind of food. Keep this in mind when you are choosing investments. You can achieve diversification through a mutual fund without the agony of reading thousands of pages of annual reports, prospectuses, and securities reports. All you need to do is invest $5000 in a mutual fund family that has several investment options.

THE DIFFERENCE BETWEEN STOCKS AND BONDS

Despite all the hype, the jargon, and the 396 million reams of paper generated each year to analyze the stock market, basically, there are only two investment choices: stocks and bonds. You can invest your dollars by making a loan to someone or by buying something that you own and control. Bonds are a loan, and stocks are ownership.

LOANED INVESTMENTS: BONDS, CDs, AND MORTGAGES

Pleasantville, USA, had a problem. The potholes on Main Street were ruining everyone's cars, the broken streetlights were causing constant traffic jams and fender benders, and the uncollected trash was attracting vermin, giving off bad odors, and upsetting the residents. Each day when the townspeople met on street corners and in coffee shops they complained to one another, saying, "Someone should do something." A committee was formed to approach the mayor, who reminded the committee that the citizens had voted down the lasts few tax increases; as a result, the town had no money to correct any of the problems. The mayor explained that if the local residents would allow him to borrow money in the name of the town, then he could fix the streets, purchase new garbage trucks, repair the traffic lights, and even build a new school. The residents would have to vote to pass a bond issue to cover the initial cost of the various projects, plus interest on the bonds. After several town meetings it was agreed that the mayor and the town clerk could hire an investment banking company to plan the bond issue for the people of Pleasantville. Within six months the town residents were voting on the new bond issue; the money was raised by selling the bonds, the streets were repaired; and the property taxes of each of the homeowners of Pleasantville were levied to cover the cost of the town debt (paying back the bondholders).

This story may seem overly simplistic, but it gives you a basic idea of how all towns, cities, states, and municipal governments all over America operate to raise money for public improvements. Taxes are levied to support the many public services and improvements that we take for granted. When you buy bonds you make an investment in public debt and also get a tax break for it. The interest income earned on municipal bonds is not taxed by the federal government because the bond is a loan you are making to a public entity.

Loaned investments are also called fixed-income investments. What you are buying is someone else's *debt* or purchasing a *debt instrument*. For the most part, people who buy bonds are conservative investors who want a slightly higher interest income than they will get at the bank but are reluctant to take the risk of uncertainty that comes in the stock market. The original dollars invested are protected by some kind of guarantee or collateral, usually in the form of assets that can be sold for reimbursement, such as property. With loaned investments, you know what you will earn in interest income before you buy. Think of all the reasons you would borrow money from your parents or the bank, or what you would ask your sister or your brother-in-law if they wanted a loan from you. Here are some questions you would want answers to before loaning money to anyone:

1. What is the money going to be used for?

2. How much do you want?

3. How long do you want it?

4. How long will my money be tied up?

5. How much interest will you pay me?

6. When will I received the interest payments?

7. How safe is my money?

8. How are you earning money so you can pay me back?

9. What collateral do you have that I can attach in case your payments stop coming in?

10. Who can guarantee that I will be paid back?

TREASURY BILLS, NOTES, AND BONDS

Buying Treasury debt from the Federal Reserve Bank is the safest loan you can make. Your funds are guaranteed by the full faith and credit of the U.S. government. (Remember that each time you pay your taxes!) The rates are not fixed; they change each week according to market conditions and are frequently set by the Open Market Committee of the Federal Reserve.

You can buy four kinds of Treasury debt: Treasury bills, Treasury notes, Treasury bonds, and zero-coupon bonds. You can buy Treasury bills in units of $10,000 (they are sold at a discount at a weekly auction). You can get them with a maturity date of 91 days, 6 months, or 1 year. Treasury notes can be bought in amounts ranging from $1000 to $5000. You can buy them with a maturity date of anywhere from 2 to 10 years. Treasury bonds can be purchased for $1000 a bond, with maturity dates of 10 to 40 years. Zero-coupon bonds come in units of $1000 and up, maturing in 2 to 20 years.

Zero-coupon bonds are called just that because that's what they pay while you hold them—nothing. They have no fixed interest rate and no income, and they are bought at a large discount; for example, a $1000 bond is bought for $218 and held for 15 years; you receive the full face value if you hold it to maturity. They simply increase in value each year until they reach maturity, but here's the nasty part—you will be taxed each year on the increased value of the bond, called the *accreted* interest, even though you don't receive any money.

This is why zeros are best used for IRAs or for a child's educational funds. You can put off paying the tax.

"LADDERED" BONDS

If you must stay with guaranteed investments, a portfolio of "laddered" Treasury bonds—Treasury bonds that keep rolling over, year after year, in intervals of 1, 3, 5, 7, and 9 years—is a better deal than CDs. At least with Treasuries, you don't have to pay state and city taxes on the interest income that you receive. You buy the notes for the varying maturity dates and let them stay with the Federal Reserve unless you need the money. Remember, though, if you cash out before the maturity date, you will lose a portion of the interest as a penalty. The 30-year bond, also called the *long bond,* is generally a poor choice because 30 years is too long a time to have your money tied up. It is best to buy a series of Treasury bills and notes in the 2- to 5-year range for the best return and the best liquidity. Stockbrokers charge a fee for setting up this portfolio for you, but you can do it yourself by getting an application for the Treasury Direct program. Write to your nearest Federal Reserve Bank or call the U.S. Bureau of the Public Debt at (202) 874-4000 for further information.

CDs

When you buy a CD, you are making a loan to the bank. CDs can be bought for as little as $500 and held for as short a time as 90 days or up to 5 years; the interest rate and principal are insured by the FDIC.

MUNICIPAL BONDS

Issued by state and city governments to raise money for schools, roads, hospitals, bridges, special projects, or general operating expenses, these bonds provide tax-free income. They can be purchased for short time periods, just like Treasury bills and notes, from 1 to 3 years. These short-term bonds are usually called tax anticipation notes (TANS), meaning that they will be paid off by future taxes collected by the government agency that issued them. The money that cities and states receive from various fees and fines covers the interest on TANS. The next time the meter maid leaves a ticket on your car, try to calm yourself by thinking of it as income for the city to cover some short-term-debt notes.

Medium-term municipal bonds are called general obligation bonds; they mature in 3 to 5 years. Your property taxes and local income taxes are used to pay back these bonds. Longer-term bonds mature in 10, 20, 25, or 30 years. Your taxes are used to pay these back too. When you see the new computers in your child's classroom, remember that this is how you paid for them.

Most longer-term bonds have a recall option. This means that if interest rates fall to a rate lower than the original interest rate at which the bond was issued, the government agency has the right to recall the bond and refinance the debt at a lower rate. In the same way that you may choose to refinance your mortgage when interest rates are lower in order to save money, public finance officials want the right to do the same thing. This refinancing movement will also lower your taxes.

When a recall option is exercised, the recall will usually be announced in several large ads in the newspaper over a 2- to 3-month period, notifying you that you must return the bond. It is useless for you to continue holding the bond, because you will not receive any further interest. When you surrender the certificate, you will be reimbursed the initial amount of money you paid when it was purchased (minus any commissions paid).

Bond interest is usually paid every 6 months. Until 1986, municipal bonds were issued with a sheet of coupons which you had to mail in to collect your interest on a semiannual basis. The coupon was the proof you needed to show you owned the bond. When you hear people say they are just clipping coupons, that means that they are collecting interest from some old municipal bonds, but very few of these old issues are still in existence. Most of them have been replaced by bonds—often called *book entry* bonds—that are registered in the owner's name. Too many problems occurred over the years with lost or stolen coupons. In the new technology era, these problems have been eliminated.

Book entry bonds work this way. The purchaser who is registered with the government agency that issued the bonds receives no coupons. When the interest is due to be paid, a check is sent to the purchaser automatically. These bonds are issued in units of $1000 but are usually sold in *lots* of 10 bonds at a time, called a *round lot*. If you buy less than a round lot, then you will be charged an extra commission for "breaking up" a lot. You can also build a portfolio of laddered municipal bonds, but this has to be done with stockbrokers who specialize in municipal securities, and they usually want you to have at least $50,000 to start this kind of program.

CORPORATE BONDS

These are the debt instruments issued for investment by large corporations. They are issued in $1000 units and purchased in round lots. The maturity of corporate bonds is similar to the maturity of longer-term municipal bonds—10 to 30 years. The interest rate is set according to the credit rating of the company. (Corporate bonds aren't the only bonds that are rated. So are municipal bonds.) The better the rating, the lower the interest rate. The ratings are set by two independent rating services: Moody's and Standard & Poor's. Table 9-2 shows the rating categories they use.

JUNK BONDS

Junk bonds are the dregs of the investment world. They were attractive for their high return in the late seventies and eighties; and they were the downfall of Michael Milken and the investment banking house of Drexel-

Table 9-2
How Bonds Are Rated by Moody's and Standard & Poor's

Bond Rating	Moody's	S&P
Best	Aaa	AAA
High quality	Aa	AA
Upper medium	A	A
Medium	Baa	BBB
Speculative	Ba	BB
Low	B	B
Poor	Caa	CCC
High risk	Ca	CC
Lowest quality	C	C
Default		D

Burnham. Since these bonds are usually rated Ba or BB and lower, they must offer an extremely high interest rate to entice investors to take the risk. The higher the interest rate, the greater the chance that the company may not be able to meet the interest payment when it is due. This is not an area for the faint of heart who worry about losing every dime.

UNIT INVESTMENT TRUSTS

A unit investment trust (called a UIT, and pronounced U-I-T) is a pool of several tax-free bonds from a single state that are packaged together by an investment manager specializing in selling tax-free bonds. Firms like Nuveen, Van Kampen, and First Trust and Kemper purchase the bonds and resell them to investors seeking tax-free income. There is no fluctuation in the initial face value of the bonds if you hold them for the full time period for which they are issued. However, if you sell the units before their maturity date and make a profit due to changes in interest rates, then the bonus income will be taxable. Some UITs are purchased at a discount, meaning that the face value of the bonds may be $1000 but the bonds really sell for $986. There is a sales charge attached to these UITs, from 2 to 5 percent, depending upon the maturity of the bonds and the amount invested. If you want to sell before maturity, the bond sponsor will purchase them from you at whatever the current market rate is for them.

MORTGAGE SECURITIES

Mortgage securities offer another kind of fixed-income investment. Mortgage bonds are bought by real estate investment trusts that specialize in mortgages on large commercial properties like shopping centers, office buildings, and industrial parks. Perhaps the most well known are GNMAs and FNMAs: These government-backed pools of home mortgages are bought from commercial and savings banks and repackaged as bonds to be sold to investors in units as small as $1000 through mutual funds and unit investment trusts. Other mortgage securities are listed in Table 9-3.

HAROLD E. DOLEY, JR.

CEO of Doley Securities, Inc.
New York and New Orleans

"When I was about six or seven years old, I used to play in my grandmother's backyard on a Saturday afternoon and people would bring her money. She would just be tending her garden, but people would come and bring her money. It took a while before she explained to me that they were coming to pay rent for the different houses she owned in the neighborhood. I was fascinated to see how she didn't have to do anything but people brought her money. I wanted to know how to get people to bring me money." That fascination led Harold Doley, Jr., to an unprecedented career in an area of financial services which had not seen any African-Americans.

At 11, when the family visited the New York Stock Exchange during a summer vacation, Doley became hooked as he stood in the visitors' gallery and watched the rabbit warren of activity below him. Men in brightly colored coats scurried about taking orders and filling sales tickets. Doley set a goal that morning that one day he would buy a seat on the Exchange. The fact that he was black and none of the men he saw there were his color did not matter to him. Doley began analyzing the stock market, and 2 years later he purchased his first shares of stock out of his savings. The stock was EDP, the data processing company that processes payroll checks. When he began studying accounting at Xavier University in his hometown of New Orleans, he already had a sizable portfolio. Immediately after graduating in 1968, Doley headed for Wall Street, driven to succeed in the securities business. His first job was as a broker trainee with Bache and Company, which is now a part of Pru-Bache & Company.

It took another 5 years to achieve his dream. In June 1973, Doley became the first African-American to purchase an individual seat on the New York Stock Exchange. It cost him $90,000. Three years later, Doley opened his own firm, Doley Securities, which specializes in selling government securities and municipal and corporate bonds and in cooperating in the underwriting of new corporate stock for large institutions. Doley left Wall Street briefly in 1982 to accept a political appointment as director of the Minerals Management Service, the second-highest source of income for the U.S. government after the U.S. Treasury. He also spent 2 years as the executive director (ambassador) of the African Development Bank and Fund. He is continuing to break new ground in the securities business. In August 1995, he opened the first African-American brokerage firm in Johannesburg, South Africa, in partnership with Lowenthal & Company, a white South African firm. Doley is also one of the few American underwriting members of Lloyd's of London.

One of Doley's role models was Madame C. J. Walker, one of America's first black millionaires. Today, he is the owner of Villa Lewaro, Madame Walker's 30-room mansion in Irvington, New York, which has been designated a national historic landmark.

"The most important thing I learned, which no one taught me, is that money is a verb. Anything with as much power and influence in the world as money has, is not a passive noun."

Table 9-3

Mortgage-Related Securities

Security	Minimum Original Denomination	Payments	Guarantee	Guarantor	Underlying Assets
Government National Mortgage Association	$25,000; $1000 in mutual funds	Monthly	Interest and principal	Federal government	Pools of FHA and VA loans
Federal Home Loan Mortgage Corp. (Freddie Macs)	$25,000; $1000 in mutual funds	Monthly	Interest and ultimate payment of principal	Federal Home Mortgage Loan Corp.	Conventional and seasoned FHA and VA loans
Mortgage-backed securities of Federal National Mortgage Association	$25,000; $1000 in mutual funds	Monthly	Interest and principal	Federal National Mortgage Association	Conventional and seasoned FHA and VA loans
Collateralized mortgage obligations of Freddie Macs and private issuers	$1000 to $25,000	Monthly or semiannually	Specified minimum obligations	Issuer	Mortgage or mortgages
Private issues by banks, thrifts, and home builders	$1000 to $25,000	Monthly	Interest and ultimate payment of principal	Private mortgage insurers	Conventional home loans

Source: courtesy of Warren, Gorham & Lamont.

OWNED INVESTMENTS: STOCKS

Owned investments are also called *equity investments.* You can earn money from them in two ways: by receiving dividends paid to shareholders and by selling the stock at a profit after they go up in value.

THE CASE OF THE XYZ CORPORATION

The XYZ Widget Corporation is a family-owned business that has been small and successfully managed for more than 30 years. The corporation has developed a new technology to make bigger and better widgets, faster and cheaper, than any other company in the widget industry. If XYZ had $20 million, it could triple the size of its plant, double its sales staff, and expand into new markets overseas; it would be so profitable, it would wipe out all its competition in the widget business. The XYZ family plans to raise the money from interested investors. To do this, the company will "go public," which means it will issue stock. The XYZ family hires an investment banking firm to help it do this. The investment banking firm examines the company's books, evaluates the company's assets, compares the profitability of the company with that of other companies in the widget industry, and decides what price the stock should be offered at and how many shares should be sold to raise the money the company needs. Once this due-diligence process is complete, the investment bankers and their attorneys file the appropriate legal papers with the Securities and Exchange Commission to get permission to sell the stock to the public. When all the legal entities give their approval and the XYZ family agrees to the terms, the stock is sold in an initial public offering.

This is where you, the general public, come into the picture as an investor and future shareholder. You have heard of the XYZ Corporation, know about its widgets, and would like to become a co-owner in the company. You buy some of the new shares when they are issued. By buying stock in XYZ, you hope to share in the profits that will come from this new expansion and development. The new stock is issued; the company gets its $20 million, minus fees to the bankers, of course; and it starts its development program. The company is no longer involved in the buying and selling of the shares.

From here on, you and your family, friends, neighbors, and any other investors (pension funds, mutual funds, or any other institutional investors) are free to sell the shares back and forth among yourselves. You bought the stock for $5 a share. By now, many other people have heard the news about the future growth of XYZ Corporation, and they also want to buy stock. Now there are more people who want to buy XYZ stock than there are shares

Table 9-4
Summary of Equity Investments

Instrument	Role in Portfolio	Liquidity	Price Volatility	Leverage Available	Investing Strategies Available	Tax Comments	General Comments
Common stock	Inflation hedge	High	Varies	Buying on margin	Stop-loss orders and/or dollar-cost averaging		Reinvestment plans available for many companies
Preferred stock	Stable income	High	Lower	Buying on margin	Dividend reinvestment	80 percent dividend exclusion for corporations only	Features are important considerations
Mutual funds	Inflation hedge and/or instant diversification	High	Medium[a]	No	Dividend reinvestment and/or dollar-cost averaging		"Families" allow flexibility
Options	Portfolio insurance and/or speculative instrument	High	Higher	Margin available under limited conditions	Can provide downside price protection	Tax liability depends on exercise date	Covered option writing can add income to investment portfolio
Commodity futures	Speculative instrument	High	High	Buying on margin	Selling short	Trading not allowed on IRAs, Keogh plans	Speculative
Stock-index futures	Speculative instrument and/or portfolio insurance	High	High	Buying on margin	Hedge against downside risk of overall portfolio	Considered capital asset by IRS	Speculative

Table 9-4 (Cont.)
Summary of Equity Investments

Instrument	Role in Portfolio	Liquidity	Price Volatility	Leverage Available	Investing Strategies Available	Tax Comments	General Comments
New issues (IPOs)	Growth or speculative instrument	Medium[b]	Higher	No margin on primary issue	Possibility for speculative gains		No commissions in primary market
Foreign equities (ADRs)	Global diversification and/or inflation hedge	Medium[c]	Varies[d]			Some countries impose local taxes	American depositary receipts remove custodial and trading inconveniences
Warrants	Speculative and/or portfolio hedge	High	Higher	Yes[e]	Warrant hedging	Considered capital asset by IRS	
Precious metals	Inflation hedge	High[f]	Higher	No		Considered capital asset by IRS	Investor should trade only with established dealer
Collectibles	Growth and/or value stability	Low	Varies	No	Significant appreciation probable only with high priced items		Significant upkeep expenses usually required

(a) Specialty or sector funds could have a less stable value than fully diversified stock mutual funds.

(b) Liquidity of a new issue in the secondary market depends on the number of shares offered, the underwriters' active marketing, and whether the issue is listed. These factors are not usually considerations for market-established instruments.

(c) Low turnover on smaller foreign exchanges—other than British, Canadian, and Japanese stock markets—could result in liquidity limitations.

(d) The combination of currency exchange and price fluctuations generally makes the value of foreign equities less stable than that of their U.S. counterparts.

(e) Transactions with overseas brokerage firms could result in time lags between order and execution, or order and delivery, in sales of securities.

(f) Platinum is much less liquid than gold or silver.

228 TALKING DOLLARS AND MAKING SENSE

available, and so the price of the stock is bid up to $10 a share. You decide to not be greedy, take your 100 percent increased shares, and sell them to another member of the public through a broker. This is basically how the stock market works.

COMMON STOCK AND PREFERRED STOCK

Stocks are issued in two classes: common and preferred.

All stock gives you a right of ownership in the company. The major difference between the two classes of stock has to do with dividends—how much you get and who gets it first. If you buy preferred stock, you always know how much you will receive in dividends because dividends are fixed at a preset rate, just like interest on a CD. Dividends are paid first to people who own preferred stock. If the company has a very good year, this can be an advantage to the people who own common stock, since their dividend is not a preset rate. Holders of preferred stock usually do not have the privilege of voting on management; those who hold common stock do. Preferred stock may be purchased from a stockbroker just like common stock, but it may be higher priced because of the guaranteed dividends. It may also be "called" (bought back) by the company and "retired" (taken off the open market).

CATEGORIES OF STOCK

Besides common and preferred, stocks can also be separated into a number of categories (see Table 9-4).

Blue chips. Blue-chip stocks are named for the most expensive poker chips. Blue-chip stocks are those issued by successfully managed companies such as IBM, General Motors, and Exxon, companies that have established themselves as mature, profitable companies that are fairly stable in most economic climates.

Defensive stocks. These are issued by companies that belong to staple industries, which even a recession won't hurt, such as food and drug companies like Coca-Cola and Pfizer.

Financial stocks. Banks, finance companies, insurance companies, and savings and loans all issue stocks and are some of the most reliable companies when it comes to paying dividends to their shareholders, but the financial industry responds to the marketplace as any other industry does, and you must be aware of that as an investor. When interest rates are low, bank stocks do very well, but not when interest rates rise; that's because almost no one buys or borrows when rates are high.

Growth stocks. Netscape, Microsoft, Starbucks Coffee, and Black Entertainment Television are examples of growth stocks. Growth stocks are stocks in developing industries—right now the hottest industries are the science and technology areas. They attract attention because of the unique nature of the product they offer, the service they provide, a patented process they own. These companies plow their profits back into expansion and development, so they don't usually pay dividends. They attract investors and push the stock price by creating innovative new products—witness the rise in Microsoft's stock price in anticipation of the debut of Windows '95.

Cyclical stocks. These stocks are in industries such as housing, trucking, steel, and airlines. These companies require long-term project commitment and expensive, heavy equipment to function. When interest rates are low, corporations build new office towers, develop new plants, and initiate long-term development projects. When the economy is in great shape, so are they; when a recession occurs, their profits and their dividends fall.

Conservative stocks. Conservative stocks are shares in older, stable companies that pay out most of their earnings in high-yielding dividends to their shareholders (see Table 9-5). Typical are utility companies—AT&T, Con Edison, your local gas company—which are part of relatively low-risk industries.

Table 9-5

50 Stocks That Never Missed a Dividend in 50 Years

Affiliated Publications	First Fidelity–New Jersey
Allied Signal	First Jersey National
American Express	First Maryland National Bank
AT&T	First National Bank–Cincinnati
Bank of Boston	Fleet National Bank
Bank of New England	Hanover Insurance
Bank of New York	Hartford Insurance
Bay State Bank	Key Bank of New York
Berkshire Gas	Eli Lilly
Boatsman's Bancshares	Midlantic Bank
Carter-Wallace	Mobil Oil
Chase Manhattan/Chemical	Norstar Bancorp
CIGNA Insurance	Pennwalt
Cincinnati Bell	PNC Financial Bank
Cincinnati Gas & Electric	Providence Energy
Citicorp	St. Paul Company
Connecticut Energy	Security Pacific Bank
Con Edison–New York	Stanley Works–Hardware
Corning Glass	State Street Bank
Continental Insurance	Traveler's Insurance
Deere & Company	U.S. Trust Company
Detroit Edison	United Virginia Bank
Eastman Kodak	United Water Resources—New Jersey
Exxon	Washington Gas Company
First Bancorp of Ohio	Wrigley's Gum

Penny stocks. Penny stocks are issued by very-high-risk small new companies. These stocks are sold over-the-counter by a limited number of small brokers. They may not even be quoted on the stock pages every day, but they are listed in the "pink sheets," which are printed up each day for the brokers who specialize in these stocks. There is such a limited number of buyers who want these shares, you may have a hard time selling them. Penny stocks usually sell for under $5 a share, and some can be bought for as little as a dime a share. If you want to study penny stocks, get a copy of *Penny Stock News* and a copy of the *Bowser Report*, which specializes in stocks that trade for less than $3 a share.

Hard assets. Hard assets are defined as anything tangible that can increase in value over time: real estate, gold, silver, coins, stamps, paintings, artwork, maps, rare books, gemstones. The problem with this type of investment is that it may be difficult to turn into cash when you want to.

WHEN YOU BUY STOCKS

Individual stocks can be bought at any brokerage firm that is licensed by the National Association of Securities Dealers and is a member of the New York Stock Exchange. You pay commission for their service whether you are a sophisticated, experienced trader with a wide range of knowledge about the market or a novice investor purchasing your first shares of stock. The amount of the commission will depend upon the services that you expect from the broker and can vary from as low as $30 to as high as $120. If you do your own research and just want to work with a broker as an order taker, then choose a deep discount broker like Waterhouse, Jack White & Co., Charles Schwab, Rose, Quick & Reilly, or Bull and Bear. If you need a great deal of advice, hand-holding, in-depth research reports, extensive literature and investment brochures, and free seminars, then you should work with one of the larger brokerage firms, such as Merrill-Lynch, Shearson, and Paine-Webber (also known as wire houses). These "extras," which appear to have no cost, are covered by the higher commissions charged by these firms. They will also keep your name on telephone solicitation lists for regular calls by new brokers trying to establish an account with you—and half of what most brokers are selling you don't need.

For a new investor with a small amount of money, there are two easy ways for you to get started in the investment game without the services of a stockbroker: dividend reinvestment plans and no-load mutual funds.

||≣ ||||≣ ||||≣ ||||≣ ||||≣ ||||≣ ||||≣||||≣ ||||≣ ||||≣ ||||≣||||≣ ||||≣ ||||≣

George and Joan Johnson began Johnson Products in 1954 by borrowing $250 to start their line of African-American grooming products. By 1960, the fledgling company had become the leading manufacturer of cosmetics for this special market, with sales of over $5 million. In 1971, Johnson Products became the first black-owned business to be listed on the American Stock Exchange, with an initial offering of 10 million shares of stock. By 1989, the company was valued at $11 million and was operating under the direction of Joan Johnson following a divorce settlement. In June 1993 the Miami-based IVAX Corporation bought the company for $67 million but retained Mrs. Johnson's services as president.

||≣ ||||≣ ||||≣ ||||≣ ||||≣ ||||≣ ||||≣||||≣ ||||≣ ||||≣ ||||≣||||≣ ||||≣ ||||≣

DIVIDEND REINVESTMENT PLANS

You think you'd like to own a piece of McDonald's, the Gap, Kellogg's, IBM, Hershey's, Sara Lee, AT&T, or your local utility company and get back some of those dollars you've spent on their products and services in dividends, but you can't afford the big expense of buying 100 shares and paying high commissions to a broker? Relax, here's the best kept secret in the investing game that can have you playing the market with the high rollers without having to sell your soul or your first-born child to get into the game.

You can make use of a DRIP—a dividend reinvestment plan. DRIPs are the best kept secret that no stockbroker will ever tell you about. They have been around for more than 50 years and are the smartest move you can make toward getting rich the slow and easy way on a few dollars a month. Once you own stock in company, the transfer agent, usually a bank, will take your dividends and use them—reinvest them—to buy more shares of stock for your account. You don't buy the additional shares through a stockbroker, so you don't pay a commission for the purchase.

Many companies require that you buy your first share of stock from a broker, for which you have to pay a commission, and you must have the stock sent directly to you. If you don't request that when you place the order for the stock, the brokerage firm will hold the stock in an account for you and keep it listed "in street name," meaning in the name of the brokerage house. And if it's not in your name, you can't use a DRIP. It takes about 5 to 10 business days for this transaction to be settled through a transfer agent, which is usually a bank that handles the documents and paperwork for the brokerage firm and the corporation.

Over 900 companies have established these investment plans for shareholders, and many utility companies make this service available to their local rate payers, without going through a stockbroker; see Table 9-6 for some of the more well-known companies that offer DRIPs. The drawback is the amount of paperwork you will find filling up your mailbox each quarter and at the end of the year.

Here's some advice if you're thinking of using a DRIP.

1. Start small. Choose one or two stocks for companies that are familiar to you.

2. Invest where you spend. Don't look for exotic stocks in strange industries that you don't understand, like biochemical technology or genetic engineering. Consider the various products you use in your daily life. What kind of car do you drive? What toothpaste do you use? Where do you do your banking? If you are willing to buy these products, why not buy their stocks? Some utility companies allow their customers to

Table 9-6
30 Well-Known Stocks That Offer DRIPs

Abbott Labs	Exxon	Philip Morris
American Express	Ford Motor Co.	Procter & Gamble
AT&T	General Electric	Quaker Oats
Black & Decker	Home Depot	Rubbermaid
Bristol-Myers Squibb	Johnson & Johnson	Sara Lee
Citicorp	Kellogg	Texaco
Coca-Cola	Kimberly Clark	U.S. Steel
Colgate	La-Z-Boy Chair	Vanity Fair
Delta Airlines	McDonald's	Wendy's
Duracell	Merck	Westinghouse

invest directly in their company stock for a minimum of $250 without even using a stockbroker for the first buy. You know you will always pay the gas and light bill, so why not get back some of that money by investing in stock:

The best research you can do on getting into DRIPs is to contact the following:

1. The National Association Investor Corporation (NAIC) at (810) 583-6242 provides its members with a monthly magazine called *Better Investing*. Each issue gives guidelines on how to start buying DRIPs from a list of over 150 stocks it recommends. NAIC will assist you with opening the account and purchasing your first share of stock. You don't have to be a member of an investment club to participate in DRIP programs, just an interested and consistent investor. NAIC also manages a no-load mutual fund that includes many of the stocks from its recommended list.

2. The MoneyPaper at (914) 381-5400 publishes an annual directory of the 982 corporations that provide DRIPs for their shareholders. It is well worth the $25 it will cost you to get a list of all the companies, addresses, phone numbers, rules, and guidelines for opening an account. If you subscribe to the *MoneyPaper* newsletter, the company assists you, for a fee, with opening your first DRIP account from its recommended list.

3. First Share at (800) 683-0743 will assist you both with buying your first single share for a fee of $30, slightly less than most stockbrokers will charge you, and with doing the research on how to continue a personal investment program.

4. *The DRIP Investor* is an excellent newsletter for newcomers to this area of investing. It's published by Charles B. Carlson, the author of *How to Buy Stocks without a Broker* and *No-Load Stocks*. For a sample copy, get in touch with:

The DRIP Investor
NorthStar Financial, Inc.
7412 Calumet Avenue
Hammond, Indiana 46324-2692
(219) 931-6480 (phone)
(219) 931-6487 (fax)

||| ≡ |||| ≡ |||| ≡ |||| ≡ |||| ≡ |||| ≡ ||||≡|||| ≡ |||| ≡ |||| ≡ |||| ≡ |||| ≡ |||| ≡ ||||≡

In June 1972, Willie Daniels and Travers Bell formed the firm of Daniels and Bell and became the first African-American stock brokerage firm on the New York Stock Exchange. They were instrumental in opening the doors for several other pioneers to enter the investment business by sponsoring them for their brokerage licenses and membership in the Exchange.

||| ≡ |||| ≡ |||| ≡ |||| ≡ |||| ≡ |||| ≡ ||||≡|||| ≡ |||| ≡ |||| ≡ |||| ≡ |||| ≡ |||| ≡ ||||≡

READING THE FINANCIAL PAGES

When you look at the stock tables in the financial pages of the newspaper, they may seem incomprehensible, but there is a key to the apparent jumble of figures. A company's up-to-the-minute activity is summarized in that one line of numbers. Here is a typical entry for AT&T:

52 Weeks		Stock	Sym	Div	Yield %	P/E	Vol 100s	Price			
Hi	Lo							Hi	Lo	Close	Change
33	24-1/4	AT&T	T	1.20	3.8	15	9772	31-1/4	31	31-1/4	—

52 Weeks Hi, Lo. These two figures show the highest and lowest prices of the stock for the previous year plus the current week.

Stock, Sym. These identify the name of the company and its ticker symbol.

Div. This figure is the annual dividend based on the last quarterly payment.

Yield %. This is the dividend as a percentage of the stock price.

P/E. P/E stands for price-earnings. The price-earnings ratio is determined by dividing the price of a share by the earnings per share. In the above example, AT&T is selling at 15 times the actual earnings of the company, which is a normal price-earnings ratio for a mature, quality stock.

Vol 100s. This is the number (volume) of shares (in 100s) sold the previous day. In the example, 9,772,000 shares of AT&T were sold.

Hi, Lo. These numbers are the high and low for the day's trading price.

Close, Change. The close is the last price the stock sold for that day. The (net) change in the stock price is the difference between the price the stock opened at (which is always the previous day's closing price) and the current day's closing price. For AT&T, the stock closed at the same price at which it opened.

STOCK MARKET INDICES

The Dow Jones Industrial Average (DJIA) is the most well-known and often quoted measure of the ups and downs of the stock market. It was created on May 26, 1896, by Charles Henry Dow, founder and publisher of *The Wall Street Journal*, to reflect the daily activity of the market in a two-page summary called the *Customer's Afternoon Letter,* and it included only 12 stocks, primarily railroad stocks. The index expanded to 30 stocks on October 1, 1928, and the closing average that day was 240.01, which is the average combined value of the 12 original stocks. Despite the hysteria of 1929, the Dow hit its lowest point, 41.22, on July 8, 1932, and it took more than 40 years to reach the landmark number of 1000 on November 14, 1972. The 2000 mark was reached on January 8, 1987; it went above 3000 on April 17, 1991; above 4000 on February 23, 1995; and above 5000 on November 21, 1995.

Despite this impressive record, the DJIA still does not offer the most accurate picture of the equity markets. It is composed of only 30 stocks: blue-chip household names with so many shares in distribution that they make up one-fifth of the trillion dollars of stocks that are traded on the Big Board. Dow-Jones stocks are chosen by the editorial board of *The Wall Street Journal* to give a broad overview of the market and American industries as a whole. Each company on the list represents a major industry, and the stocks of the companies are widely held by large institutions like mutual funds and pension funds and by many individual investors. They are recognized as offering relative stability and quality in a highly volatile environment. Only 13 companies from the original list are still included in the index: Among them are EXXON (originally it was called Standard Oil), General Electric, Sears Roebuck, General Motors, and Texaco. Dow Jones also maintains an index of transportation stocks and utility stocks. See Table 9-7.

Other market indices offer a more accurate measure of market changes:

Standard & Poor's 500. This index is a much broader barometer of the stock market because it focuses on the *Fortune* 500 companies, including 400 manufacturers, 40 financial stocks, 40 utilities, and 20 transportation stocks. Because of the broader coverage of stocks, it provides a much more realistic gauge of how the market is performing on a daily basis. When the Dow moves up 50 points, this index may move up only 6 points.

Value Line Index. The Value Line Index indicates a much broader reach of market activity than even the Standard & Poor's 500, following 1700 companies. The Value Line does not focus on specific industry groups or sectors.

NYSE Composite Index. This index follows the approximately 2100 stocks listed on the New York Stock Exchange, without consideration of other trading exchanges.

AMEX. The American Stock Exchange lists over 2000 smaller companies not listed on the NYSE.

NASDAQ. The National Association of Securities Dealers Automated Quotations system is where you find the "penny"

Table 9-7
The Dow Jones Stocks

Industrials (30)	Transportation (20)*	Utilities (15)*
Allied Signal	Alaska Air	American Electric Power
Alcoa	AMR Corporation	Centerion Energy
American Express	Airborne Freight	Consolidated Edison
AT&T	American President Lines	Consolidated Natural Gas
Bethlehem Steel	Burlington Northern R/R	Detroit Edison
Boeing	Conrail	Houston Industries
Caterpillar	Consolidated Freight	Niagara Mohawk
Chevron	CSX Corporation	North America Corporation
Coca-Cola	Delta Airlines	Pacific Gas & Electric
Dupont	Federal Express	Panhandle Eastern Electric
Eastman Kodak	Illinois Central	People's Energy
Exxon	Norfolk Southern	Peco Energy
General Electric	Roadway Systems	Public Service Enterprises
General Motors	Ryder Systems	SCE Corporation
Goodyear	Southwest Air	Unicom Corporation
IBM	Union Pacific Group	
International Paper	USAir Group	
J. P. Morgan	XTRA Corporation	
McDonald's	United Air Lines	
Merck	Yellow Corporation	
Minnesota M&M		
Philip Morris		
Procter & Gamble		
Sears Roebuck		
Texaco		
Union Carbide		
United Technologies		
Walt Disney		
Westinghouse		
Woolworth		

*The 20 transportation stocks (airlines and railroads) were added to the index on January 5, 1970, and the index of the 15 utilities (gas and electric) began on January 2, 1929.

stocks and many other newly issued inexpensive stocks of over 5000 small companies selling from 10 cents to $10. NASDAQ has been around for 25 years as of February 8, 1996. The stocks listed on NASDAQ are primarily IPOs, or initial public offerings. Some are dogs; some, however, turn out to be the largest and most profitable growth stocks in the country—like Apple Computer, Netscape, Microsoft, and Starbucks. If you like risk, here it is.

Wilshire 5000. This index tries to give a daily performance average of all the stocks on all the exchanges in the United States.

INVESTMENT CLUBS

For the past 3 years, the 11 members of the Ten Percenters Investment Club have met on the tenth of each month, regardless of the day of the week, to discuss the status of their portfolio and the monthly report circulated before the meeting by their presiding partner, Elizabeth Waller. The club has two basic parts to its investment philosophy: (1) to become more investment-oriented, rather than consumer-oriented as individuals, and (2) to keep at least 50 percent of its investment dollars in African-American-owned companies. The members have modeled their club on another group, the Fundi Investment Club, a group of African-American brothers who have been meeting since 1988, have invested $100 a month since then, and now have a portfolio of over $126,000 in stocks. Fundi is a Kiswahili word that means "passing knowledge down from one generation to another."

Corporate research reports are a shared responsibility among the Ten Percenters group. Any member is free to choose a company, get the annual report, analyze the industry data and the products made, and share the information with the other members. After a report is prepared, it is forwarded to each member for review and recommendation, taking into consideration what other stocks the club has purchased, sold, reviewed, or added to the club's portfolio. The members are invited to submit stock recommendations and offer suggestions, comments, and questions about the status of the portfolio based on the information they have received during the month.

At their latest meeting, Wayne Hicks, the finance partner, offers a report on the status of dues and expenses, which is then reviewed and discussed. Two members have recently resigned, and the impact of their resignation on the club's treasury is evaluated. Wayne also offers a suggestion for purchasing a new technology stock that he has been researching.

Wayne's mother, Liz Hicks, a schoolteacher, has been an active club member from the time of the first meeting, which was held on the first day of Kwanzaa in 1993. Liz recommends that the group buy Pepsi-Cola. She has seen a favorable earnings report and read about some positive investment moves that the company has made to support the developing South African market. Pepsi has also received good press in the black media because of its new financing arrangements offered for franchises to African-American entrepreneurs.

This is a typical scenario of what happens in most investment club meetings, with one notable difference. With the exception of Wayne and Liz Hicks, who have a family relationship, none of the brothers and sisters in the Ten Percenters have ever met each other. The Ten Percenters Investment Club is conducted strictly by e-mail on the PRODIGY system. All dues, financial reports, research and legal documents are transmitted by fax machine or sent by U.S. mail.

Investment clubs are the hottest new social strategy that is catching on in the African-American community among working professionals interested in building a sense of personal financial well-being and a strong economic sense of community. To start your own investment club, contact the National Association Investor Corporation (NAIC) at (810) 583-6242.

THINK ABOUT INVESTING IN MUTUAL FUNDS

Joe Richardson woke up to the sound of his *Panasonic* clock radio, turned on the light, and remembered that he hadn't paid the *Con Edison* bill. He took a quick shower with *Coast* soap, brushed his teeth with *Colgate* toothpaste, used his *Schick* deodorant, and shaved with his *Gillette* razor before stepping into his *Dockers*, *Reeboks*, and new sweatshirt from *The Gap*. He rushed into the kitchen and grabbed a bowl of *Kellogg's Corn Flakes*, a cup of *Maxwell House coffee*, a glass of *Tropicana* orange juice, and a *Centrum* vitamin before heading out the door to get into his new *Ford Taurus*. He stopped at a *Mobil* gas station and used his *Nynex* cellular phone to call his office. Next, he stopped at the *First Nation's Bank* to get some cash from the *Diebold* automated cash machine and then returned some videos to the *Blockbuster* video store. Finally, he picked up a *Hallmark* card for his mother's birthday.

Like most people, Joe is such a busy character that he doesn't have time to think about investing any money, although the idea is attractive to him, and he has no idea which stocks to buy. He is missing one obvious and commonsense approach to where he should put his investment dollars—in the same products that he spends money on each day. The phone company, the utility company, the products and services that you use on a daily basis are the best place to start looking at products and services for investing. If you drink the same orange juice, use the same deodorant, buy the same detergent year after year, then you must be happy with the product to keep making repeat purchases. Start looking at those companies as reasonable stocks to invest in if they are publicly traded. If you don't have the time to do the research yourself, then open a mutual fund account that includes many of these products in their portfolio. Mutual funds are made up of stocks and/or bonds from a number of companies (see Figure 9-5). If Joe Richardson wanted to invest $1 a month in each of the products that he uses on a daily basis, he could easily do it with a stock mutual fund.

GETTING INTO MUTUAL FUNDS

Mutual funds are not a new idea. They have been around since 1924 when the large Boston bankers and trust fund managers suddenly discovered that they were managing the investment portfolios for several members of the same wealthy family. Many of the descendants of wealthy families, who had earned their money from whaling, shipping, and textile mills (and probably the slave trade), had individual trust funds managed by the various banks. With each succeeding generation, the size of the trust funds shrank and the bank trust departments realized that they were duplicating the paperwork

SAMPLE MUTUAL FUND PORTFOLIO

AEROSPACE / DEFENSE
Boeing Company	$ 9.00
Lockheed Corporation	$12.00
Rockwell International Corporation	$ 4.00

APPAREL
Liz Clairborne, Inc.	$13.00
Sears	$12.00

AUTOMOBILES & TRUCKS
Chrysler Holding Corporation	$10.00
Ford Motor Company	$10.00
General Motors Corporation	$13.00

CHEMICALS
Avery International Corporation	$ 8.00
Dow Chemical Co.	$12.00
Sherwin - Williams Paints	$ 9.00

COMMUNICATIONS
Capital Cities / ABC, Inc.	$17.00
Commerce Clearing House, Inc.	$ 6.00
Dun & Bradstreet Corp	$10.00
Walt Disney Company	$15.00

DISTILLING & TOBACCO
Philip Morris	$12.00
RJR Nabisco, Inc.	$18.00
Seagrams Co., Ltd.	$21.00

ELECTRONIC & ELECTRICAL EQUIPMENT
Corning Glass Works, Inc.	$13.00
Hewlett - Packard, Co.	$16.00
Raychem, Inc.	$31.00
Texas Instruments, Inc.	$ 6.00
Westinghouse Electronic Corporation	$15.00

ENERGY / PETROLEUM
Ashland Oil Company	$12.00
Atlantic Richfield	$19.00
Royal Dutch Shell Petroleum, Corp.	$25.00

ENVIRONMENTAL PROTECTION
Browning-Ferris Industries, Inc.	$18.00
Waste Management, Inc.	$14.00

FINANCIAL SERVICES
American Express	$14.00
Citicorp	$21.00
Household Finance International	$13.00

HEALTH CARE & COSMETICS
Abbott Laboratories	$19.00
Baxter Travenol Laboratories	$ 7.00
Bristol-Meyers, Inc. (Alka-Seltzer)	$28.00
Johnson & Johnson, Inc.	$21.00
Merck and Company, Inc.	$26.00
Pfizer, Inc.	$25.00
Scherring-Plough (Dr.Scholl's etc.)	$22.00
Tambrands (Tampax, etc.)	$20.00

MULTIFORM INDUSTRIES
Fuqua Industries, Inc.	$15.00
Gulf & Western	$12.00
ITT Corporation	$10.00
Loews Corporation	$12.00
Textron Corporation	$12.00

PACKAGING & CONTAINERS
Crown, Cork & Seal Co., Inc.	$22.00

PAPER & FOREST PRODUCTS
Georgia-Pacific Corp	$10.00
Mead Paper	$10.00
Scott Paper Co.	$12.00
Weyerhauser Co.	$ 9.00

PHOTOGRAPHIC EQUIPMENT
Eastman Kodak	$18.00
Polaroid Corporation	$12.00

PRINTING & PUBLISHING
R.R. Donnelly	$12.00
New York Times	$12.00

RETAILING
American Greetings Card Corporation	$15.00
Great A&P Tea Company	$ 9.00
Kmart Corporation	$12.00
Mercantile Stores, Co.	$15.00
Nike, Inc.	$12.00
Sara Lee	$10.00

TIRE & RUBBER
Goodyear Tire & Rubber	$10.00

TRANSPORTATION
AMR Corporation	$16.00
Union Pacific Corporation	$22.00
Northwest Airlines,Inc.	$15.00
United Airlines	$11.00
TOTAL INVESTMENTS	**$996.00**
Cash and cash equivalents	$ 4.00

Figure 9-5. If you invest $1000 into a mutual fund, here's how it would be divided.

and transactions for several members of one family because they were required to keep all transactions separate.

A law was passed in the Commonwealth of Massachusetts which allowed the banks to pool the funds of several members of one family into a mutual fund management portfolio as long as the same percentage of shares of ownership were maintained. This management decision marked the creation of the mutual fund industry. Even though there are several investment management companies that have been successfully managing funds for more than 50 years, mutual funds have only become popular for the small investor in the last 30 years. Mutual funds have grown since then from $24 million to an industry of over $3 trillion, and most of that has developed in the last 3 years through retirement-plan investments in stock and bond funds. Besides investing in mutual funds to save for your retirement, you can use mutual funds for other goals, such as saving toward the down payment on a house or your child's college education.

TYPES OF MUTUAL FUNDS

There are many funds with different investment objectives. The Investment Company Institute, the trade organization for all funds, divides firms into 22 categories according to their investment objective. Here are the most common types that you'll see.

1. *Aggressive growth funds.* They seek to give you maximum capital gains and growth, and they speculate in stocks and sometimes use high-risk investing techniques. These funds are high-risk and rarely pay dividends.

2. *Growth funds.* The main purpose of growth funds is to achieve an increase in the value of the investment, but they also pay small dividends. Growth funds buy stocks of companies that are expected to grow faster than average. These companies include large established companies, as well as smaller, emerging companies with quiet prospects. Growth funds are much less volatile than aggressive growth funds.

3. *Growth and income funds.* These funds strike a balance between long-term growth stocks and stocks that produce current income. Growth and income funds invest primarily in companies whose stocks are rising but that also have a solid record of paying dividends. Growth and income funds tend to be more stable than growth funds.

4. *Equity income funds.* These funds seek current income by investing in companies with a good, long-term track record for paying dividends on a quarterly basis. Equity income funds are considered very conservative investments.

5. *Bond funds.* Remember, bonds are debt. Bond funds seek a high level of current income by investing in a mixture of corporate bonds and government bonds. Bond funds are also considered conservative investments.

6. *High-yield bond funds.* This is another name for junk bond funds. These funds invest in a high percentage of lower-rated bonds which are quite risky but will pay a higher interest rate, when they do pay dividends. Needless to say, these funds are risky.

7. *Sector funds.* Sector funds focus on a single industry. Therefore they don't offer you quite the same diversification that you would generally get in a mutual fund. They will concentrate on perhaps only health companies, or drug companies, or high-technology companies, or financial-service companies. They choose one industry and buy companies only in that industry. The risk is much higher for sector funds because the diversification is lower. If the industry has a bad year, there are no other stocks in the fund to counterbalance the loss.

8. *International and global funds.* These funds spread the risk of overseas investing and foreign exchange. They may specialize in

regions such as the Pacific Basin or Latin America, or they may diversify into Europe, Asia, and Australia. The annual report will give you a detailed breakdown by country and by company as well as an idea of the costs of currency arbitrage, which is a big expense in these funds.

9. *Country funds.* Like international and global funds, these funds invest by geography. But they only buy the stocks of companies that are located in one particular country. Examples are the Japan Fund, the Korea Fund, the India Fund, the Turkey Fund, the Mexico Fund, the Spain Fund, and the France Fund. The Third Century Fund, managed by Maceo Sloan of NCM Capital [(919) 688-0620], and the Calvert New Africa Fund [(800) 368-2748] focus on emerging companies in Africa and are open to small investors for a $1000 minimum investment. Look at what a fund is doing in a country and what you know about the country's economy. If you're comfortable with it, go with it.

10. *Money-market funds.* Money-market funds are an excellent place to put away some money for short-term savings goals, and you still have the privilege of writing a check in an emergency if you need cash. In addition, you'll get a slightly higher yield than you'll get from a savings account at the bank. Money-market funds invest in the same thing that a bank will—CDs, Treasuries, and banker's acceptances—but the funds aren't insured. Some funds may also invest in higher-yielding corporate commercial paper securities, which also are not insured; the prospectuses will tell you that. Some funds also do not return your original checks to you for your records.

11. *Index funds.* These funds are made up of stocks listed in the Standard & Poor's 500 stock index, which accounts for roughly 70 percent of the value of all U.S. stocks.

12. *Balanced funds.* Balanced funds aim for three objectives: to conserve the investor's initial principal, to pay current income, and to promote long-term growth of both principal and income. A balanced fund will have a mixture of stocks and bonds.

MORE ABOUT MUTUAL FUNDS

Mutual funds are bought in shares and are listed in the daily newspaper by their net asset value, just like stocks are. As the prices of the stocks within the fund change each day, so will the prices of the shares of the mutual fund. You can read this movement in the financial pages each morning.

When should you invest in a mutual fund and how much should you invest? Don't listen to the market gurus who tell you that they have a system for timing the market and can always find the right time to get into or out of a stock or a mutual fund. Most of those strategies don't work; and if you're a small investor, you can't afford their services. That's why you "hire" a professional money manager who runs a mutual fund portfolio. Let him or her do the thinking for you when it comes to the technical analysis.

DOLLAR-COST AVERAGING

For the novice investor who wants to build a well-diversified portfolio beginning with a small amount of money, dollar-cost averaging is a "no-brainer" approach using mutual funds. This is a time-tested investment strategy that requires no more than a clear-minded commitment on your part and consistent, disciplined payments regardless of the share price of the fund. After you decide which mutual fund family fits your goals, you open an account with usually a minimum of $1000 and set up an automatic monthly investment arrangement having automatic withdrawals taken from your bank account or your paycheck through a payroll deduction plan. Regardless of the ups and downs of the market, you invest the same amount each month—$50, $100, or whatever you can afford. Here's how it works.

Monthly Investment	Share Price	Shares Purchased
$100	$10	10
$100	$12	8.33
$100	$15	6.67
$100	$13	7.69
$100	$ 9	11.11
$100	$11	9.09
Totals $600	$70	52.89

AVERAGE COST/SHARE—Total investment/divided by shares purchased = $11.34
AVERAGE PRICE/SHARE—Total share price/divided by number of investments = $11.66

This works well when you also have a large lump sum to invest and want to even out the price fluctuations that occur on a regular basis in the market.

ADVANTAGES OF INVESTING IN MUTUAL FUNDS

Investing in a mutual fund has several advantages.

1. *Diversification.* The average stock mutual fund will own about 50 to 80 companies at one time, plus the fund also has cash available to buy more shares. If you tried to purchase at least 100 shares of each of the companies that are owned in a large, diversified, blue-chip stock mutual fund, you'd probably have to spend about $120,000 for the share prices and the commissions! This is perhaps 100 times more than you would pay for a share of a fund, which gives you ownership in all these companies.

2. *Professional management.* You don't have to go through the hassle of deciding which stock to buy, when to buy it, and when to sell it. The investment decisions are made by experienced managers and stock analysts who are well trained in their field. You get their expertise for about one-half of 1 percent, which is taken out of your invested funds as a management fee.

3. *Record keeping.* You receive one statement detailing your fund transactions, including purchases, sales, dividends, capital gains

distributions, and your current holdings. If you have a money-market mutual fund, you have the privilege of check writing. Many of these funds will allow you to write a check whenever you need to as long as the check is for at least $500.

4. *Automatic reinvestment.* At your request, all your dividends and your capital gains will be used to buy new shares in the fund. If you're retired and want regular monthly or quarterly income, you also have the benefit of automatic withdrawal. You simply arrange with the fund ahead of time where the check should be sent, how much money you want out of your account, and how often.

5. *Fund switching.* You can switch from one fund to another within the same fund family simply by making a phone call if your investment objectives change. This lets you switch from a long-term investment to a short-term money-market fund, where you can get access to the proceeds by writing a check.

6. *Liquidity.* Mutual funds are liquid investments; this means that the shares can be bought and sold daily. This is very different from investing, say, in real estate, where you would have to go through lengthy negotiations with brokers, buyers, sellers, banks, and lawyers before you could get your money.

7. *Low start-up costs.* A mutual fund allows you to open an account with a minimum investment of anywhere between $250 and $1000 (see Table 9-8), and your subsequent investment can be made on a monthly basis for $25, $50, or $100.

8. *Access to high-cost investments.* When you buy a mutual fund, you have access to investments that would normally require you to invest much larger amounts. For example, if you buy a Treasury bill, you need $10,000. But if you buy into a government securities fund that owns Treasury bills, you only need $1000.

Table 9-8

Twenty Funds with $500 Minimum Investment for Small Investors

The investment objective for these funds varies from aggressive growth and international to equity income and corporate bond income, but the funds are a starting point for you to consider if you want to begin with a small account.

Fund Name	Load/No Load	800 Number
AARP Growth	No load	322-2282
AIM Constellation	5.50%	347-4246
Alliance Quasar	4.25%	221-5672
Berger Growth	No load	333-1001
Capstone Medical	No load	262-6631
Compass Capital	4.50%	451-8731
Delaware Trend	4.75%	523-4640
Evergreen Growth & Income	No load	807-2940
Excelsior Managed Income	4.50%	233-1136
Federated Liberty Equity Income	5.50%	245-2423
Franklin Growth	4.50%	342-5236
Phoenix Worldwide	4.75%	243-4361
Piper Emerging Growth	4.00%	866-7778
Putnam Equity Income	5.75%	225-1581
Sierra Emerging Growth	4.50%	222-5852
Strong Total Return	No load	368-1030
SunAmerica Small Company A	5.75%	858-8850
United New Concepts A	5.75%	366-5465
VanKampen Corporate Bond A	5.75%	421-5661
Vanguard STAR—Index	No load	635-1511

9. *Easy monitoring.* Mutual funds can be tracked as easily as stock prices. They are listed in the financial pages of most daily papers, where you can look up the change in their net asset value each day. Many mutual funds also get quarterly updates and annual reviews in major financial publications such as *Barron's, Forbes,* and *Money* magazines.

FEES

Funds come in two basic groups: load funds and no-load funds. A load is a sales charge. That's the fee that the broker earns for assisting you with any research, information, and support service that you request when opening an account and buying a fund. Loads can vary from as low as 2 percent to as high as 8.5 percent of the price you pay for the stock. No-load funds have no sales charge, but you will also have to take full responsibility for your investment decisions and do all of your own research. All the money that you put in goes directly into the investments. No-load funds have been bought directly from the management. So far there has been no proof that there is a difference in performance between load and no-load funds. Just the same, choosing a fund strictly because it does not have a load is a foolish idea for buying a fund.

The criteria should take three things into consideration: how the fund has performed, although there is no guarantee that it will continue to perform as it has in the past; how experienced management is; and does the fund's investment philosophy match your personal investment goal. If you feel you are able to pick a mutual fund on your own, then do your homework and follow through. If you need help, you're going to have to pay a fee to a planner or advisor or a commission to a broker. All funds, load and no-load, have fees and expense charges that can be as low as 0.75 percent or as high as 2.25 percent. Fees and expenses are how the mutual fund management company pays for all those free brochures, free phone calls, the staff or portfolio managers, and the cost of research to determine which stocks to buy and sell. Read the prospectus carefully to see what it will cost you on an annual basis and on a long-term basis.

FUNDS AND THE IRS

The fund management is responsible for reporting your earnings and losses to the IRS whether the money is in an IRA or not. (Did you think you could leave your favorite uncle out of this transaction?) And capital gains and dividends paid out to you will be reported and are going to be taxed as ordinary income. Your fund will send you and the IRS a tax form called a 1099 detailing which payouts were dividends and which were capital gains.

FUND FAMILIES

Mutual funds come in families. If you select a mutual fund on the basis of management, here's where you would start. A family of funds is managed under the "umbrella" of one investment management company, such as Fidelity, Vanguard, T. Rowe Price, or Dreyfus, which manages well over 50 funds. There may be a growth fund, a growth and income fund, a high-risk fund, a municipal bond fund, and a money-market fund all under the same umbrella. If you're buying a load fund (one that charges a sales commission), be sure that the family of funds will let you switch from one fund to the other without an extra charge. That way, when the stock market turns down, you can painlessly move your money to a bond fund or a money market fund while you wait for the market to improve.

When you choose a family of funds, you need to look at the services that are provided. Does it have an 800 number that you can call 24 hours a day? Does it have automatic reinvestment of dividends? Will you get regular quarterly statements? Does it have a frequent withdrawal plan? Does it also have an automatic investment plan where you can write your checks and have them automatically deducted from your bank account every month? Answers to these questions will help you narrow down your choice of a fund.

How do you make the final choice? As noted earlier, choose a fund on the basis of how the fund is managed, what the fund's objective is, and what track record it has. Don't make your choice on the basis of what it is going to cost you. Too many people look at the load and decide that's as far as they should look. But load is *no* indication of what kind of return you will get from a fund, and total return should be your main concern.

Let's look at a mutual fund's average annual return between 1985 and 1995:

		1 Year	5 Year	10 Year
(Debt)	Money-market funds	6.00%	7.61%	6.90%
(Debt)	Taxable bonds/GNMA funds	12.69%	17.23%	10.18%
(Debt)	Tax-free bond funds	14.80%	8.00%	8.20%
(Equity)	Total-return fund	17.22%	20.13%	13.69%
(Equity)	Capital appreciation/growth stocks	13.18%	15.56%	17.39%
(Equity)	International funds	8.60%	11.00%	12.40%

Note that a 3 percent difference in return every year equals 50.83 percent more money in 15 years. That can make one's retirement years more comfortable or a college education much more affordable.

WHAT IS TOTAL RETURN?

Mutual funds and stocks are frequently discussed and evaluated in terms of their overall total return, but that is not clearly explained in the annual reports and prospectuses that you will read. There are some complicated formulas used by the technical analysts, but for your purpose there is a plain and simple answer. You buy a share of stock on January 2 (the market is closed on New Year's Day) for $10 a share. On December 31 of that year, the stock you bought has gone up to $15 a share. Your investment now has gone up, or appreciated in value, by 50 percent. But that's not all. At year-end, the company declares a dividend of $1 a share, so you also have earned some income from owning that share of stock. The $1 dividend divided by the $10 original investment = 10 percent return on your money. Add this to the 50 percent appreciation value, and you get a total return for the year of 60 percent!

Earnings from dividend income are taxed each year as you receive them even though you may choose to reinvest those dividends in new shares or partial shares of the stock. The increased value of the shares is not subject to taxes until you sell the shares, which could be several years in the future. Then you have a capital gain on the share price, which is taxed at the same rate as your ordinary income. When you sell stock at a profit, then you have a tax liability, which can reduce your total return by about 30 percent.

|||☰||| *Chance has never yet satisfied the hope of a suffering people. Action, self-re-* |||☰|||
liance, the vision of self and the future have been the only means by which
the oppressed have seen and realized the light of their own freedom.
MARCUS GARVEY

ETHICAL INVESTING

Social activists who want to ensure that their investment dollars won't pay for polluting the environment or supporting the manufacture and sale of nuclear weapons will be interested in a small group of mutual funds that follow a set of broad, socially conscious investment guidelines. The definition of socially conscious investing may or may not be as narrowly defined as you want it to be, but a careful reading of the fund's prospectus and a few calls to the investor relations office will answer your questions about any funds in which you are considering investing. Most socially conscious funds avoid investing in companies that:

- are connected with tobacco, alcohol, or gambling

- sell artillery or military weapons

- pollute the environment

- have been sued for sex and race discrimination

- have been charged with unfair labor practices

Here is a list of mutual funds that specialize in ethical investing.

Ariel Appreciation (Ariel is the only mutual fund company owned and managed by African-American investment managers and advisors.)	(800) 292-7435
Calvert Social Investment Equity	(800) 368-2748
Domini Social Index Trust	(800) 762-6814
Dreyfus Third Century Fund	(800) 645-6561
Pax World Fund	(800) 767-1729

ETHNIC ART AND COLLECTIBLES

||≣|| *A people without knowledge of their history is like a tree without roots.* ||≣||
MARCUS GARVEY

Investing in African-American art has become a big business in the last three decades as more and more middle-class African-Americans can afford to purchase sculpture and artwork that had been beyond their reach. The increased effort of the media, more and more cultural centers that display the works of African-American masters, and retrospectives in museums and libraries have stimulated an interest in these items.

African-American collectibles cover an enormous range of items; some of which depict a heritage that some African-Americans would like to forget ever occurred. Some collectibles spark intense controversy since some African-Americans (and other Americans) see them as being offensive and reinforcing stereotypical images that should be forgotten. Items such as Dixie Boy posters and Aunt Jemima salt and pepper shakers are collected, as well as movie posters from the "race" films of Oscar Michaux and autographs signed by Joe Louis, Jack Johnson, Willie Mays, and Hank Aaron. The many items available in this area represent a broad cross-section of interests and tastes that vary as widely as the items themselves. The values assigned to each item depend upon their age, condition, scarcity, and desirability.

Collecting African-American art and memorabilia should not be done as an investment, but as a hobby, for the joy of collecting, for the preservation of an aspect of our culture that is rapidly disappearing. If you happen to make some money from the items that you possess, then consider it an added bonus. Enjoy looking at them, playing with them, sharing them with friends, family, and visitors, but don't buy these items with a profit motive in mind.

A quiet market for items of the slave trade also exists among collectors, black and white. Handbills for slave auctions, reward posters for runaway slaves, and leg-irons and shackles have grown in value over the years as they have become more scarce. Given the perversity of racism, the more bizarre the instrument, the higher the price it demands. Iron masks and tongue guards

In 1946, the U.S. Mint issued the first of 3 million Booker T. Washington commemorative half-dollar coins, showing the profile of the educator who started the Tuskegee Institute and the National Negro Business League. In 1951, another coin featuring the twin profiles of Washington and George Washington Carver was released. Although 5 million of the half-dollar coins were authorized, only 3 million were ever issued. The present value of these 50-cent pieces varies from $10 up to $800 based on what condition they are in and where they were minted.

which punished a slave by not allowing food or water are more expensive to purchase than shackles or neck braces.

Rare books autographed by W. E. B. DuBois, Booker T. Washington, Langston Hughes, Carter G. Woodson, and several noted black scholars of the early twentieth century now command prices of as much as $500 or more per volume.

Black dolls are a long-standing collector's item that is still popular with all age groups and have sparked conventions, clubs, and newsletters as well as some big-ticket prices at major auction houses. Boy dolls are much more valuable than girls dolls since there were so few of them manufactured.

The U.S. Postal Service is helping to create black memorabilia with its limited editions of postage stamps that feature noted African-American figures from jazz singers and rock stars to scientists and poets. The recent spate of Legends of the West stamps series included a stamp that bore the wrong picture of Bill Pickens. This stamp is now worth over $300. Stamps are also an attractive and educational hobby for children.

For further information about a newsletter and national convention that focuses on collecting black memorabilia, contact The Black Memorabilia Collectors Association at 2482 Devoe Terrace, Bronx, New York 10468; or call (718) 584-1737.

INVESTING GUIDELINES

1. Decide how much risk you can live with and what is comfortable for you.

2. Do your homework. Read everything you can get your hands on; make sure you understand the type of risk you are taking. Spend an afternoon in the business section of the library studying Value Line and Moody's industry reports and get objective information from independent sources.

3. Get the annual report and prospectus for several funds, and read them very carefully. Ask questions. Many large companies have shareholders' relationships offices that specialize in providing information for investors. Call them if you want more information. Go to the library and read the Standard & Poor's industry reports to see how your chosen company compares with its competitors.

4. When you are researching a company, look at the Value Line report on the company for historical (past) earnings, dividend history, and stock-price performance. Learn the fundamentals of the company, its financial history, the products and services it offers, and its corporate structure. Value Line also gives safety ratings on stocks and their timeliness for upward growth.

5. Decide how long you are willing to wait for a profit. Three years? Five years? Ten years? Don't look for a once in a lifetime hot stock tip to make you rich overnight. Real wealth doesn't grow that way. Patience is the only way to achieve the long-term growth you are seeking. If you want to sell out after 6 months when the stock price drops 2 points, then you are not an investor!

6. Choose a stock that you like and follow the prices in the newspaper on a daily basis for a month. Imagine that you own 100 shares. How would you feel if the price went up $5? Down $3?

7. Apply the *rule of 72*. Whatever the rate of interest you receive on a CD, passbook account, or money-market fund, divide that

interest rate into the number 72. The result tells you how many years it will take to double your money at that interest rate. For instance, a 9 percent investment will take you 8 years to double your money (9 divided into 72 equals 8).

8. Don't open any accounts or write any checks unless you fully understand what you are doing and why. If you have a queasy knot in your stomach when you are writing the check, STOP!

CREATING A DIVERSIFIED PORTFOLIO

If you win the lottery, get an inheritance, or want to diversify all those CDs you've been hoarding in the bank for several years, here's a rule of thumb for how to do it and have a comfortable sense of well-being and profitability. Let's take the hypothetical case of a couple in their mid-fifties who have just inherited $100,000 and are looking for additional income in 7 to 10 years to supplement their retirement income. What are their choices?

- A bank instrument (money market, certificate of deposit)

- A unit investment trust/individual bonds

- A mutual fund

- A real estate investment

- An annuity

- A cash-value insurance policy

This hypothetical couple should invest their money in a broad array of investments. The percentage of money in each category will vary depending upon the age of the investor. A diversified portfolio for this couple might look like this:

Amount	Investment	% of Portfolio
$10,000	Liquid/cash investments (money markets and savings)	10
$20,000	Unit investment trusts/bonds (5-year and 10-year, tax free)	20
$25,000	Growth and income mutual funds (total return and appreciation)	25
$10,000	Leveraged real estate	10
$15,000	Annuities ($10,000 fixed, $5000 variable)	15
$20,000	Single-pay life insurance	20
Results:	Debt issues = 60%	
	Equity issues = 40%	
	Taxable income = 35%	
	Tax free or deferred = 65%	

This mixture provides approximately $12,650 annual income generated through interest, dividends, and systematic withdrawals.

Go back to your net worth statement in Chapter 4 and look at the assets that you have which are growing in value. What portion of them are in savings instruments? What is the chance that they will grow in value and keep up with inflation? Decide how much more you want to learn about the various areas of investments that have been discussed. Take a look at mutual funds. Every investment goal you have can be fulfilled with the broad range of mutual funds that now exist.

STARTING YOUR INVESTMENT EDUCATION

The first investment you should make should be in educating yourself. Before you start filling out applications and writing checks, spend your first $100 on your financial education. Know what you're doing before you get into it. It is better to lose an opportunity than your capital.

1. Take advantage of every opportunity to learn about investing—attend seminars, enroll in a continuing education course at a junior college, or take a night school class.

2. Make a list of the questions you have and spend an afternoon in the public library searching for answers. While you're there, explore some of the many financial newsletters and publications available.

3. Subscribe to a personal finance magazine for a year and read it regularly.

4. Start reading the financial section of the newspaper and watch the many financial information shows on television on a regular basis.

5. Make an appointment with a financial professional. Many of them offer a free consultation for half an hour to get to know you and answer your questions; don't, however, expect him or her to solve all your problems and educate you fully in one brief visit.

After reading, studying, and talking to an investment professional, keep in mind three basic concepts before you start writing checks and opening investment accounts: clarity, common sense, and commitment. Are you clear about what you're doing? Does this investment make sense for you when you reflect on your financial goals? Can you explain it to your spouse, to your children, to your accountant, and to yourself? Are you committed to staying with this investment for the long term?

Investing can become a lifetime hobby that can build a solid financial foundation for yourself and your heirs. Building a dynasty starts with a commitment to the future and to yourself, and it can be done a dollar at a time.

Jerome Hartwell Holland, the former president of Hampton Institute, Hampton, Virginia, became the first African-American member of the Board of Governors of the New York Stock Exchange in 1972. The former All-American football player was a star athlete during his years at Cornell, where he received his bachelor's and master's degrees. Holland studied for his Ph.D. at the University of Pennsylvania and was appointed president of Delaware State College shortly after his graduation. After 10 years as president of Hampton Institute, Holland was appointed by President Nixon to serve as ambassador to Sweden for 2 years. His son, Joseph Holland, an attorney and a graduate of Harvard Law School, was the first African-American to purchase a Ben & Jerry's franchise, located on 125th Street in Harlem. The ice cream store is managed and staffed by homeless African-American men from a nearby shelter, Harkness Homes, which was established and funded by Joseph Holland.

IO

||||≡ ||||≡ |||| ≡ |||| ≡|||| ||||≡ ||||≡||||≡ |||| ≡||||≡ |||| ≡|||||

RETIREMENT: CAN YOU
AFFORD IT?

"Papa always taught us that with every dollar you earn, the first ten cents goes to the Lord, the second goes in the bank for hard times, and the rest is yours, but you better spend it wisely. Well, it's a good thing we listened because we're living on that hard-time money now, and not doing too badly."

Sarah Delany, age 105, and Dr. Elizabeth Delany, age 103
from their family memoir, Having Our Say

Sarah and Bessie Delany had no idea when they were working in New York City as a schoolteacher (Sarah) and as a dentist (Bessie) in the 1930s, 1940s, and 1950s that they would end up living 40 years beyond retirement age. Becoming the subject of a family memoir that was a best-seller and later a hit Broadway play was an added perk gained as a benefit of longevity. Unless you have a crystal ball and know the predetermined date of your departure from this earthly plane, you'd better put some money away for those later years. Census data and a recent statement from the American Association of Retired Persons confirm that the fastest-growing age group in the United States is composed of people over the age of 85. If you make a modest effort to take care of yourself, you can expect to be an octogenarian at the least. And you don't want to be looking for a minimum-wage job behind the counter at the nearest fast-food franchise at that age, so start planning for retirement now.

Retirement planning is a luxury that most African-Americans have not always been able to consider. Most of the parents of today's generation were too busy with the day-to-day survival issues to focus on any financial matters greater than keeping food on the table, clothes on our backs, and the rent and the phone bill paid. A black middle-class lifestyle needed two wage earners to maintain a decent standard of living that included having a mortgage on a house, owning a car, and being able to take an occasional vacation. Any extra dollars went to send the children to college, care for an elderly parent, and help out a relative who fell on hard times. A long-term goal was to make it to next year and still have what you started out with last year.

The 1990 U.S. Census data also support the fact that life-expectancy in the African-American community makes the idea of retirement planning somewhat of a distant fantasy. Few black men live beyond the age of 64—if that long—so they rarely survive long enough to draw too many social security checks. Black women fare a little better with an average life-expectancy of age 72. Every church group and apartment building in the African-American community has at least one or two elderly sisters who manage to get by on little or nothing beyond a pittance from social security. But now as African-Americans earn higher incomes, have better medical care, and enjoy healthier lifestyles, a longer life span is becoming a reality and merits an expense item in the family budget.

III≡III *The future must be planned for today. We may never see it in our lifetime,*   III≡III
but the success of our ventures will impact future generations.
L. DOUGLASS WILDER
former governor of Virginia in Ebony, April 1988

With the "last-hired, first-fired" scenario faced by most African-Americans in the job market, the idea of long-term career planning was an academic exercise to be read about and witnessed for white counterparts. Accumulating enough money to build a nest egg or staying employed long enough to qualify for a company pension just didn't happen. For most African-Americans, the jobs of choice after World War II were civil service, the military, the post office, government agencies, or public-sector jobs, like school teaching, nursing, or social work where a guaranteed pension was put aside for you if you were lucky enough to last 30 or 40 years and collect it. Government employees did not contribute to the social security system until recently, and government pensions did not come with investment choices or contribution options so there was no need to review the plans—just keep punching the clock and wait until you were eligible to collect.

Nearly 40 percent of African-Americans who are now retired have only been able to do so after years of long-term employment as civil-service workers, teachers, postal workers, or military personnel. Many of those jobs are rapidly disappearing for the under-40 generation of African-American government employees as federal and state bureaucracies, public-sector agencies, and nonprofit social-service organizations where many African-Americans are employed are falling on hard times and are being forced to downsize and restructure themselves.

BUT CAN YOU AFFORD TO RETIRE?

||≣|| *The cost of living is going up and the chance of living is going down.* ||≣||
FLIP WILSON
As his character "Geraldine"

Most African-Americans agree with the adage that there are only two sure things in this world: death and taxes. Now there's a third—retirement. The increased income that is now flowing into the African-American community means that many of us will be here far longer than we ever expected.

If you think your budget is tight today, wait until you see what you'll have when you retire. Let's suppose that you are now 30 years old, are earning $36,000 a year, and are doing fairly well at your job. You've heard about the company retirement plan, and one day you'll get around to reading the brochure, but first you want to pay down the student loans, treat yourself to a new car, and put a down payment on a house or a condo so you can have a tax shelter and finally own your own four walls. Thinking about retirement can wait until next year, right? Wrong! Each year you postpone the decision to invest in a retirement plan makes you about $5000 poorer in future dollars.

If you're comfortable living on $3000 a month now, that amount will provide little more than one week's living expenses by the year 2025. With 4 or 6 percent inflation, $3000 in today's dollars will have to grow to $15,781 in 2025 to equal that same amount of purchasing power (see Table 10-1). If you need added incentive to put away money for retirement, take a look at Table 10-2 to

Table 10-1

Inflation Rate Comparison Chart

In case you haven't noticed, the cost of everything is constantly going up!

Items	1955	1975	1995
Newspaper—*Chicago Defender*	.25	.50	1.00
Movie ticket	3.00	5.00	8.00
Ebony magazine	.75	1.50	2.25
Gallon of gas	.27	.45	1.19
Minimum wage	.75	2.10	4.25
New car	2,450.00	4,875.00	14,630.00
New house	10,825.00	39,780.00	99,300.00
Bus fare	.35	.75	1.50
Gallon of milk	.88	1.52	3.20
Sneakers	2.99	19.95	89.95
First-class postage stamp	.03	.10	.32
Cup of coffee	.25	.50	1.00
Dow-Jones Average	416.58	925.93	5,505.25

see what social security projects as future income if you're lucky enough to collect it in say, 30 years, when you retire. Will this be enough for you to retire on comfortably in 30 years? Assuming a 6 percent inflation rate and the same current living expenses, how much will you need?

Whether your retirement is several decades away, less than 10 years ahead, or just around the corner, there *are* some basic decisions you will have to make. Fill out Figure 10-1 to see how much you will need. Pay attention and

Table 10-2

Future Social Security Retirement Benefits

If This Is What You Earn Now	These Are the Monthly Social Security Payments You Will Collect in 30 Years
$20,000	$ 780
$30,000	$1047
$40,000	$1183
$50,000	$1308
$60,000	$1448

Note: These are 1994 dollars. Can you live on these monthly payments in the future if you need $3000 a month now?

Future Retirement Needs Based on Current Living Expenses

Choose one of the inflation rates to figure your retirement needs over 30 years. For instance, if you are currently paying $750 a month for mortgage or rent, etc., multiply that amount by the 4 or 6 percent inflation factor to determine your future cost of living.

Years to Retirement	Inflation Rate	
	4%	6%
5	1.216	1.338
10	1.480	1.791
15	1.801	2.397
20	2.191	3.207
25	2.665	4.292
30	3.243	5.743

Fixed Payments: Payments for the same amount which must be made each month (or quarterly, annually, etc.) with or without income.

Rent or mortgage payment $_____
Car payment $_____

Loans
   Personal loans $_____
   Other $_____

Insurance
   Health $_____
   Homeowner's $_____
   Other $_____

Payroll deductions
   Insurance $_____
   Savings $_____

Flexible Payments: Necessities that vary in cost from month to month, year to year

Food $_____
Clothing $_____
Laundry and dry cleaning $_____
Personal grooming $_____

Utilities:
   Telephone $_____
   Electricity and gas $_____

Transportation
   Gas and oil $_____
   Taxi, bus, subway, railroad $_____

Figure 10-1. How much will you need?

Medical expenses (not covered by insurance)
Dentist $_____
Medicare $_____
Other $_____

Taxes
Savings $_____

Real estate/property tax $_____
Other$_____
Discretionary Spending: Modifiable luxury items
Eating out $_____
Vacations and weekend trips $_____
General entertainment
Movies $_____
Books and magazines $_____
Courses, seminars, workshops $_____
Maid service $_____
Charitable contributions $_____
Other $_____

Figure 10-1. *(Cont.).*

investigate any company option that may be available to you today! Most of us won't be able to afford to retire if we haven't started contributing to an IRA, a Keogh, a 401(k) plan, or something that will grow tax-deferred over the next few decades. (See Figure 10-2.) Figure 10-3 shows us that the earlier you start investing, the more income there will be when you retire.

IIIᴇIII   *The present will always contribute to the building of the future.*   IIIᴇIII

FRANTZ FANON
Black Skin, White Masks, *1967*

SOURCES OF RETIREMENT INCOME

So where's it going to come from, this future cashflow that's going to make it possible for you to sit home and relax once you become a senior citizen? The expected pay out will come from four basic resources: social security, employer-sponsored pensions or profit-sharing plans, IRAs, and personal savings.

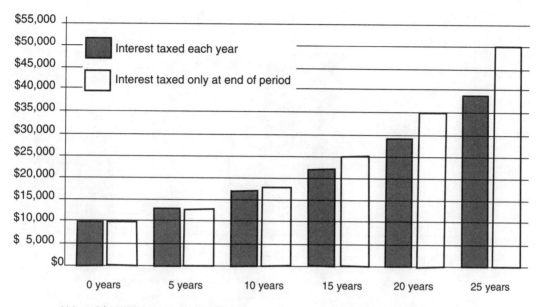

Value of $10,000 investment yielding 8% annually with a 31% marginal tax rate.
IP 23 © Copyright Ibbotson Associates 1996

Figure 10-2. Benefits of deferring taxes.

1. SOCIAL SECURITY

The first person to collect social security was Ida M. Fuller of Ludlow, Vermont. She received check no. 00000001 on January 31, 1940, for $22.54. Ms. Fuller had been a bookkeeper for more than 30 years at one of the textile mills in the area. She had invested less than $100 in FICA contributions before she retired. She lived for another 23 years, collecting a check each month until she died. The way the system is going now, none of us will be as lucky as Ida.

The Roosevelt administration hadn't counted on this kind of longevity and the generational imbalance we have now which is depleting the government trust fund that started more than 50 years ago. The picture looks bleak for the future of social security, as all the economic pundits and notable think tanks predict that the next generation is going to bankrupt the system. With

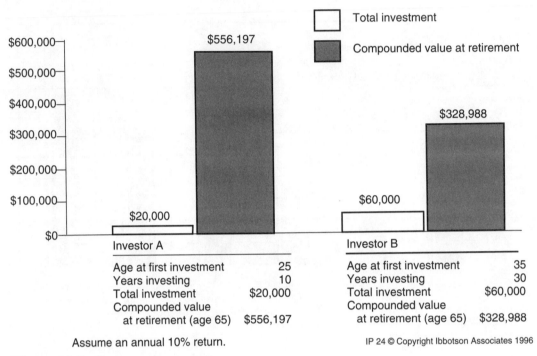

Figure 10-3. Compounding over time.

the budget debacle out of Washington and the constant "borrowing" from the Social Security Trust Fund, the baby boomers now turning 50 will be lucky to collect anything at all beyond the year 2030.

If you're part of the next wave of wage earners, you'd better start thinking about doing as much as possible for yourself as you can. The dollars you're giving up in social security payments you may never see again. If you're turning 50 this year, there's a chance that by the time you need to collect social security, you will get a reduced benefit and it will only last for about 5 years. If you're under 40 (people born after 1960), when you reach 67 (your new retirement age) and need to draw on the system, it will be bankrupt and you may not see a dime of all those FICA contributions you're making now. Assuming that a solution is found, here are the rules on allowing you to collect retirement benefits.

||≣ |||||≣ |||||≣ |||||≣ |||||≣ |||||≣ |||||≣|||||≣ |||||≣ |||||≣ |||||≣ |||||≣ |||||≣
*Amos Fortune (1721–1801) was a slave who was granted his freedom at
age 60. He went on to read law and establish a successful tanning
business. Fortune also founded the first town library in Jaffrey, New
Hampshire, as well as a school that trained black and white apprentices in
the bookbinding business. The Amos Fortune Forum in the Town Meeting
House still hosts a summer educational series today.*
||≣ |||||≣ |||||≣ |||||≣ |||||≣ |||||≣ |||||≣|||||≣ |||||≣ |||||≣ |||||≣ |||||≣ |||||≣

You have to have worked for at least 40 quarters, meaning 10 years, in
order to be eligible to collect. That 40 quarters could be a string of summer
jobs, several short-term consulting gigs, 2 years of teaching, and 5 years in a 9-
to-5 position behind a desk. If your total time adds up to the required 40 quarters and you earned at least $2500 in a year, then you're eligible to collect so-
cial security.

How Much Will You Collect?   Write to the Social Security Administration [or
call (800) 772-1213] and request a Statement of Earnings (Form SSA-7004) to
see how much is in the fund for you so far. The administration takes an average of your income from age 22 to 62, not counting the 5 years that you made
the least money. After you send the form in, it will take about 6 weeks for you
to get an answer.

2. EMPLOYER-SPONSORED PENSIONS OR PROFIT-SHARING PLANS

If you have a pension plan, congratulations. At least 40 percent of all businesses, particularly small businesses, have no pension plan. How much you
will have at retirement depends on the type of plan that your company has.

- *Defined-benefit pension plans.* These plans are being phased out
because of the tremendous expense they are for large
corporations that provide most of them. They are the only plans
that can tell you exactly what amount you will receive at
retirement based upon your current salary—assuming that you
stay with the company until age 65. If you're still in one of these

dinosaur plans, you should receive a statement each year from your employer telling you how much you have coming to you. If you've been throwing your yearly statement in a drawer and ignoring it, take it out and study it. Talk to your employee benefits counselor for an explanation. These plans are also among the few that are guaranteed by the Pension Benefit Guaranty Corporation in Washington, D.C., but only for a maximum annual payment of $31,000 as of 1995.

■ *Profit-sharing plans.* These are uncertain plans and depend upon the whim of your employer if he or she wants to fund it that year. The amount that goes into the plan each year depends upon how profitable the company was that year and if your employer feels like adding funds to the account that year. The amount can be as little as 2 percent or as high as 15 percent of your salary. Everyone gets the same percentage rate.

■ *401(k) plans.* These plans are the wave of the future. They were established in 1982 and named for the section of the Internal Revenue Code which created them. The money from these plans is the only money that most people will have in their golden years. Your employer has to sponsor your 401(k) and agree to do the paperwork and set up fees to get it started. You have the option to contribute to the plan, thereby reducing your current take home income and your taxable income. Tax on the money you put into the plan is deferred until you're ready to start drawing the money out.

Most employers match the amount that you put into the plan to encourage you to contribute—50 cents on the dollar is the usual amount, up to 6 percent of your income—but you have to put in the first dollars. Think of it as free-found money from the boss. The maximum amount you can contribute is also based on your salary. For 1996, the ceiling is 15 percent of your income or $30,000, whichever is lower. This limit increases each year to adjust for inflation.

Investing in Your 401(k) Plan. This is probably the first investing experience that most people are exposed to and the one where they make the biggest mistake in their investment choices. The brochure that comes to you has a lot of legalese mumbo-jumbo and charts about how the 401(k) plan has been set up and where you are allowed to allocate the money you contribute to it. The array of choices is like the menu at a financial supermarket—from 4 to 14 mutual funds, including stock funds, bond funds, money-market funds, international funds, are not uncommon. Choosing the safest investment option—a guaranteed income contract, known as the GIC option—is a mistake, especially if you're young and have at least 30 years before you call it quits. The younger you are, the more risk you should take. The pie charts in Figure 10-4 give you an idea of how you should diversify your choices for the maximum return over time. The higher the return on your money, the more you will have when you retire. Being too safe is unprofitable. The 3 percent difference between a 4 percent return and a 7 percent return over 30 years is $53,073. (See Figure 10-5.) It is your money and your future! With each dollar you are making a commitment to yourself, so make the best of it.

Some plans allow you to purchase company stock through the 401(k) plan. This is a fine idea if you truly believe in the future profits of your em-

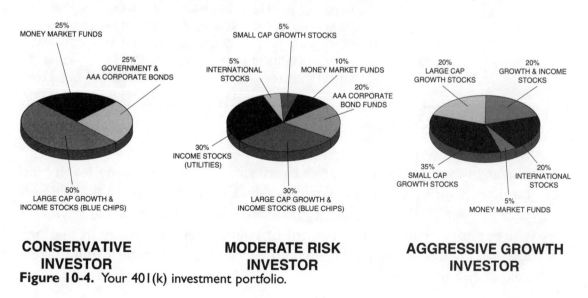

CONSERVATIVE INVESTOR   **MODERATE RISK INVESTOR**   **AGGRESSIVE GROWTH INVESTOR**

Figure 10-4. Your 401(k) investment portfolio.

Monthly Investment	Years to Retirement	Total Monthly Investment Through Age 65	4% Rate of Return	6% Rate of Return	8% Rate of Return	10% Rate of Return
$50.00	40	$24,000.00	$59,098.07	$99,574.54	174,550.39	$316,203.98
	35	21,000.00	$45,686.55	$71,235.51	$114,694.12	$189,831.90
	30	$18,000.00	$34,702.47	$50,225.75	$74,517.97	$113,024.40
	25	$15,000.00	$25,706.48	$34,649.70	$47,551.32	$66,341.67
	20	$12,000.00	$18,338.73	$23,102.04	$29,451.02	$37,968.44
	15	$9,000.00	$12,304.52	$14,540.94	$17,301.91	$20,723.52
	10	$6,000.00	$7,362.49	$8,193.97	$9,147.30	$10,242.25
	5	$3,000.00	$3,314.95	$3,488.50	$3,673.84	$3,871.85
$100.00	40	$48,000.00	$118,196.13	$199,149.07	$349,100.78	$632,407.96
	35	$42,000.00	$91,373.09	$142,471.03	$229,388.25	$379,663.81
	30	$36,000.00	$69,404.94	$100,451.50	$149,035.94	$226,048.79
	25	$30,000.00	$51,412.95	$69,299.40	$95,102.64	$132,683.34
	20	$24,000.00	$36,677.46	$46,204.09	$58,902.04	$75,936.88
	15	$18,000.00	$24,609.05	$29,081.87	$34,603.82	$41,447.03
	10	$12,000.00	$14,724.98	$16,387.93	$18,294.60	$20,484.50
	5	$6,000.00	$6,629.90	$6,977.00	$7,347.69	$7,743.71
$200.00	40	$96,000.00	$236,392.27	$398,298.15	$698,201.57	$1,264,815.92
	35	$84,000.00	$182,746.19	$284,942.06	$458,776.50	$759,327.61
	30	$72,000.00	$138,809.88	$200,903.01	$298,071.89	$452,097.58
	25	$60,000.00	$102,825.91	$138,598.79	$190,205.28	$265,366.68
	20	$48,000.00	$73,354.93	$92,408.18	$117,804.08	$151,873.77
	15	$36,000.00	$49,218.10	$58,163.74	$69,207.64	$82,894.07
	10	$24,000.00	$29,449.96	$32,775.87	$36,589.21	$40,969.00
	5	$12,000.00	$13,259.80	$13,954.01	$14,695.37	$15,487.41

Figure 10-5. Watching it grow.

ployer, but sometimes you can go overboard and take company loyalty too far. Keep your investment in company stock down to no more than 20 percent of your 401(k) portfolio. If the stock suddenly takes a nosedive and you're sitting with 45 to 50 percent of your retirement money in that one area, you're in gloomsville until you see some recovery, which could take a year or two or longer.

Borrowing from Your 401(k) Plan. This is an option that is available to you without the tax penalty you would have to pay if you took money out of your IRA. You are allowed to borrow up to 50 percent of your balance in your 401(k) account or $50,000, whichever is less, if you need the money for one of three things: (1) unexpected medical emergencies, (2) college tuition, or (3) the down payment on a house. But don't do this if you can possibly find another way to get the money. You are forced to pay interest on the loan, even though the loan is your money, usually at the prime rate plus 1 to 3 percent, and you have 5 years to pay the money back. If it is not repaid in that time, then the IRS will consider it a full withdrawal, tax it as income, and sock you with the extra 10 percent penalty. If you leave your job before the loan is paid back, it becomes due in full immediately. Consider borrowing elsewhere.

403(b) Plans. These are similar to 401(k) plans, but they are only for people who work in schools, hospitals, and nonprofit organizations. The maximum annual contribution can be $9500 or 20 percent of a person's salary, whichever is less. The drawback here is that most nonprofit organizations do not have a plan in place, and if they do have one, they are not required to match the amount of money that you invest in them. 403(b) plans are not a requirement in school districts and nonprofit agencies, and the expense of managing them is becoming prohibitive so many plans are being eliminated or reduced.

3. INDIVIDUAL RETIREMENT ACCOUNTS (IRAS)

If you work for a company that doesn't have a 401(k) plan or any other retirement plan option, you can still choose to do an IRA but you'll have to discipline yourself to use these accounts. An IRA is a tax concept created by the IRS to let you put away money for your retirement savings. It is not an investment in and of itself; it is the tax category that you designate when you open the account. Your earnings are tax-deferred. The investment choices for IRAs are just about anything available out there in the financial supermarket with the exception of gold, real estate, and tax-free investments:

Bank CDs and Treasury notes

Bank money-market accounts

Money-market mutual funds

Stock mutual funds

Zero-coupon bonds

Insurance annuities

Individual stocks

Here are the rules for who can have an IRA:

- If you have no retirement plan at your job, you can put away up to $2000 a year and deduct it from your current taxable income.

- If you're married and your spouse is unemployed, then $250 can be invested in a spousal IRA.

- If you earn less than $25,000 a year, even if you do have a 401(k) plan available at work, you can still contribute to an IRA and get the full deduction.

Once the money is deposited in an IRA investment account, you must be prepared to leave it there until you reach age 59½. If you touch it before reaching that age, you will pay a hefty penalty to the IRS—a 10 percent tax penalty—as well as the regular state and federal taxes you would have owed if you had taken the $2000 a year as ordinary income.

Talk with an accountant or work out the numbers before you start writing checks to see if you can still take the deduction for the IRA. Even if you can't, you should still consider the long-term benefit and the tax-deferred earnings.

|||≣|| *My future depends mostly upon myself.* |||≣|||

PAUL ROBESON
October, 1924

4. PERSONAL SAVINGS

This is what's going to make the difference if you can manage it for your future comfort. If you max out on your 401(k) contributions, then you're one of only 4 percent of the people in the United States who have that much money available to them in extra dollars. If you want to keep looking for some form of tax-deferred growth and have some extra dollars, then investigate tax-deferred annuities (see Table 10-3). They come in two flavors: fixed and variable.

The fixed income annuity is the insurance company's version of a CD. You purchase a contract and get a 1-year rate of interest. That rate rolls over

Table 10-3

The Value of Tax-Deferred Growth

$50,000 Investment in a Fixed Annuity, 8% Return Compounded Annually

End of Year	Earnings Taxed at 28%, Cumulative Value	Earnings Tax-Deferred, Cumulative Value
5	$ 66,157	$ 73,466
10	$ 87,536	$107,946
20	$153,249	$233,048
30	$268,295	$503,133

Variable annuity—This is what most 401(k) plans really are:

You select from several options:

Money-market account
Fixed account
Corporate bond portfolio
Guaranteed income contract
Common-stock portfolio

Additional features

- 100 percent of your money goes to work.
- All earnings accumulate tax-deferred until withdrawn.
- You may change your investment options.
- You can avoid probate because proceeds are payable to a named beneficiary.
- There is a guaranteed death benefit—this is an important benefit that protects your principal.

and is renewed each year, like your 1-year CD. The interest you earn grows tax-deferred. Some fixed annuities allow you to withdraw the interest each year on the anniversary date, but it is pointless to buy an annuity contract if you're going to draw the interest out each year. These are not places where you park a lump sum of money for only a year or two; they are long-term commitments—10 to 15 years—for retirement savings so you get the tax advantages, not the quick turnover. Annuities come with buried sales commissions, surrender charges, and penalties that can reduce your interest income if you decide to cancel the contract in less than 7 years. Ask the insurance agent or financial consultant who is selling it to you to explain the withdrawal options and penalties.

But a variable annuity is like investing in a group of mutual funds under the umbrella of an insurance company that manages these contracts. The advantage of a variable annuity is that you postpone paying taxes on the investment returns on your dollars until you need those dollars. The same rules apply with the 59½ age limit on the tax penalty as for an IRA. That $50,000 lump sum your Aunt Martha left you could be invested in an annuity to supplement your "golden years" planning.

RETIREMENT PLANNING CHECKLIST

Take a few minutes now to review the following checklist, so you can start planning for a comfortable retirement:

1. Look at your list of assets and liabilities and review your current living expenses. Look again at Figure 10-1.

2. Set specific investment and savings objectives and review them whenever the economy changes.

3. Create a cashflow plan and determine your fixed and variable spending. What can be changed? Where can you squeeze out an extra few dollars a month to add to a 401(k) or a tax-deferred variable annuity?

JAMES HUNT IV, FINANCIAL ADVISOR

Hunt Investment Advisors
Dallas, Texas

Each week on his radio show on KKDA-AM in Dallas, Jim Hunt finds a way to enlighten his listeners about the importance of managing money and putting dollars away for the future. His quizzes and contests on the basics of investing and concepts of financial planning are offered with streetwise humor and a "down home" commonsense approach that draws callers who keep the phones lit up long after he has left the studio. Hunt is determined to spread the gospel of financial awareness by any means necessary and has found the secret of helping his listeners to get serious about their lives financially.

Hunt knows well the need for such advice in the African-American community. He learned it the hard way. Even though he has a degree in political science from Howard University and 5 years in corporate sales and banking, it was the sudden illness of his father that made him realize how little he knew about the financial side of life. "My father was a funeral director and my mother taught school. Mom's paycheck had gone to cover tuition bills for my brother and me, so she hadn't put away much for retirement. They gave us an education and a comfortable middle-class life in the suburbs but we knew nothing of the family finances." The stroke and a heart attack severely disabled Hunt's father for several years until his death. His illness was a financial drain on the family resources. The small insurance policies of less than $30,000 and a few pieces of real estate that were barely profitable were a revelation to Hunt about how fragile his parents' financial circumstances were. He began to explore financial services as a career.

The sign on the office door reads "Investment Advisor," but Jim Hunt is really a financial educator. He writes a weekly column in a Dallas paper, does his radio show, and commits as much spare time as possible to teaching courses and seminars in the African-American community. Hunt talks to anyone who will listen—a high school class, a women's investment club, young parents at a church convention, small-business people at a fund-raising dinner. He and his wife, Noelle Green-Hunt, who is also a financial-services professional, frequently host seminars to inform and educate their peers.

Hunt sees too many African-Americans stuck in some antiquated thinking about the old way of sitting back and hoping that the government will come through with a decent pension, or that some income from a couple of small pieces of real estate will supplement our social security check, but that's not how it is anymore.

" Too many African-Americans are sleeping through this period of financial change that is going on in the country. It's tough with so many "real world" obligations pulling at us and so little time to absorb it all. Plus the financial news is so confusing and negative it's easier to not listen and concentrate on real estate because that's what we've seen in the past, but we owe it to our children to create new financial lives for them and ourselves. We deserve to try a new approach. **"**

4. Make a firm decision about where you want to retire. Then investigate the tax laws for that location. Do you really want to sell the house and move to a new area away from friends, family, and the familiar neighborhood where everyone knows you? The weather in Florida may be great, but how many people do you know there?

5. Interview several financial advisors and compare the information they give you. Decide what you need to do and stay aware of changing laws and options.

6. Choose a financial professional to review your personal situation and determine what your new retirement tax situation will be.

7. Ask the Social Security Administration for a benefit estimate for your social security income.

8. Meet with the benefits counselor of your company and review your payment options. Is the lump-sum distribution a realistic option for you, or do you want to leave the choice of managing your retirement fund to the company? Thinking about this now will let you avoid being under financial pressure later.

9. Move your IRA or Keogh if you are dissatisfied with its performance.

10. Draft a financial plan for your retirement. Now draft an alternate plan for comparison. Review your plan annually to see if it still meets your needs.

EARLY RETIREMENT

If you have the dream of retiring before age 65, then you better start putting away a hefty portion of your income from the day you start working. A 40-year-old person who wants to retire at age 55 with an annual income of $40,000 has to put away $8280 a year for the next 15 years. See Table 10-4.

Table 10-4

If You Want to Retire Early

For retirement income of:	You'll have to save this much each year to retire at:	
	Age 55	Age 62
$30,000		
Present age 35	$ 6,018	$ 2,776
45	$ 19,010	$ 7,183
Total saved:`	$297,420	261,840
$60,000		
Present age 35	$ 12,036	$ 5,551
45	$ 38,020	$14,367
Total saved:	$594,840	523,680

Note: The table assumes that at retirement accumulated assets are used to buy an 8 percent annuity with payments made until death, based on life-expectancy. Contributions to savings are made at the beginning of the year and yield 8 percent in tax-free interest. Social security benefits start at age 62 but are not included. No adjustment has been made for inflation.

|||≣||| *I don't believe in planning for the future. I believe in planning for now.* |||≣|||
RAY CHARLES, 1978

RETIREMENT PLANNING FOR THE SELF-EMPLOYED

OK, you've been shuffled through the human recycling bin of outplacement, or you saw it coming and got out early. Smart you, to make the big break from corporate America, start your own enterprise, and call the shots as your own boss. Now you're working flexible hours from your new office, you earn enough not to miss the benefits package, and you and your spouse are managing quite well without the bureaucracy, with one exception—nobody is putting away any money for your retirement.

For small-business owners, the constant temptation is to keep plowing profits back into the business to make it grow faster, but that isn't serving their retirement planning. You have more options as an entrepreneur to put away retirement money, but you need to supply the discipline factor, which isn't always there. A common belief among small-business owners, African-Americans included, is the assumption that they will be able to sell the business for a hefty profit and retire with a large nest egg. Big mistake. Your product or service business may not be as attractive an operation without you at the helm. Better start looking at retirement plans while the ducats are coming in. Here are the frequently asked questions about plans for the self-employed.

RETIREMENT PLANNING OPTIONS

KEOGHS

What Is a Keogh Plan?　A Keogh plan is a special retirement program for individuals who are self-employed as sole proprietors or partners in business. The advantages of a Keogh plan include these:

- You reduce your federal income tax because the amount of your contribution, within specified limits, may be claimed as a tax deduction.

- You probably reduce your state income tax because the majority of states do not impose an income tax on the amounts contributed to a Keogh.

- You also reduce your federal and state income tax for current years because the earnings on a Keogh are exempt from taxation until they are withdrawn. The money must stay in the account until you are 59½ to avoid the 10 percent early-withdrawal penalty imposed by the IRS.

- You might pay a smaller amount of income tax when the funds in your Keogh are distributed to you because, by then, you will likely be in a lower tax bracket and/or distribution might qualify you for a special low rate of taxation.

- You are providing for your own retirement, and you have a wide choice of investment alternatives.

What Do I Need to Know about Keogh Plans?　If you have any earnings from self-employment, you need to know how a Keogh plan will affect your business operations and allow you to reduce your current income taxes while you accumulate funds for your retirement. You also need to know what types of Keogh plans there are, how much you can contribute each year, what your obligations are toward any employees that you may have, and how payments from your Keogh plan are taxed.

Am I Eligible to Open a Keogh Plan?   Generally, if you are self-employed and have a profit, you are eligible to open and contribute to a plan. In order for you to be considered self-employed, you must render some personal service to the business. If you merely provide financial backing for a business and receive a share of the profits, you are not eligible because you are considered a silent partner who is not involved in the daily management of the business. You do not have to be self-employed on a full-time basis, but the amount invested in the Keogh plan cannot exceed the amount of your earnings from being self-employed.

Are There Any Disadvantages to Opening a Keogh Plan?   Yes. If you have employees, you are required to provide them with the same or a similar form of retirement planning and investing which you have created for yourself.

What Are the Different Types of Keogh Plans Available?   There are two main types used by most businesses:

1. *Defined-benefit plans.* Business owners are required to put away for themselves and for their employees the smaller of $118,800 or 100 percent of the plan participants' average taxable compensation for their highest consecutive years. You can see why most of these plans are being phased out.

2. *Defined-contributions plans.* These are the more popular plans for small-business owners and self-employed professionals. These plans include:

   ■ *Money purchase plans.* In this type of plan, a set dollar amount or set percentage of earnings is put aside each year in the plan, regardless of the level of profits earned in the business or professional practice. The annual deductible contribution to each Keogh plan participant is the lesser of $30,000 or 20 percent of taxable compensation for the self-employed person and $30,000 or 25 percent for employees.

- *Profit-sharing plan.* Contributions are made only if there are profits. A percentage of profits is set aside in the Keogh plan. The annual deductible amount for each Keogh plan participant is the lesser of $30,000 or 15 percent of taxable compensation for the employees and $30,000 or 13.0435 percent for the business owner. That difference is accounted for by the FICA (Social Security) contribution.

When May I Make Contributions to the Keogh?   If your plan is opened before the end of your taxable fiscal year, you may make your contributions at any time before your income tax return for that year is due (including extensions). New plans must be opened by December 31 or on the last business day of the employer's tax year.

How Do I Set Up a Keogh Plan?   Before you begin making contributions to a Keogh, you must apply to the IRS for approval of the plan after it has been developed by an actuary or a pension consultant. A separate tax form must be filed each year regarding the amount of funds contributed each year for each employee participating in the plan. Participants must also receive annual reports indicating the amounts contributed for them, the way the funds are invested, and the current value of the amount invested.

Who Will Manage the Investments of the Keogh?   Most Keoghs are sold by insurance agents, financial planners, stockbrokers, and bankers as prepackaged retirement plans where the bulk of the paperwork has been predetermined for you. The plans are usually structured and managed by a third-party trust, which, in turn, monitors the funds going into the investment accounts and the paperwork.

When a trust is used, a formal legal document is required by the IRS, and title to the funds is transferred to the third-party trustee (usually a bank or an investment company) that holds the funds for the benefit of those participating in the retirement program. The person or company that initiates the plan still retains the power to direct the investments.

SIMPLIFIED EMPLOYEE PLANS (SEPs AND SAR/SEPs)

Simplified employee plans (SEPs), or super-IRAs, as they are often called, were introduced in 1978 to assist small-business owners and self-employed individuals with setting up relatively simple retirement plans. They provide an alternative to Keoghs, which require detailed planning and analysis by an actuary, who must then submit documents to the IRS for approval (a process that can take up to 3 months and can cost from $600 to $3000, depending upon the size of the company). Congress is trying to phase these plans out, so be sure after 1996 to speak with your accountant to see if they are still available to you. If you already have a SEP, then you can continue to contribute to it under the "grandfather" rules that apply here.

> ■ SAR Simplified Employee Pension Plan (SAR/SEP). This is a salary reduction business IRA plan, like a 401(k) plan, where the employer takes the money from the employee's paycheck and puts it into the plan for the employee. Contributions must be in an amount proportionate to annual compensation and may not exceed 15 percent of taxable compensation. An advantage of this plan is that it requires less paperwork than other more complex plans and the reporting procedures are simpler. Many small-business owners choose to set up a combination of the two plans, SEPs and SAR/SEPs, which allows them more flexibility in the amount of funds invested each year.

Through SEPs, small companies with less than 26 employees can avoid a lot of unnecessary fees, setup costs, and annual trustee expenses usually charged by pension fund administrators. In addition to the plan's primary purpose of providing retirement income, a SEP can also be used to reduce a business's taxable income, since the earnings from the concern can be used to make the payments into the SEP.

To open a SEP account, an employee establishes an IRA through a bank, mutual fund, or other financial institution of his or her choice. The employer agrees to make an investment contribution each year into the employee's IRA and signs IRS Form 5305-SEP. This form is kept on file by the employer, and a copy is given to the employee and to the financial institution that will serve as the trustee for the account.

The trustee is responsible for all the paperwork, including reporting to the IRS each year. Fees, which are usually charged to the employee's account, vary, but they usually run from $25 to $50 for setting up each account in the SEP, and there is a $5 to $10 surcharge per year for each participant in the plan. Employees have contributions to SEPs deducted from their salaries in the same manner as with a 401(k) plan or a tax-sheltered annuity.

The same rules apply to SEPs as they do to Keoghs: Employers can contribute up to $30,000 a year per employee or 15 percent of the employee's gross income, whichever is less. There can be no unequal contributions to the SEP in favor of senior employees or owners. Employers are also not allowed to discriminate among employees; everyone who is over 21 years of age, has earned at least $300 in the last calendar year, and has worked with the company for at least 3 of the last 5 years must be allowed to join the plan. However, employees who are covered by union contracts and nonresident aliens can't participate.

Once the accounts are set up and the SEP deposits are made to the employee's account, the plan operates in much the same way as other retirement plans. The same rules regarding withdrawals, penalties, and taxation of withdrawals all apply. Bear in mind, though, that while the SEP is an employer-contributed plan, it is also similar to an IRA in that the account can be opened as late as April 15 and the deduction can still be credited to the prior tax year. Remember, also, that with a simplified employee plan, your investment options are the same as with any other IRA.

III≣III *All futures are erected out of a past.*   III≣III
ASA HILLIARD, Kemet and the African Worldview, 1986

IRAs ARE STILL A GOOD IDEA

If you're self-employed, temporarily unemployed, and don't have a clear job title, like many African-Americans who are now temporary workers, independent contractors, part-time consultants, etc., without clear long-term employment goals, you gotta do at least an IRA.

If you have been making regular annual contributions to an individual retirement account in order to reduce your taxable income or to supplement your retirement income, but have decided you won't bother anymore because they're no longer deductible under the new tax laws, think again.

The income that is earned on an IRA will continue to grow at a faster pace, since the interest on this investment is compounded and not taxed until after retirement. Usually most people are in a lower tax bracket then, which can make a big difference in retirement income. Most other investments will increase your taxable income each year and give a lower net return on your money.

Even with the changes brought about by the new tax code, many of the old rules will still apply to IRAs. For example, you are limited to a total contribution of not more than $2000 a year, you may not withdraw the funds until you reach age 59½, and you must begin withdrawing them by April 1 of the year after you reach age 70½.

Here's where things changed. Under the old tax law, if you needed to withdraw money from your IRA early, both the 10 percent penalty and the tax due applied to the interest earned as well as to the original dollars invested that had not been taxed. With the new tax rules, taxes and penalty do not apply to the nondeductible contribution because you already paid the taxes on that money in the year it was earned.

Suppose you were to continue making nondeductible IRA contributions, investing $2000 a year at 8 percent. Five years from now you would have $12,672 in your account ($10,000 plus $2672 interest). Then let's say you find the condo of your dreams and decide to withdraw the money for the down payment. Since you have already paid income taxes on $10,000 ($2000 for 5 years), that money is yours to do with as you please; the IRS is only interested in the tax-free interest of $2672. You would pay taxes of $748.16 on that amount assuming you were in a 28 percent bracket, plus a penalty of $267 (10 percent of the $2672) for making an early withdrawal. Nondeductible IRAs require that you keep accurate records until you start withdrawing the funds.

Let's assume that you're married and that you and your spouse file taxes jointly and have an adjusted gross income of $45,000. This puts you in the new 28 percent tax bracket. You have analyzed your budget, and your goal is to continue to put at least $2000 a year in some form of retirement fund to supplement your pension and social security. Here's how the numbers work for someone in the 28 percent tax bracket when the $2000 annual IRA investment is compared—after 10 years—with other vehicles.

Total Outlay	Annual Yield	With IRA	Without IRA
$20,000	8%	$31,291	$27,568
	10%	$35,062	$29,904
	12%	$39,309	$32,449

The difference is due to the taxes that must be paid each year on the interest earned. As you can see, even though an IRA investment is no longer deductible, the long-range interest, dividends, and capital gains continue to grow as untaxed income until you make a withdrawal. This is the most practical reason an IRA continues to be an attractive investment even when you can't deduct the contribution.

|||≡||| *When I was forty and looking at sixty, it seemed like a thousand years away.* |||≡|||
But sixty-two feels like a week and a half away from eighty. I must now get on with those things I always talked about doing but put off.
HARRY BELAFONTE, *December 15, 1989*

STARTING LATE AND CATCHING UP

If you're getting started late in the retirement game, there's still hope if you're willing to risk it. Aggressive growth funds are the only funds that have a long-term history (over a 20-year period) of giving the best bang for your buck. This is the only solution to building a nest egg that will mean something unless you know you're going to inherit Fort Knox.

Some financial planners and advisors suggest that when you finally retire, your income needs will decrease, but nothing could be further from the truth. Government studies show that although your expenses for going to work—commuting, lunches, clothing, etc.—may be eliminated, you will have increased expenses for many of the things that retirees have often wanted to do: travel, hobbies, and educational interests. There is also the increase in medical expenses that come with the aging process.

Your primary concern is having enough income to fill the gap between pension, social security, and savings. You have little choice about the fixed-income aspect of how much you receive from social security, if it is still available, and from your pension. The two major income choices you control are in the investment area and in your home, if you own one.

Some retirement advisors suggest that the cheapest way to live rent-free during retirement is in a house that is fully paid for. However, the value of your house may be costing you money with the interest income that you are losing on the equity that is locked in those four walls. Suppose you bought your house 30 years ago for $40,000, when you needed every inch of space in those four bedrooms, three baths, finished basement, family room, dining room , and two-car garage. You could be just as happy with a two-bedroom condo in a small retirement complex where someone else worries about the roof leaking, the faucet that drips in the bathroom, the furnace that needs to be serviced, and the grass that needs to be cut. The house is now easily worth $300,000, and you don't really need all that space. Since you are over the age of 55, you qualify for the $125,000 net capital gains exemption allowed to homeowners on profits from the sale of the home. Have the children all moved away, bought their own homes, and created new lives for themselves? Is it important to leave the property to the heirs or are you more interested in attaining a simpler, aggravation-free lifestyle and having the equity in the house in the bank instead earning some extra interest for you?

If you sold your $300,000 house and purchased a smaller residence with the $125,000 you are entitled to under the capital gains exemption, you would still have to pay taxes on the remaining $175,000. Assuming a 30 percent tax rate you would still have $122,500 available to invest in a conservative retirement portfolio of blue-chip preferred stocks, insured municipal bonds, and Treasury notes that would give you some extra income. The major decision is: Do you want to sell the house?

REVERSE-ANNUITY MORTGAGES

For many retirees, their home is their biggest asset after working and paying off the mortgage. It is also the most illiquid investment that you may own. If you have already retired from the job market and have limited income for your living needs, but your house is fully paid for, you may want to consider a reverse-annuity mortgage, particularly if you have children who have moved away and are not interested in inheriting your property. The idea is that the bank pays you "mortgage payments" and, in turn, ends up with your house.

First, the bank appraises your house and gives you a valuation. Then the bank sets up a payment plan, which is usually quite low, with your property as security—in other words, a mortgage. The bank pays you (rather than you pay it) a fixed sum each month as income for you to use in any way you see fit. The payments are set up to continue for what they bank presumes to be the rest of your life. When you die, the bank owns the title to your house and will resell it to interested buyers. If any family members appear and wish to purchase the property, they must be prepared to repay the loan. The biggest problem with these loans is what happens if you outlive the expected date of death that the bank projects for you? If you live too long, then you have to start paying the bank back, which puts you right back where you started—broke and in debt.

Reverse-annuity mortgages are not available at all banks or in all states. They are becoming more popular as the federal government begins to support the concept for these loans through the FHA and Fannie Mae.

Fannie Mae expects 100 lenders, covering most states, to offer reverse mortgages this year for retirees who need the additional income. For details, call Fannie Mae at (800) 732-6643.

The National Center for Home Equity Conversion (NCHEC) offers a list of reverse-mortgage lenders too. Send $1 and a stamped, self-addressed, business-sized envelope to:

NCHEC
7373 14th Street, West
Suite 115
Apple Valley, Minnesota 55124

|||☰||| *A man of character is a man of wealth.* |||☰|||
                                    EGYPTIAN PROVERB

RETIREMENT IS ALSO ABOUT FULFILLMENT

Retirement can be the beginning of another phase of life, not the end of your productive years. When Allen Allensworth (1842–1914) retired from his 30-year position as an Army chaplain after World War I, he had one special dream that he wanted to fulfill. Allensworth and his brother had escaped from the plantation where they were slaves in Alabama. They made it to Missouri where they were sheltered and educated by a family of free blacks. The two boys grew up there, and after Emancipation, they opened a restaurant that was quite successful. Allensworth had joined the Union Army during the Civil War, after which he returned to the South to be with his family and start a school near the plantation where he had once been enslaved.

After several years of teaching, in 1871, he went to the seminary and became an AME minister and worked as a circuit preacher in Kentucky and Illinois. The Army asked him to reenlist in 1896, and he did so as a chaplain, serving in the Army during the War of 1898 and traveling to Cuba and the Philippines. After 20 years of service, he retired in 1906 and moved to California to pursue his dream. His travels and his years of service convinced him that he needed to find a place where he could create a community of comfort away from the racism and hostility that he had seen so much of in the South as he had grown up in Alabama.

In 1908, using his life savings, he established the first black town in California, called Allensworth, in Tulare County, which lies halfway between Los Angeles and San Francisco. He invited blacks to move to California to take advantage of the climate and the job market. In the first 6 years, the town grew to over 200 families, and there were fruit and dairy farms, a hotel, a post office, railroad station, and a black-owned bank. Unfortunately, with Allen Allensworth's sudden death in a motorcycle accident in 1914, along with the lure of better jobs in the San Francisco Bay Area, the town began a slow decline. Problems with the water supply and the closing of the railroad station finally hastened the decline until in 1990 fewer than 30 families remained in residence. The site along California Route 43 has been designated as the Allensworth State Historical Park by the state of California.

IIIＥIII *Let the Afro-American depend on no party, but on himself for his salvation.* IIIＥIII
Let him continue toward education, toward character, and above all, to put money in his purse. When he has money, and plenty of it, parties and races will become his servants.

IDA B. WELLS, 1892

Aging is a guaranteed step in the life process, and it is your decision how to plan for it properly. At 60, you should be thinking about coasting into a financial comfort zone rather than how you will meet the mortgage payments, the car note, do you have enough insurance, and can you afford to go to the dentist. All financial news reports from AARP to the Social Security Administration and several Congressional committees have voiced the concern about how to support the coming surge in demand for services for the aging American population. The warnings of gloom and doom may seem a bit hysterical, but they are well-founded. You have to consider all these messages as a clear-sighted effort to make you aware that you must be prepared to handle your portion of the responsibility for your own retirement planning process.

FINAL LEGALITIES

"It is important and right that all privilege of the law be ours, but it is vastly more important that we be prepared for the exercise of these privileges."

Booker T. Washington, 1932

William Alexander Leidesdorff (1810–1848) is recorded as being the first African-American millionaire in the United States, but technically that is questionable. He was born in the St. Croix, Virgin Islands, to Anna Maria Spark, a free African woman. Leidesdorff was legally acknowledged by his father, a Danish merchant and landowner, and sent to Europe for his education. In his early twenties he came to New Orleans and started out as a cotton broker and tobacco trader. His pale skin and straight dark hair allowed him to blend in quite comfortably with the growing merchant class of Creoles that controlled a considerable amount of business in the city.

Leidesdorff built a respectable fortune for himself there and owned several ships to support his business. According to local folklore he was engaged to be married to a young white woman, and when he disclosed the truth about his parentage, her family forced her to break off the engagement and she committed suicide. True or not, Leidesdorff sailed for California on a ship, the *Julia Ann,* in the spring of 1841. It was the beginning of the golden age of California and the economic possibilities were enormous. Leidesdorff was captivated by the mixture of Mexicans, Native Americans, and immigrants from the East. He settled in a tiny village that bore the Mexican name of Yerba Buena; only 33 families lived there, along the shores of a large bay at the northern stretch of the Monterey coast.

He used his skills in the new territory, which was still governed by Mexico, to establish a trading business, a general store, and a restaurant in the growing area. He purchased his first property at the corner of Clay and Kearney Street, where he built the city's first hotel. He was elected to the town council and was instrumental in developing the first public school system in California. Leidesdorff found it expedient to change his citizenship and become a Mexican citizen, entitling him to one of the many land grants being made by the new governor of the territory. He received 360,000 acres of land in the Sacramento Valley along the American River across from Sutter's Mill, which he developed into a large cattle breeding ranch.

Leidesdorff was hired as the U.S. vice consul in 1845 to assist in the negotiations between Mexico and the United States for control of the region. This position allowed him to have exclusive control of the sale of all meals and provisions supplied to the U.S. Army, which added to his wealth. When the U.S. Army finally secured the new territory, Leidesdorff was released from his position as vice consul, and he returned to his business development activities. Yerba Buena officially changed its name to San Francisco. Gold was discovered on his ranch on March 15, 1848. Two months later, Leidesdorff died suddenly of typhoid fever at the age of 38. He left no wife, he had no children, and his only surviving relative was his mother, who still resided in St. Croix. He also did not have a will.

Without a will, Leisdedorff's enormous business holdings and property came under the control of the courts. Some historians want to believe that there was resistance to allowing the property to pass into other hands because Leidesdorff was passing for white, but other documentation from professional colleagues dismisses that concept, confirming that because of his light skin he was perceived as being of Mexican descent. The question that had to be resolved was whether a non-U.S. citizen could inherit or pass on property in the United States. Leidesdorff had not changed his citizenship, and his mother was considered a Danish subject since Denmark ruled the Virgin Islands at the time. Thomas Larkin, the former U.S. ambassador to Mexico and Leidesdorff's business colleague, asked to be made administrator of the estate, promising to maintain the properties and pay the taxes until matters could be resolved. James Folsom was the Army quartermaster in San Francisco, and he had done business with Leidesdorff. Folsom knew the potential value of the estate, and in 1849 he made a trip to St. Croix to meet with Anna Spark, Leidesdorff's mother. He spent several weeks trying to convince her to sell her interest in the properties to him. After many meetings for negotiation she sold her rights to her son's estate for $75,000.

The estate, which included the huge cattle ranch and 309 San Francisco city lots, was finally settled by the California High Court in 1852 when title was transferred to James Folsom. Taxes, mortgages, debts, and court expenses charged against the property amounted to $63,000. Final valuation of all properties was listed as $1,442,000. The cattle-breeding ranch on the banks of the American River became the town of Folsom, California. The only remaining evidence of Leidesdorff's presence in California is his grave at the Mission Dolores and a small street that is named for him in the business district of downtown San Francisco.

III≡III   *Too often in the black community when the family dies, the company dies.*   III≡III
A. G. GASTON
1988

The lesson of William Leidesdorff's life is that if you want to pass on your property to your family and your heirs, you have to write your wishes down. That means facing up to your own mortality and working with an attorney to put your house in order, and most people do not want to do that. It is amazing how many African-Americans often go out of their way to avoid any situation that requires dealing with lawyers, courts, and legal matters, but we do this to our detriment, particularly in the area of wills and estate planning.

DYING WITHOUT A WILL

To die without a will is to die intestate, and that leaves a nightmare of problems for your family and makes the courts and lawyers quite wealthy. Without a will, a public administrator is appointed, who divides up your property and decides who gets what according to some very specific predetermined rules that might have you turning in your grave.

The rules are different in each state, but here's a general outline of how the distribution can work. If you have a spouse but no children, then the spouse takes everything. If you're married and have children, your spouse may only get one-third or one-half of everything. The rest may go into a trust for your minor children. If you have children only, then the estate is split between them equally. Married people without children will be surprised to find out that in some states surviving parents and brothers and sisters are entitled to as much as half of their estate. If you have no spouse and no children, then your parents get it all. If your parents are not alive, then your siblings get equal shares of whatever you left behind. If your siblings have not survived you, then their children will receive your property. If there are no nieces and nephews, then your grandparents come into line for your inheritance.

Many single African-American women are building comfortable nest eggs for themselves by investing in a house, mutual funds, and retirement plans, but they are ignoring this important document. Your total assets could end up supporting some relatives whom you have not spoken to in decades, or worse, whom you have never met. If you have nieces, nephews, cousins, or adopted children you would like to support, you must write it down. If there is a university alumni association that can benefit from your estate or some non-profit organization that you admire that would benefit from your estate, you must put the bequest in writing.

The biggest problems of intestacy occur when there are young children, and 70 percent of all Americans under 40 who have children do not have wills. If, through some strange quirk of fate, both parents were to die simultaneously in an accident, who would take care of the children? Ironically, this is the question that stops many a person from writing a will at all—not being able to decide who should be the children's guardian. But this is the very reason why you should write the document, even if you have nothing to leave your children. The courts may separate your children or designate different relatives in a distant state as their guardian when you might have preferred that they live with close friends in a community they call home.

If you have been legally separated for years and have never bothered to get a divorce, that surviving spouse whom you haven't seen in decades is also entitled to a share of your estate, regardless of your feelings. If this is the case, make an appointment with an attorney tomorrow.

Dr. Martin Luther King, Jr., died intestate at age 39, and the bulk of his estate went to his wife and children. However, the major earnings came to him after his death in the form of royalties from his writings. Without a will, there was no provision for the remainder of his property, which had to be administered by the courts. Thousands of dollars of royalty income was held by the publishers until final decisions were made by public administrators.

"Estate planning" may sound as if you need to own massive assets and a long list of properties like William Leidesdorff, but that is a totally erroneous assumption. It is also amusing to hear people approach the task of making a will by starting with the phrase "If I die ...." It may seem morbid or insensitive to talk about cemetery plots, funeral arrangements, and testamentary trust agreements while you're young and healthy, but death is not an optional clause at the end of a long happy life. Death is definitely an irrevocable guarantee that you can bank on, and it may not wait until you are old and gray and over 65.

Very few people relish the thought of planning for their death, but from a historical perspective, we don't get out of this life alive so we may as well be realistic about the inevitable. This means making some effort to plan for how you want things to be done at the end. In other words, write a will.

||☰|| *Death cannot put the brakes on a good dream.* ||☰||
MARVA COLLINS, August 1986

WRITING YOUR WILL

Some of the misconceptions and reluctant attitudes expressed by people of all races and from all walks of life about writing a will border on the bizarre or the superstitious, and African-Americans are no exception to the rule.

1. "If I don't think about death and don't make a will, then it won't happen." You're going to die one day anyway. Why don't you plan for it to be handled the way you want it to be?

2. "I don't really have anything to leave anybody, so what difference will it make?" This is the lazy way out of facing up to the inevitable, and that attitude has made a lot of lawyers rich. Probate fees and court costs, no matter how little you have, can be from 2 to 5 percent of whatever you have accumulated before your family can touch a dime of it. And the process can take from 6 months to 5 years if you leave no final instructions about how you want your affairs handled. A lot of this can be avoided by writing a will. It leaves clear instructions about how you want to dispose of what you own, who should take care of your children until they are adults, and what should happen to your property.

3. "I'm not old and sick, so I don't have to think about dying." Obviously, William Leidesdorff felt the same way—he was only 38 years old. Even if you have nothing more than your car, your furniture, and a small savings account, you should have a will, especially if you are single. You have a right to decide who gets the car or your grandmother's ring. If you don't, the state in which you live will decide—at your expense. That savings account will be eaten up immediately by fees for a court-appointed lawyer, and other assets may even have to be sold to pay the court costs. If you want a favorite niece or nephew to have your antique silverware or your computer, write it down!

4. "I'll just put my spouse's name [or my brother's name, sister's name, everybody's name] on all of my accounts, and then I won't need to write a will." Wrong again. You still can't avoid probate this way.

5. "I don't want some stranger to know all my business!" Strangers will make the final decisions about how to dispose of your assets after you're gone, and charge a lot more for the experience after you're dead, so you may as well work with someone before the fact and have your affairs arranged the way you want them to be. Prior planning also costs a lot less.

WHERE THERE'S A WILL, THERE'S A RELATIVE

Take a few minutes to consider the *advantages* of leaving a will:

1. Your instructions for the distribution of your possessions are carefully carried out precisely the way you want. If you want Aunt Sylvia to take your cats, then say so.

2. You name your own executor to carry out your instructions. If your sister-in-law is an attorney and you trust her as being honest and ethical, discuss it with her.

3. You decide who will be the guardian of your minor children.

4. Your assets are distributed to your heirs without confusion. The court bureaucracy is another issue.

5. You specify the exact amounts you want to give to each of your heirs. It will limit unnecessary family fights. You're already dead, so they can't yell at you if they didn't get what they wanted.

6. You reduce some of the expensive legal and probate costs by writing it all down.

THREE TYPES OF WILLS

Basically, there are three types of wills. First, there is the holographic, or handwritten, will. If you want to, you can sit at your kitchen table with paper and pen and get your next-door neighbor to witness your declarations. However, such a document can still be angrily contested by relatives who may be left out. Many lawyers discourage the "do-it-yourself" method. In fact, if your assets are substantial, it's worth the expense to pay an expert to prepare a proper will. Too many handwritten wills have been declared null and void because of confusion in the language or for improper witnesses.

The second type of will is a noncuperative will. A product of the video age, this is an oral will—usually recorded on videotape. It still requires two witnesses in order to be accepted as legal, and not all states are totally will-ing to accept this type of will in court, but it is becoming more and more popular.

Finally, there is the formal will, which is a written document that con-forms to the laws of the state in which you live. It is prepared by an attorney and is tailored to your particular needs. Ask yourself the questions listed in Figure 11-1. Gather together a record of your assets and liabilities. Use the bal-ance sheet and net worth statement you prepared in Chapter 4 as a guideline to review your assets. Go down the list and start putting names next to vari-ous items. Aunt Sylvia gets the book collection; your son will inherit your house; the life insurance has a designated beneficiary, but do you want to change that? Think it through and write it down!

BASIC REQUIREMENTS: BEFORE AND AFTER

In order to write a will, there are some basic requirements. You must be an adult and show some sense of awareness about the list of assets and the re-sponsibility of the document. Usually two witnesses are required; some states require three. They must all be there together and see you sign the will. A no-tary must also notarize the signature of the witnesses on the affidavit. These are called self-proving wills, meaning that the witnesses need not appear in court to support your statements.

After getting it written, you should leave the original in possession of your attorney and keep a copy for yourself—in your safe deposit box. Burial instructions should not be in the will. It may not be read for several weeks, and usually the law requires that your body has to be disposed of in 5 days, so pre-pare a separate letter of instructions for funeral arrangements. Safe deposit boxes are a mistake for original documents like these. The box is usually sealed as soon as the bank knows that you have passed on, and it will not be opened until a representative from the IRS (it gets its share even in death) and a rep-resentative from the state banking commission are present with your attorney and executor to document the contents of the safe deposit box. It could take several weeks or months to arrange such a meeting.

Here's a basic list of questions you will need to answer before you make an appointment to draw up a will.

1. To whom do you generally want to give your assets after your death?

2. If your first choice as a beneficiary is your spouse, who would be your second choice if he or she dies before you do?

3. Are there any special items (jewelry, cars, cats, your stamp collection, etc.) that you would like to give to special people?

4. Are there any special family members or friends that you would like to give extra cash or gifts to?

5. If your children are still minors, when do you want them to get the cash, insurance money, or property that you would leave to them? If money, would you like it paid to them in a lump sum or spread out over several years?

6. Do you want to give any gifts to your favorite church or charity?

7. Whom do you wish to manage the assets for the children if they are minors?

8. Have you left enough money available to pay any taxes, funeral expenses, and legal fees that may be owed on your estate?

9. If your assets add up to more than $600,000, are you willing to make special arrangements using various trusts to decrease the taxes?

10. If none of your children are living at the time of your death or after your spouse's death, who would be your next choice as a beneficiary?

11. Whom have you chosen as your:
Executor?
Coexecutor?
Trustee?
Guardian for your children?

12. Who should get the "remainder" of your estate—those items that may be paid to you after your death? For example, who should get the lottery ticket you bought the day before your death, a house deeded to you by a parent whose estate gets settled after your death, that manuscript you sent out that gets optioned for a movie after you're deceased, a lawsuit that is settled in your favor after you're gone?

Figure 11-1. Who should get what?

‖☰‖ *When brothers fight to the death, a stranger inherits their father's estate.* ‖☰‖
Nigerian proverb

CHOOSING AN EXECUTOR

Writing a will also requires that you choose an executor. This is the person who you feel will be responsible enough to carry out your instructions as

PIERRE VINCENT, ATTORNEY-AT-LAW

Philadelphia, Pennsylvania

"People need to know that hearses don't have U-Hauls with them and since they don't, if you own anything that won't perish with you, then you need to speak for it. And you don't need to speak for it so much as to designate who should get it, but so that your family can stay intact. So many families have broken apart because things were not placed in someone else's hands by the person who owned them. And the more wealth you have or are perceived to have, the bigger the fights that ensue."

Pierre Vincent is a rare gem in the African-American community as a specialist in the area of trusts and estates law. After graduating from Howard University (with a degree in French), Golden Gate University (with an M.A. in public administration), and Syracuse Law School, Pierre spent 4 years in the army and moved to Philadelphia to become a city solicitor. During his tenure in the court system, he saw how deficient the African-American community was in estate planning. Many African-American families and business partners were coming through the court system too often, suffering long-term bureaucratic delays and expenses, paying lawyers who were clearly mismanaging estates, and encountering unnecessary problems that arose from not knowing what should be done and how probate should be handled.

Vincent set up an office, starting out on a part-time basis, working with African-American accountants, bankers, insurance agents, and other attorneys, and began to pursue the educational approach. He has spent 7 years working evenings and weekends teaching the fundamentals of estate planning. Teaching seminars and workshops whenever someone would listen to him, Vincent has worked with churches, civic organizations, schools, and community groups with a goal to get the word out about how to preserve what a family has worked so hard for. Getting the information out there is his goal, by any means necessary. Wherever he can find a platform to speak about it with families and small business owners, he takes it.

"Traditionally we haven't had the knowledge, and for most African-Americans the concept of having something to leave behind is a new idea. The attitude among most of us was 'I don't have anything so as long as we could pay for the funeral who cares about the rest?' That's changing and writing it down is such a simple concept but also a frightening experience for people. I try to make it as clear and simple as possible so they can relate to the idea a bit more comfortably. There is so much they don't know that can make the process easier."

"Our fears and lack of trust in the court system may be well-founded for other reasons, but in this case we need to learn to use it to keep what little we have and build on it. Wealth is a perception, and it encourages friends and family to start so many needless fights because they don't know what you have. A will is a legal document, a contract between you and your possessions, and it becomes a law unto itself that cuts down on all the fights that may ensue after you're gone."

you have requested them. Choosing a lawyer, accountant, or financial planner who is familiar with your family assets may sound like a good idea, and he or she may be able to remain more objective and not be swayed by your relatives, but not all lawyers, accountants, or financial planners are as competent or as proficient in the area of probate. Choosing a relative as executor is also risky; times of grief often create mixed emotions, perhaps keeping the relative-executor from being a far cry from objectivity. Your executor should be someone who is not named in the will and preferably young enough to outlive you. A coexecutor should also be named as a second choice, in case the executor dies unexpectedly.

The executor's job is time-consuming and paper-intensive, so think twice before asking someone to accept such a responsibility. The executor is responsible for making certain that all the deceased's assets are gathered, debts paid, and taxes filed on time. If the total assets are less than $600,000, then no federal taxes are required. State taxes are a separate matter. For example, in New York, if total assets add up to more than $108,000, then estate taxes start at 2 percent and up.

The executor is likely to be asked to post a surety bond to ensure that he or she is financially and legally aware of the nature of the executor's obligation. This is required because the deceased's family has the legal right to sue the executor for mismanagement of the estate or mishandling of assets. If this happens, the surety bond is there to reimburse the estate for any losses that are proven.

Before choosing your executor, discuss the responsibility frankly. Executors and attorneys are often entitled to fees of up to 5 percent of the total estate. Check Appendix A for available publications on the role of the executor.

CREATING A LIVING WILL

With the development of modern medical technology, many people who would have died in the past can now be kept alive by artificial means. Artificial feeding, mechanical ventilation, antibiotics, dialysis, and resuscitation can now be used to maintain a comatose patient indefinitely. The moral and ethical questions arising around this issue have also prompted a new legal vehicle that each of us may make use of—a living will (see Figure 11-2).

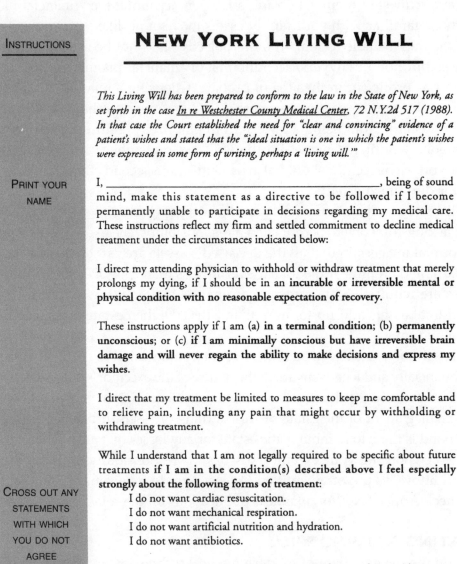

NEW YORK LIVING WILL

This Living Will has been prepared to conform to the law in the State of New York, as set forth in the case <u>In re Westchester County Medical Center</u>, 72 N.Y.2d 517 (1988). In that case the Court established the need for "clear and convincing" evidence of a patient's wishes and stated that the "ideal situation is one in which the patient's wishes were expressed in some form of writing, perhaps a 'living will.'"

PRINT YOUR NAME

I, _____, being of sound mind, make this statement as a directive to be followed if I become permanently unable to participate in decisions regarding my medical care. These instructions reflect my firm and settled commitment to decline medical treatment under the circumstances indicated below:

I direct my attending physician to withhold or withdraw treatment that merely prolongs my dying, if I should be in an **incurable or irreversible mental or physical condition with no reasonable expectation of recovery.**

These instructions apply if I am (a) **in a terminal condition;** (b) **permanently unconscious;** or (c) **if I am minimally conscious but have irreversible brain damage and will never regain the ability to make decisions and express my wishes.**

I direct that my treatment be limited to measures to keep me comfortable and to relieve pain, including any pain that might occur by withholding or withdrawing treatment.

While I understand that I am not legally required to be specific about future treatments **if I am in the condition(s) described above I feel especially strongly about the following forms of treatment:**
   I do not want cardiac resuscitation.
   I do not want mechanical respiration.
   I do not want artificial nutrition and hydration.
   I do not want antibiotics.

   However, I **do want** maximum pain relief, even if it may hasten my death.

CROSS OUT ANY STATEMENTS WITH WHICH YOU DO NOT AGREE

© 1993
CHOICE IN DYING, INC.

Figure 11-2. Example of living will.

ADD PERSONAL INSTRUCTIONS (IF ANY)

Other directions:

These directions express my legal right to refuse treatment, under the law of New York. I intend my instructions to be carried out, unless I have rescinded them in a new writing or by clearly indicating that I have changed my mind.

SIGN AND DATE THE DOCUMENT AND PRINT YOUR ADDRESS

Signed _____ Date _____

Address _____

WITNESSING PROCEDURE

I declare that the person who signed this document is personally known to me and appears to be of sound mind and acting of his or her own free will. He or she signed (or asked another to sign for him or her) this document in my presence.

YOUR WTINESSES MUST SIGN AND PRINT THEIR ADDRESSES

Witness 1 _____

Address _____

Witness 2 _____

Address _____

Courtesy of Choice In Dying   11/93
200 Varick Street, New York, NY 10014 1-800-989-WILL

PAGE 2

Figure 11-2. *(Cont.).*

A living will is a legal document drawn up while in good health which states what your wishes are in the event of an accident or illness that leaves you in a vegetative state dependent upon life-maintenance for the duration of your existence. It must be signed and notarized. Usually, it is then attached to a medical power of attorney, which specifies which family member or medical professional you have chosen to make the final decision about whether you continue on life-support. Living wills may also be used to stipulate which vital organs, if any, may be donated to another individual.

It may sound gruesome to think about, but what would you prefer if you're in an accident and end up in a coma for 3 years? Do you want to be kept alive on life-support systems forever? If not forever, for how long? If the doctor's verdict is that you have permanent brain damage and you will never wake up again, have you chosen someone to exercise your medical power of attorney to make the final decision? A medical power of attorney (see Figure 11-3) is a document that is approved in most states and is becoming more and more accepted in medical circles. The original should be given to a lawyer, one copy should be given to a medical professional who attends you, and a copy should be given to at least one family member. These people can't ask you what you want once you're unconscious.

So far, 38 states and the District of Columbia have passed laws allowing residents to make such statements, even offering them direction if a court decision became necessary. However, the following states have not enacted such legislation: Kentucky, Massachusetts, Michigan, Minnesota, Nebraska, New Jersey, North Dakota, Ohio, Pennsylvania, Rhode Island, and South Dakota. For further information on living wills, contact Choice in Dying, 200 Varick Street, New York, New York 10014, (212) 366-5540.

POWER OF ATTORNEY

You've just received that coveted promotion, and it requires that you move to Florida. You make plans to sell your house and get a fresh start by buying a new house in your new tropical home. There's just one big problem: The real estate agent tells you that the market is soft, and it may take 6 months to sell your property—but within 2 months' time, you have to be in Florida.

The solution to this dilemma may be simpler than it seems. You can give your attorney, accountant, real estate broker, or brother your power of attorney to complete the contract for you. This rather uncomplicated legal document gives another person the right to act as your "agent" or "attorney-in-fact" when conducting fiscal affairs in your absence. In an agreement with your broker or attorney, you spell out all the terms and conditions for selling your current property, such as the amount of down payment, the contract terms, and the signature responsibilities during the process of closing and forwarding the funds. The advantages of this arrangement are clear. It saves you the time and expense of constant trips back and forth to your former residence for contract meetings and closings with buyers.

THE FLEXIBILITY FACTOR

Powers of attorney are very flexible and can be written to suit any situation—from selling your home or car to managing your personal affairs while you are away on sabbatical. The major advantage is that in case of a long-term illness or extended vacation, your attorney-in-fact gains fiduciary responsibilities to immediately conduct your business affairs as well as handle any unexpected business opportunities that may arise if you have furnished the appropriate instructions. There are different types of powers of attorney for different types of situations.

A general power of attorney allows your agent to conduct all financial matters, including the payment of bills, the handling of investments, the selling of property, and withdrawals from bank accounts. By signing this document, you are giving your agent unlimited power and must be absolutely sure that your friend, relative, spouse, or business manager is completely trustworthy. By not keeping a close eye on their trustees, a number of famous stars and sports figures such as the late boxer Joe Louis, Melba Moore, Flip Wilson, the late Redd Foxx, and Kareem Abdul Jabar lost their fortunes. You have to be absolutely certain that this person will not do anything that you wouldn't do and is always thinking of *your* best interest and not his or her own.

<table>
<tr><td>

INSTRUCTIONS

PRINT YOUR
NAME

PRINT NAME,
HOME ADDRESS,
AND TELEPHONE
NUMBER OF
YOUR PROXY

ADD PERSONAL
INSTRUCTIONS
(IF ANY)

© 1993
CHOICE IN DYING, INC.

</td><td>

NEW YORK
HEALTH CARE PROXY

(1) I, _____, hereby appoint:
(name)

_____
(name, home address and telephone number of proxy)

_____

as my health care agent to make any and all health care decisions for me, except to the extent that I state otherwise.

This Health Care Proxy shall take effect in the event I become unable to make my own health care decisions.

(2) Optional instructions: I direct my proxy to make health care decisions in accord with my wishes and limitations as stated below, or as he or she otherwise knows.

(Unless your agent knows your wishes about artificial nutrition and hydration [feeding tubes], your agent will not be allowed to make decisions about artificial nutrition and hydration.)

</td></tr>
</table>

Figure 11-3. Example of medical power of attorney.

PRINT NAME, HOME ADDRESS, AND TELEPHONE NUMBER OF YOUR ALTERNATE PROXY

(3) Name of substitute or fill-in proxy if the person I appoint above is unable, unwilling or unavailable to act as my health care agent.

_____

(name, home address and telephone number of alternate proxy)

_____

ENTER A DURATION OR A CONDITION (IF ANY)

(4) Unless I revoke it, this proxy shall remain in effect indefinitely, or until the date or condition I have stated below. This proxy shall expire (specific date or conditions, if desired): _____

_____

SIGN AND DATE THE DOCUMENT AND PRINT YOUR ADDRESS

(5) Signature _____ Date _____

Address _____

WITNESSING PROCEDURE

Statement by Witnesses (must be 18 or older)

I declare that the person who signed this document is personally known to me and appears to be of sound mind and acting of his or her own free will. He or she signed (or asked another to sign for him or her) this document in my presence. I am not the person appointed as proxy by this document.

YOUR WITNESSES MUST SIGN AND PRINT THEIR ADDRESSES

Witness 1 _____

Address _____

Witness 2 _____

Address _____

© 1993
CHOICE IN DYING, INC.

Courtesy of Choice In Dying   11/93
200 Varick Street, New York, NY 10014 1-800-989-WILL

PAGE 2

Figure 11-3. *(Cont.).*

IIIƎIII *Three kinds of people die poor: Those who are divorced, those who incur* IIIƎIII
debts, and those who move around too much.

SENEGALESE PROVERB

LOOKING FOR A LAWYER

There are two major problems you'll encounter when doing your estate planning. The first will be finding an African-American attorney who has the experience you seek. Over 65 percent of all African-American attorneys are specialists in criminal law, which is not surprising when you review the justice system; therefore many African-Americans may reject the idea of using black counsel and will be tempted to resort to "the white man's ice is colder" syndrome. The last decade has allowed more and more young African-Americans to attend law school and develop diverse backgrounds and experience which can provide the broader service you require. Make the effort to contact the local bar association or write or call the National Bar Association to find someone who can assist you.

The second problem will be the attitude of resistance many African-Americans have about paying fees for financial and legal services to other African-American professionals. The issues of respect, fear, distrust, and anxiety often steer us back into looking for the white professional who, it is incorrectly assumed, is more competent and knowledgeable and capable of rendering better services. Keep in mind that many African-American professionals have had to work twice as hard to get half the professional recognition they deserve for the services they can provide. You have a right to seek good and competent service for the dollars you will spend, but the attorney also has the right to be respected for his or her professional qualifications and paid fairly.

Before making an appointment with an attorney, it is perfectly acceptable for you to ask for references and get referrals from accountants and bankers. Make a list of the questions you need to have answered at the first appointment. For writing up the will and the trust, will the attorney charge you a flat fee or an hourly rate? How long will the process take? What information will be required? Will there be an additional fee for any changes or codicils that may have to be added later?

You have worked too many years to accumulate assets, struggled too hard to manage your affairs properly. Economic empowerment begins with you and your family. Personal financial well-being begins with the desire to preserve your assets and pass them on. Building a dynasty starts and grows one day at a time, one dollar at a time. It is up to you to create and follow a plan that works for you and the generations to come which are expecting to stand on your shoulders to move up the economic ladder.

‖≣‖   *We've got to decide if it's going to be this generation or never.*   ‖≣‖
DAISY BATES
Little Rock, Arkansas, 1957

CONCLUSION

"*It is time for every one of us to roll up our sleeves and put ourselves at the top of the commitment list.***"**

Marian Wright Edelman

If you have gotten this far in the book, then you have made a serious commitment to becoming a financially aware person and to learning how to control your own financial destiny. By now you should be aware that your personal financial goals and choices will also become the example for broader economic change within your community.

If you need some additional guidelines to follow, clip this list and put it up on the bathroom mirror.

TEN FINANCIAL RESOLUTIONS FOR AFRICAN-AMERICANS TO FOLLOW

1. Educate yourself about money. There is a whole world of possibilities and opportunities waiting for you, but you must look for them and set some realistic goals for achieving financial well-being. Begin with a personal finance magazine. Go to a free seminar. Attend a one-day workshop at a community college. Call an 800 number for some of the free literature that is available. It's up to you to find out what is so easily available for so little.

2. Get out of unnecessary debt. Live within your means and stop using credit cards to enhance your lifestyle. Credit cards are an unhealthy use of your life's energy. Borrowing is only useful when it supports an asset that is giving you a reasonable return on your time and your money.

3. Get adequate insurance, but don't overpay for it. You have worked too hard not to protect your property, your income, and your business. It is also impossible to pass on any assets to your heirs and leave your family intact without adequate health and life insurance.

4. Make a written plan to achieve your financial goals. They don't become real to you until you see them on paper and put a timetable to achieving them. Refer to them monthly, quarterly, annually; the same way your boss evaluates your professional performance on the job, you should evaluate your financial goals on a regular basis and make changes when your life situation changes.

5. Include savings in your monthly budget. If you don't put yourself on your own payroll, who will? Make yourself your number one creditor. You owe it to yourself to begin saving today—even if it begins with one dollar!

6. Use African-American professionals wherever possible. There are many accountants, doctors, lawyers, financial advisors, and other well-trained professionals available to help you achieve your financial goals. Start by giving them the opportunity to support you in your effort. They will probably work with you with a level of respect, sensitivity, intelligence, and awareness of your true feelings that you will not get from anyone else!

7. Contribute to every retirement plan available to you. In all likelihood, you will live much longer and be in better health than your parents and no one is going to take care of you the way you can do it for yourself. There is so much free information available to you about 401(k) plans, IRAs, SEPs, etc., all you have to do is look for it. Don't expect the federal government to rescue you when you're 80. Use time wisely and invest for that long-term comfort now.

8. Invest regularly. Start with $20 a month, and don't be afraid of the risk of the stock market. Starting small and staying in for the long haul is the only way to beat inflation. Join an investment club, or create your own DRIP program. Give a portion of that money to a black investment company if you wish, but get started now!

9. Adopt a positive attitude about money. The fears about financial well-being will not go away until you begin to change how you see yourself and examine the possibilities of change for yourself and your community. No one else is responsible for your situation but you, and when you begin to realize the strength in that, then you will accomplish a new sense of freedom, self-esteem, and profitability.

10. Stop procrastinating! Talking and thinking about change will not create change. Action is the only way to accomplish the goals you set for yourself. Take each step one day at a time, but get started!

|||≣||| *Education is our passport to the future, for tomorrow belongs to people who* |||≣|||
prepare for it today.

MALCOLM X

Appendix A

‖‖‖‖ ‖‖‖ ≡ ‖‖‖ ≡ ‖‖‖ ‖‖ ‖‖‖‖‖ ‖‖‖ ≡ ‖‖ ≡ ‖‖‖ ‖‖‖

FINANCIAL LEARNING LIST

"If it is to be, it is up to me."

Traditional saying

Here's how to conquer your fears and procrastination about making financial decisions. Knowledge of personal financial planning techniques can improve the use and enjoyment of your personal income. Reading one or more articles about personal money management over a period of time will make you familiar with a variety of financial topics and may be helpful in solving a present or future problem and keep you informed about changes in the economy, investment opportunities, and tax laws. The criteria for selection was quality and availability at newsstands and public libraries.

NEWSPAPERS

The New York Times. "Personal Finance" and "Investing" appear in the Sunday business section each week. Sunday's edition also has "Consumer Rates," which gives average current interest rates on mortgages, passbook savings, money-market funds, personal loans, and tax-exempt bonds. The Saturday *Times* often carries a useful column called "Your Money."

USA Today. "Taxtalk," "Business Travel," "The Economy," "Moneytalk," and "Real Estate" appear throughout the week in the *Money* section of this national daily paper.

The Wall Street Journal. "Your Money Matters" is a Friday column that is found on the front page of Section 3, "Money and Investing."

New York Daily News. The Sunday edition has a pull-out section on business including personal finance topics and investing.

Barron's. This weekly newspaper on investing summarizes the past week on Wall Street and includes articles on new stock issues, trends in

313

investing, and industry overviews as well as editorials by well-known financial columnist Alan Abelson.

Investor's Business Daily. Like *The Wall Street Journal,* this daily offers detailed charts, graphs, and industry reports on investing.

Many local and regional newspapers have personal finance sections and include nationally syndicated columnists such as Jane Bryant Quinn and Andrew Leckey.

MAGAZINES

Several magazines of general interest also provide financial columns and news about money issues. Choose one to subscribe to in the next year to broaden your financial knowledge.

GENERAL INTEREST MAGAZINES

American Woman. Has a bimonthly column "Jobs & Money."

Black Enterprise. Has a brief monthly "Moneywise" column on personal finance and occasionally in-depth money-management topics. Every April and October, this magazine is devoted to personal money management.

Family Life. Has a bimonthly column "Family Strategist" focusing on family financial issues.

Good Housekeeping. Provides a monthly question-and-answer column entitled "Your Money."

GQ. Has a monthly financial column "Money" that examines various issues on this subject.

Mademoiselle. Has a monthly question-and-answer column "Money."

McCall's. Has a monthly "Consumer News" column that focuses on personal finance matters.

New Woman. Prints regular monthly articles on financial topics and short items of current financial information. The October issue usually has a special section called "Career and Money News."

Newsweek/Family Circle. Publishes a regular biweekly column by Jane Bryant Quinn.

Parenting. Prints a monthly column "Your Money's Worth" that addresses money issues.

Self. Has a column "Money & Job Journal" that appears in its monthly issue.

Working Woman. Offers in-depth articles with a very personal approach, found in the monthly column "Life & Style: Money." Recent issues followed a couple for 6 months through a complete financial makeover in a financial workshop series.

FINANCIAL MAGAZINES AND NEWSLETTERS

Business Week. Offers a weekly Personal Business Department featuring a financial topic under the heading of "Smart Money." It also covers finance, economic analysis, and international business. 30 issues for $27.95.

Consumers Digest. Features a department called "Money Watch" which provides information on many different issues. It also offers special sections like "The Complete Guide to Mutual Funds." Six issues for $15.97.

Consumer Report. Devotes its monthly issues to personal finance and consumer issues. It offers a "Your Money" department, product updates, as well as regular financial features. A one year subscription costs $24.

Entrepreneur. Features a "Money Department" that examines various financial topics. A one year subscription costs $19.97.

Forbes. Offers advice from five columnists in the "Money and Investments" section of this biweekly magazine. Additional topics covered include management strategies, trends, computers/communications technology, and law and issues. 17 issues for $23.95.

Fortune. Offers a "Personal Fortune" Department examining a variety of financial topics. The April issue offers a special report on taxes. "Portfolio Talk," "Smart Spending," and "Investment Strategy" are regularly featured sections in this biweekly magazine. 20 issues cost $43.80.

Kiplinger's Personal Finance. Offers "How I did it" personal finance anecdotes and regular features on saving and investing, smart shopping, career changing, health and fitness, mutual funds, and financial technology in this monthly magazine. One year subscription costs $19.95.

Money. Published monthly, it provides useful personal finance tips and features as well as regularly covered topics such as "Smart Spending,"

"Idea of the Month," "Fund Watch," and a "Money Helps" question-and-answer column. 13 issues for $19.95.

Retire with MONEY. Is a monthly newsletter from the editors of MONEY discussing the steps to take now to build your wealth plan for the later years of financial well-being. Call toll free: 1-800-225-2002 for free sample issue. 12 issues for $29.95.

Smart Money. Is The Wall Street Journal Magazine of Personal Finance. It offers columns like "Me and My Money" as well as the regularly featured column "Ten Things," which discusses topics such as Ten Things Your Credit Card Company Won't Tell You. A one year subscription costs $15.

Worth. Has a Personal Adviser Department devoted to issues such as family finance, taxes, and banking. It also has regular features on investing strategies, mutual funds, and global markets, in addition to general business stories. One year subscription costs $14.97.

Your Money. Is a monthly magazine examining a variety of financial concerns, including how to save more and investment tips. 12 issues for $15.97.

BOOKS

GENERAL INFORMATION

Anderson, Claud. *Black Labor, White Wealth.* Baltimore, Duncan & Duncan, 1995.

Applegarth, Ginger. *The Money Diet.* New York, Penguin Books, 1995.

Berg, Adrienne G. *Your Wealth-Building Years: Financial Planning for 18-to-38-Year Olds.* New York, Newmarket Press, 1990.

Berger, Esther M. *Money Smart: Take the Fear Out of Financial Planning.* New York, Avon Books, 1993.

Berger, Esther M. *Money-Smart Divorce.* New York, Simon & Schuster, 1966.

Bodnar, Janet. *Kiplinger's Money Smart Kids (and Parents, Too!).* Washington, D.C., Kiplinger's Books, 1993.

Boston, Kelvin. *Smart Money Moves for African-Americans.* New York, Putnam, 1996.

Bowman, Linda. *Freebies and More for Folks over Fifty.* Chicago, Probus Publishing, 1991.

Briles, Judith. *Money Phases: The Six Financial Stages of a Woman's Life.* New York, Simon & Schuster, 1985.

Bryne, Bill. *Habits of Wealth.* New York, Berkley Books, 1992.

Chamblis, Darden H., Jr. *The Bank of America's Guide to Making the Most of Your Money.* New York, Dow Jones-Irwin, 1990.

Chilton, David. *The Wealthy Barber: Everyone's Common Sense Guide to Becoming Financially Independent.* Rocklin, California, Prima Publishing, 1996.

Collins, Victoria F., and Wall, Ginita. *Smart Ways to Save Money During and After Divorce.* Berkeley, California, Nolo Press, 1994.

Diamond, Ann B. *Fear of Finance: The Women's Money Workbook for Achieving Financial Self-Confidence.* New York, HarperCollins, 1994.

Dolan, Ken, and Dolan, Daria. *Smart Money.* New York, Berkley Books, 1990.

Dominguez, Joe, and Robin, Vicki. *Your Money or Your Life.* New York, Penguin Books, 1992.

Drew, Bonnie, and Drew Noel. *Fast Cash for Kids.* Hawthorne, New Jersey, Career Press Book, 1995.

Eisenberg, Richard. *The Money Book of Personal Finance.* New York, Warner Books, 1996.

Farrell, Paul B. *Investing Guide to the Net: Making Money On-line.* New York, John Wiley & Sons, 1996.

Forman, Norm. *Mind over Money: Curing Your Financial Headaches.* New York, Doubleday, 1987.

Gallagher, Stephanie. *Money Secrets the Pros Don't Want You to Know.* New York, American Management Association, 1995.

Gardner, David, and Gardner, Tom. *The Motley Fool Investment Guide.* New York, Simon & Schuster, 1996.

Godfrey, Neale S. *Money Doesn't Grow on Trees.* St. Louis, Missouri, Fireside Books, 1994.

Heady, Christy. *The Complete Idiot's Guide to Making Money on Wall Street.* Indianapolis, Indiana, Alpha Books, 1994.

Lewin, Elizabeth. *Financial Fitness for Newlyweds.* New York, Facts on File, 1984.

Lieberman, Annette. *Unbalanced Accounts.* Boston, Atlantic Monthly Press, 1987.

Lynch, Peter. *Learn to Earn.* New York, Simon & Schuster, 1995.

Lynch, Peter. *One Up on Wall Street.* New York, Penguin Books, 1990.

Malkiel, Burton. *A Random Walk down Wall Street.* New York, Norton, 1990.

Oliver, Melvin L., and Shapiro, Thomas M. *BLack Wealth/White Wealth.* New York, Routledge, 1995.

O'Neil, Terry R. *The Life Insurance Kit.* Chicago, Dearborn Financial Publishing, 1993.

Strayer, Robert. *Debt Free in Four Years.* Bayside, New York, Barclay House, 1995.

Travis, Dempsey. *Real Estate Is the Gold in Your Future.* Chicago, Urban Research Press, 1988.

Tyson, Eric. *Investing for Dummies.* San Mateo, California, IDG Books Worldwide, 1996.

Tyson, Eric. *Personal Finance for Dummies.* San Mateo, California, IDG Books Worldwide, 1994.

Van Caspel, Venita. *Money Dynamics for the 1990's.* New York, Simon & Schuster, 1988.

Weinstein, Grace. *Men, Women & Money.* New York, Signet, 1987.

Weiss, Geraldine, and Lowe, Janet. *Dividends Don't Lie: Finding Value in Blue Chip Stocks.* Chicago, Dearborn Financial Publishing, 1989.

Wolff, Michael. *Net Money: Your Guide to Personal Finance Revolution on the Information Highway.* New York, Random House Electronic Publishing, 1995.

MONEY ATTITUDES

Brown, Frederick S. *Money & Spirit.* Virginia Beach, Virginia, A.R.E. Press, 1995.

Foster, Richard J. *Money, Sex & Power: The Challenge of a Disciplined Life.* New York, Harper & Row, 1985.

Slater, Philip. *Wealth Addiction.* New York, E. P. Dutton, 1980.

Weinstein, Grace. *Men, Women & Money.* New York, Signet, 1987.

White, Shelby. *What Every Woman Should Know about Her Husband's Money.* New York, Random House, 1995.

MONEY MANAGEMENT

Applewhite, Richard C. *Clear Your Credit & Get Out of Trouble.* Sugar Land, Texas, JaCee Publishing, 1994.

Boroson, Warren. *The Ultimate Stock Picker's Guide.* New York, Times Mirror Higher Education Group, 1996.

Carlson, Charles B. *Buying Stocks Without a Broker.* New York, McGraw-Hill, 1992.

Case, Samuel. *The First Book of Investing.* Rocklin, California, Prima Publishing, 1994.

Dionisi, David J. *Perfect Money Planning.* Dallas, Texas, Taylor Publishing, 1995.

Dolan, Daria, and Dolan, Ken. *The Smart Money Family Financial Planner.* New York, Berkley Books, 1992.

Dorf, Richard C. *The New Mutual Fund Investment Advisor.* Chicago, Probus Publishing, 1991.

Dotto, Dave D. *How to Make Nothing but Money.* New York, Simon & Schuster, 1990.

Dover, Benjamin F. *Life after Debt.* Fort Worth, Texas, Equitable Media Services, 1993.

Dunnan, Nancy. *How to Invest from $50 to $5,000.* Bristol, Indiana, Cloverdale Press, 1995.

Gelb, Eric P. *Personal Budget Planner.* New York, Career Advancement Center, 1991.

Humphrey, Phyllis. *Wall Street on $20 a Month: How to Profit from an Investment Club.* New York, John Wiley & Sons, 1986.

McGee, Adolph. *How to Correct Your Own Credit!* New York, Goshen, 1988.

Meriwether, Crystal K. *The Record Keeper: The Workbook That Helps You Organize Your Life.* New York, Dembner Books, 1985.

Phillips, David T., and Wolfkiel, Bill S. *Estate Planning Made Easy.* Chicago, Dearborn Financial Publishing, 1994.

Pollan, Stephen M. *How to Borrow Money.* New York, Simon & Schuster, Cornerstone Library, 1983.

Rosenberg, Jerome R. *Managing Your Own Money.* New York, Newsweek Books, 1985.

Thomsett, Michael C. *Getting Started in Bonds.* New York, John Wiley & Sons, 1991.

Wall Street Journal Guide to Understanding Money & Markets. New York, Prentice-Hall, 1989.

Weinstein, Grace W. *The Lifetime Book of Money Management.* Detroit, Michigan, Visible Ink, 1993.

RETIREMENT

Benna, R. Theodore. *Escaping the Coming Retirement Crisis.* Colorado Springs, Colorado, Pinon Press, 1995.

Brenner, Lynn. *Building Your Nest Egg with Your 401(k).* Washington, Connecticut, Investors Press, 1995.

Coyle, Joseph S. *How to Retire Young and Rich.* New York, Warner Books, 1996.

Kaplan, Lawrence J. *Retiring Right.* New York, Avery Publishing Group, 1996.

Newman, Joseph. *Teach Your Wife to Be a Widow.* Washington, D.C., U.S. News & World Report, 1984.

Orman, Suze. *You've Earned It, Don't Lose It: Mistakes You Can't Afford to Make When You Retire.* New York, Newmarket Press, 1994.

Ottenburg, Robert K. *Kiplinger's Retire & Thrive.* Washington, D.C., Kiplinger's Washington Editors, 1995.

TAXES

Crouch, Holmes F. *Keeping Good Records.* Saratoga, California, Allyear Tax, 1995.

O'Leary, Timothy. *The Tax Realities of Divorce.* Gahanna, Ohio, R. J. Publishing, 1986.

WILLS

Clifford, Denis. *The Simple Will Book.* Berkeley, California, Nolo Press, 1995.

VIDEOS

The Beardstown Ladies Cookin' Up Profits on Wall Street. Learn about investing from the investment club members who wowed Wall Street and also get tips on making a mean apple pie. (60 minutes) $29.98

Meg Green's Financial Workout. Simple exercises and basic concepts to get your financial life in shape with no-nonsense workout tips. (59 minutes) $49.98

Money and Marriage. Probes the key financial issues in establishing this lifelong partnership and the process of managing money together. (50 minutes) $24.98

Preparing Your Home to Sell. Presents easy ways to help you enhance the value and appearance of your home to make it attractive to potential buyers. (45 minutes) $19.98

Sell It Yourself. Step-by-step advice on how you can increase your profits by selling your home yourself. (30 minutes) $29.98

Stock Market: Understanding the Basics. Discusses what stocks are, why you should buy them, and how to analyze and track them. (110 minutes) $49.98

Understanding Wall Street. Explains how the stock market works and how to buy and sell stocks and bonds. (110 minutes) $49.98

An Economic Primer. Write to:
Geanine D. Thompson
Thomson McKinnon Securities, Inc.
Public Relations—17th floor
Financial Square
New York, New York 10005
(212) 804-6522
(20 minutes) $19.95

Your Personal Financial Guide to Success, Power, and Security. The only personal finance video that focuses on the African-American financial experience. Contact:

In the Black Productions, Inc.
P.O. Box 1229
New York, New York 10185
(212) 864-0318
$29.95 plus $4 shipping

The Stock Selection Guide Video
National Association Investors Corporation
P.O. Box 220
Royal Oak, Michigan 48068

FOR THE COMPUTER CROWD

YOUR PC AND THE INFORMATION SUPERHIGHWAY

Women's Wire. This on-line service gives women the opportunity to post questions to its financial forum, "Women & Investing." The forum is primarily educational. The on-line service is $9.95 a month. For more information, call (415) 378-6500.

SOFTWARE PACKAGES

Kiplinger's CA—Simply Money. It shows you in three simple steps how to balance your checkbook and your credit card statements. Also, it can forecast annual budget expenses and update prices on your investments. It's available for both DOS and Windows. (800) 225-5224.

Quicken. This package, available from Intuit, provides you with features to pay your bills, reconcile many types of financial accounts, and create financial records and a custom-tailored investment portfolio. (800) 624-8742. Intuit has also created an Investor Insight program which gives historical data on over 5000 stocks. For a 30-day trial, call (800) 624-2106.

Street Smart. It's available through Charles Schwab & Co. and is used primarily for creating and monitoring your investment portfolio. In addition, it allows you to keep up with current financial news and obtain research reports from investment analysts. (800) 334-4455.

Mortgage Analyzer. This software helps you determine whether or not you can qualify for a mortgage or refinance your mortgage and provides you with information about the different types of mortgages available and how they affect your taxes. (801) 295-1890.

Buy or Rent. It analyzes for you, based on your tax rate and housing costs, whether or not to buy a home. Try it before you apply for a mortgage. (800) 289-6773.

PC Life Services. Everything you ever wanted to know about your insurance needs is answered with this software. It explains the different types of insurance products available. (212) 408-0529.

Scudder Tuition Builder Kit. It estimates how much college costs will be in the year you send your child to college and tailors an investment program to meet those costs. (800) 255-2470.

College Cost Explorer. This financial software program allows you to access a database of thousands of private sources of scholarships, financial aid packages, and loans. (800) 323-7155.

TAX PLANNING

Kiplinger TaxCut. This is easy-to-use software that not only lets you fill out your federal and state returns but also project the tax consequences of your actions before you take them. (800) 365-1546.

Turbo Tax. It will print out your completed federal and state tax returns after you complete a number of tax preparation exercises. This software package lets you file your return electronically, too. (800) 964-1040.

RETIREMENT PLANNING

Harvest Time. This software package will help you calculate how much you'll need to save toward retirement. Also, it tracks different types of retirement-oriented investment products. (800) 397-1456.

T. Rowe Price Retirement Planning Kit. It allows you to estimate your retirement expenses and figure out how much you're going to need to save based on current earnings and savings. (800) 638-5660.

Similar software programs are available from Vanguard (800) 876-1840 and Fidelity (800) 457-1768. Each program costs from $15 to $17.

ESTATE PLANNING

Home Lawyer. User-friendly software, this package allows you to write your own will, a residential lease, an employment agreement, and other frequently used legal documents. (800) 288-MECA.

Willmaker. It takes you through a step-by-step process of writing a will. You can also create different types of trusts as you are working on your estate plan. (800) 992-NOLO.

It's Legal. This software provides power-of-attorney forms, estate planning worksheets, different types of wills, and a living trust. (800) 223-6925.

Appendix B

||||| |||| ||||| |||| ||||||||||| ||| ||| ||| ||| |||| |||||

WHERE TO WRITE OR CALL FOR MORE INFORMATION

"To those incurable optimists among you, the age of miracles is over. The age of slogans is over. The age of progress without a plan is over. The age of studying without a strategy, running without a reason, and flying without a plane is over. The waters of reaction are not going to turn into the wine of justice. Not today. Not tomorrow. Not ever, if we do not come together."

Richard Hatcher, mayor of Gary, Indiana,
March 16, 1974

CREDIT

For a list of inexpensive bank credit cards, write to or call:

BankCard Holders of America
524 Branch Drive
Salem, Virginia 24153
(540) 389-5445

To find a good debt counseling agency in your area:

Consumer Credit Counseling Service
National Foundation for Consumer Credit
8701 Georgia Avenue, Suite 507
Silver Spring, Maryland 20910
(301) 589-5600 or (800) 388-2227

INSURANCE

James Hunt has written a helpful publication called "How to Save Money on Life Insurance," which can be obtained from:

National Insurance Consumer Organization
121 N. Payne Street
Alexandria, Virginia 22314
(703) 549-8050

These three agencies will give you comparable insurance rate quotes:

Insurance Quote Services
3200 N. Dobson Road
Building C
Chandler, Arizona 85224
(800) 972-1104

Insurance Information Inc.
134 Middle Street
Lowell, Massachusetts 01852
(800) 472-5800

SelectQuote Insurance Services
140 Second Street
San Francisco, California 94105
(800) 343-1985

Lost a policy or want free brochures on how to buy insurance and annuities? Contact:

American Council of Life Insurance
1001 Pennsylvania Avenue, N.W.
Washington, D.C. 20004-2599
(202) 624-2000

If you are a military officer or part of a military family, you have access to an insurance company that offers some of the best rates available:

USAA
9800 Fredericksburg Road
USAA Building
San Antonio, Texas 78288
(800) 531-8100

MONEY MANAGEMENT

These money-management booklets:

"Your Financial Plan"

"Managing Your Credit"

"Children and Money Management"

"Your Food Dollar"

"Your Housing Dollar"

"Your Travel Dollar"

"Your Savings & Investment Dollar"

"Your Insurance Dollar"

can be obtained, at $1 each, from:

Money Management Institute
Household Financial Services
2700 Sanders Road
Prospect Heights, Illinois 60070

RETIREMENT

For $2, you can get "A Guide to Understanding Your Pension Plan" if you write to:

Pension Rights Center
918 16th Street, N.W., Suite 704
Washington, D.C. 20006

For the free booklet "Know Your Pension Rights," contact:

American Association of Retired Persons
601 E Street, N.W.
Washington, D.C. 20049
(202) 326-4000 or (800) 424-3410

To get a free copy of "Your Pension: Things You Should Know about Your Pension Plan," write:

> Public Affairs Department
> Pension Benefit Guaranty Corporation
> 2020 K Street, N.W.
> Washington, D.C. 20006

To order "Consumer's Guide to Long-Term Health Care," write:

> Health Insurance Association of America
> P.O. Box 4155
> Washington, D.C. 20018

For at-home health care, call:

> National Association of Home Care
> Visiting Nurses Association
> (800) 452-2547

To find out how much social security you will get, ask for "Request for Earnings Benefit Estimate Statement"—Form SSA-7004. Contact:

> Social Security Administration
> Department of Health and Human Services
> Baltimore, Maryland 21235
> (800) 772-1213

Need a social security number for your child? Call the Social Security Administration at (800) 772-1213.

INVESTING

> *Shopping for a Better World.* Lists 1300 household products that do not pollute the environment, meet affirmative-action quotas, and do not use animal testing. Contact:

> Council on Economic Priorities
> 30 Irving Place
> New York, New York 10003
> (212) 420-1133

Investing for a Better World. Monthly newsletter on socially responsible investments. Call or write:

Franklin's Insights
711 Atlantic Avenue
Boston, Massachusetts 02111
(800) 548-5684

Better Investing. Monthly small investor's magazine for members only. Write:

National Association of Investors Corporation
1515 E. Eleven Mile Road
Royal Oak, Michigan 48068
(810) 583-6242

Gemline Recovery Service. Offered by the American Gemological Society, this service povides documentation on authenticity and testing of gemstones. Call (212) 704-0727. You can also obtain a free brochure on investing in gems from the Society.

If you think a jeweler has cheated you, write:

Jewelers Vigilance Committee, Inc.
1180 Avenue of the Americas
New York, New York 10036

TAX HELP

To order tax forms, call (800) 829-1040. This number provides 24-hour recorded announcements of over 100 topics and a complete general guide to tax forms and filing procedures for tax information.

To find a tax preparer, contact:

National Association of Enrolled Agents
16952 Ventura Boulevard
Encino, California 91316

National Association of Black Accountants
7249-A Hanover Parkway
Greenbelt, Maryland
(301) 474-NABA (phone)
(301) 474-3114 (fax)

DISCOUNT INVESTMENT BROKERS

Bull & Bear (800) 262-5800

Charles Schwab (800) 222-5321

Fidelity Investments (800) 544-6666

Quick & Reilly (800) 999-8924, ext. 2711

Jack White (800) 431-3500

Waterhouse Securities (800) 550-3535

If your brokerage firm goes out of business, write to:

Securities Investor Protection Corporation
900 17th Street, N.W., Suite 800
Washington, D.C. 20006
(202) 223-8400

If you have a complaint against your broker, call the National Association of Securities Dealers at (202) 728-8000 or write to:

Office of Consumer Affairs and Information Services
Securities and Exchange Commission
450 5th Street, N.W., Room 2111
Washington, D.C. 20549

If you want the SEC's free brochures "What Every Investor Should Know" and "Investigate before You Invest," write:

The SEC Publications Section
Public Reference Branch Stop 1-2
Washington, D.C. 20549

GENERAL FINANCIAL INFORMATION: PAMPHLETS TO WRITE FOR

Many of these are free. Include a stamped, self-addressed, legal-size envelope.

To get a copy of "Consumer Handbook on Adjustable Rate Mortgages," write to any Federal Reserve Board office (12 regional locations) or ask at your local bank for the address nearest you.

For "Helping Stabilize Budgets and Lives" and "When Tragedy Is a Stack of Bills ...," write to:

> Budget and Credit Counseling Service
> 55 Fifth Avenue
> New York, New York 10014

To obtain "Everybody's Money Answers Your Home Equity Loan Questions," write to:

> The Credit Union National Association
> Public Relations Department
> P.O. Box 431
> Madison, Wisconsin 53701

To order "How to Read an Annual Report, Power of the Printed Word," contact:

> International Paper Co.
> Department 8
> P.O. Box 900
> Elmsford, New York 10523

For a copy of "Ideas to Help You Manage Money," write to:

> Investor's Diversified Services
> IDS Tower, Department 3359
> Minneapolis, Minnesota 55402

For a free copy of "Instruments of the Money Market," write to:

> Federal Reserve Bank of Richmond
> 701 Byrd Street
> Richmond, Virginia 23219

To get a free copy of a bibliography on investment, write:

> Brooklyn Public Library
> Business Library
> 280 Cadman Plaza West
> Brooklyn, New York 11201

For $4 total or $1 each, you can order these pamphlets:

"The New York Stock Exchange"

"Bonds and Preferred Stocks"

"Convertible Securities"

"The Questions to Ask before You Buy Stocks"

by writing to:

New York Stock Exchange, Inc.
Publication Section
11 Wall Street
New York, New York 10005

To get a free copy of "The Smart Investor's Guide to Successful Money Management," write:

Merrill Lynch
225 Liberty Plaza
New York, New York 10080

For a free copy of "A Translation: Turning Investment-ese into Investment Ease" and "What Is a Mutual Fund?" write:

Investment Company Institute
1600 M Street, N.W.
Washington, D.C. 20036

You can obtain "Tax Exempt Unit Investment Trusts: An Investor's Guide" from:

Public Securities Association
One World Trade Center
New York, New York 10048
(212) 466-1900

To get "What Everyone Should Know about Consumer Banking," write:

New York State Bankers Association
485 Lexington Avenue
New York, New York 10017

For $1, you can get "Your Guide to Mutual Funds without Sales Charges" from:

No Load Mutual Fund Association, Inc.
Straus Association, Inc.
655 3rd Avenue
New York, New York 10017

For 75 cents each, you can order "What You Should Know about Probate" and "About the Executor" from:

National Resource Center for Consumers of Legal Services
1444 I Street, N.W., 8th floor
Washington, D.C. 20005

"Probate: A Practical Guide for Settling an Estate" is published by HALT, an organization created to limit the need for lawyers. Membership is $15. Write to:

HALT
1319 F Street, N.W., Suite 300
Washington, D.C. 20005

Looking for a certified financial planner? Call or write:

The Institute of Certified Financial Planners
Two Denver Highlands
10065 E. Harvard Avenue, Suite 320
Denver, Colorado 80231-5942
(800) 242-PLAN

International Association of Financial Planning
Two Concourse Parkway, Suite 800
Atlanta, Georgia 30328

TOP 22 MUTUAL FUND FAMILIES

These are by no means the only mutual funds that you should consider for your investments. The ones listed here have all been in the business of managing money successfully for at least 10 years—some more than 50 years.

Alliance Capital Management ($250 minimum, load)
(800) 227-4618

Van Kampen–American Capital Incorporated ($500 minimum, load)
(800) 421-5666

American Funds Group ($250 minimum on some funds; $1000 on others, load)
(800) 421-4120

Benham Management Corporation ($1000 minimum, no load)
(800) 472-3389

Berger Funds Group ($250 minimum, no load)
(800) 333-1001

Calvert Management Group ($1000 minimum, Ariel Fund, $2000 minimum, load) (socially responsible investments)
(800) 368-2748

Colonial Management Associates ($1000 minimum, load)
(617) 426-3750 or (800) 345-6611

Delaware Group ($25 minimum on stock funds, $1000 minimum on government funds, load)
(215) 988-1333 or (800) 523-4640

Dreyfus Corp. ($2500 minimum, load on some stock funds)
(800) 648-9048

Fidelity (minimum varies from $500 on some funds for IRAs to $2500 on others, load on some funds)
(617) 523-1919 or (800) 544-8888

Kemper Financial Services ($1000 minimum, load)
(800) 621-1048

Keystone Custodian Funds ($250 stock funds, $1000 bond funds, load)
(617) 621-6100 or (800) 343-2898

Massachusetts Financial Services ($1000 minimum, load)
(800) 637-2929

Montgomery Funds ($1000 minimum, no load)
(800) 572-3863, ext. 114

Neuberger & Berman Mgt. ($500 minimum, Partners Fund; $1000 others, no load)
(800) 877-9700

Oppenheimer Management Corp. ($1000 minimum, load)
(800) 525-7048

Phoenix Investment Counsel ($500 minimum, load)
(800) 243-0436

Putnam Management Co. ($500 minimum, load)
(617) 482-1400 or (800) 225-1581

T. Rowe Price Associates ($1000 stock funds; $2000 government funds, no load)
(301) 547-2308 or (800) 541-8462

Franklin-Templeton Investment Group ($500 minimum, load)
(813) 823-8712 or (800) 342-5236

Twentieth Century Investors ($1 minimum! no load)
(816) 531-5575 or (800) 345-2021

Vanguard Advisors, LP (varies from $1500 to $3000, no load)
(800) 962-5102

USEFUL 800 NUMBERS

CREDIT CARD NUMBERS

To report lost or stolen cards, call:

American Express (800) 528-2121; cash emergency locations (800) CASH-NOW
Diner's Club, (800) 234-6377
Discover Card, (800) 347-2683
MasterCard, (800) 826-2181
Visa, (800) 336-8472
Chevron, (800) 243-8766
Phillip, (800) 331-0961
Shell, (800) 331-3703
AT&T, (800) 225-5288
Sprint, (800) 877-4646

MAJOR SERVICE AND APPLIANCE MANUFACTURERS

Apple Computer, (800) 538-9696
Atlas Van Lines, (800) 457-3705

Avon Products, (800) 445-2866
Carrier Air Conditioning, (800) 227-7437
Cuisinart, (800) 243-8540
Eastman Kodak, (800) 242-2424
Electrolux, (800) 892-5678
Frigidaire Appliances, (800) 451-7007
General Electric, (800) 626-2000
Gibson Appliances, (800) 458-1445
Kelvinator, (800) 323-7773
Polaroid, (800) 343-5000; in Massachusetts, (617) 577-2000
Sunbeam Oster, (800) 597-5978
Tappan, (800) 537-5530
Texas Instruments, (800) 842-2737
United Van Lines, (800) 325-3870
Westinghouse, (800) 245-0600
Whirlpool, (800) 253-1301

CAR-SERVICE PROBLEMS

AAMCO Transmission, (800) 523-0401
Meineke Discount Muffler, (800) 275-5200
Midas Muffler, (800) 621-0144
Audi, (800) 822-AUDI
Buick, (800) 521-7300
Chevrolet, (800) 222-1020
Nissan, (800) 647-7261
Peugeot, (800) 345-5549
Pontiac, (800) 762-2737
Toyota, (800) 331-4331

MISCELLANEOUS NUMBERS

U.S. Savings Bonds, (800) US BONDS

To order postage stamps by phone, call (800) STAMPS-24. This number provides 24-hour "charge it" on Visa or MasterCard ($3 service charge).

For student loan problems, call:

Federal Student Aid Information, (800) 433-3243
Student Aid Funds, (800) LOAN-USA
Nellie Mae Loans, (800) EDU-LOAN

GLOSSARY

Accumulation plan   A plan for the systematic accumulation of mutual fund shares through periodic investments and reinvestment of income dividends and capital gains distributions.

Adjustable rate mortgage (ARM)   A mortgage with an interest rate tied to a financial index, such as the 6-month Treasury bill rate, that can go up or down at specific intervals.

Adjusted gross income   Gross income, reduced by allowable adjustments, before calculation of federal income tax. The deductions from gross income that determine adjusted gross income are called *above the line* deductions.

Administrator   An administrator is a person appointed by the court to settle an estate.

Amortization   The reduction of the principal of a loan by regular payments. In general, a method for reducing debt or for recovering the cost of intangible assets. This includes such practices as depreciation, depletion, prepaid expenses, and deferred charges.

Annuitant   The person who has a contract with a life insurance company to receive periodic payments for a specific number of years, or perhaps for life.

Annuity   A contract sold by life insurance companies that guarantees the purchaser fixed or variable future payments, usually upon retirement. Earnings grow tax-deferred within the annuity until the contract begins paying out.

Assets   Something of value. Fixed or permanent assets include buildings, land, and machinery; liquid assets are cash or investments that can be easily converted into cash; intangible assets, such as patents, goodwill, and copyrights, have no physical existence but are worth money.

Averages   Various ways of measuring the trend of stocks listed on exchanges. Formulas, some very absolute, have been devised to compensate for stock splits and stock dividends and thus give continuity to the average. In the case of the Dow Jones Industrial Average, the prices of the 30 stocks are totaled and then divided by a figure that is intended to compensate for past stock splits and stock dividends and that is changed from time to time.

Back-end load   The redemption fee charged when a shareholder withdraws or redeems a mutual fund's shares; typically 1 percent.

Balanced mutual fund A fund whose objective is to minimize risk while obtaining high returns through a portfolio of common and preferred stocks as well as bonds.

Balloon clause A clause in an installment loan contract calling for a final payment substantially larger than the earlier payments.

Balloon payment or note A loan in which both principal and interest must be paid in a lump sum upon maturity, that is, at the end of the loan period.

Basis point One hundredth of one percentage point. When interest rates rise 25 basic points, they move up one-fourth of one percentage point.

Bear market A declining stock market.

Beta A technical analyst's estimate of how much a stock price will react to the volatile changes in the stock market. A beta of 1.00 means the stock's price is expected to fluctuate along with the Standard & Poor's 500, whereas a stock with a beta under 1.00 would fluctuate less than the market, and one with a beta over 1.00 would fluctuate more.

Bid and asked price The *bid* is the highest price a prospective buyer will pay for a security; the *asked* is the lowest price at which a seller will sell a security.

Big Board A popular term for the New York Stock Exchange, Inc.

Binder A receipt for money paid to secure the future right to purchase real estate, in accordance with terms already agreed to by buyer and seller.

Blue-chip stock A high quality stock of a financially sound, well-known corporation whose shares are widely held by individual investors and institutions.

Blue-sky laws A popular name for laws enacted by various states to protect the public against securities frauds. The term is believed to have originated when a judge ruled that a particular stock had about the same value as a patch of blue sky.

Bond An IOU or certificate representing debt issued by a corporation, municipality, or the federal government. The issuer promises to pay back investors (lenders) the full loan amount (known as the face value), at a stated time (called the maturity date). In addition, the issuer pays lenders an annual fixed rate of interest (known as the coupon rate) at regular intervals, usually every 6 months.

Bond fund A mutual fund invested completely in bonds.

Bond ratings A system used by two independent services, Moody's and Standard & Poor's, for grading the financial condition of corporations and municipalities issuing bonds. Aaa or AAA are the highest ratings, while D indicates the issuer has defaulted on its financial obligations.

Book value The value of a company found by subtracting total liabilities from total assets. It is also known as shareholder's equity because it theoretically indicates a company's worth if its assets were sold, its debts paid off, and the net proceeds distributed to shareholders. It is used to identify undervalued companies.

Bull market An advancing stock market.

Buy order   An order placed with a stockbroker to purchase a specific stock, bond, option, or commodity at the mart (that is, at the best price available) or at another specified price.

Cafeteria plan   A written qualified plan under which all employee participants may choose among two or more benefits consisting of cash and statutory nontaxable benefits.

Call   An option to buy 100 shares of a stock at a certain price for a stated period of time. Calls are purchased in anticipation of a stock going up in price.

Callable   Refers to a bond or preferred stock that can be bought back from the investor by the issuer before the maturity date. Precise call dates must be stated in the offering prospectus.

Cash value   The dollar amount you may borrow against a life insurance policy. The amount increases over time as dividends and premiums accumulate.

Certificate   The actual piece of paper that is evidence of ownership of stock in a corporation. Loss of a certificate may cause, at the least, a great deal of inconvenience.

Churning   Illegal and excessive buying and selling of securities by a commission-hungry stockbroker.

Closed-end fund   An investment company whose funds are pooled for common investment, and whose shares are bought and sold on a stock exchange or over the counter. It's called "closed-end" because the number of shares is fixed.

Collateral   Securities or other property pledged by a borrower to secure repayment of a loan.

Commercial paper   Short-term loans, like a postdated check. These promissory notes are issued by "well-known" corporate borrowers and accepted by large banks or brokerage houses to meet corporate cash needs. Most have varying maturity periods, from 30 to 180 days. Most of these notes are bought by money-market funds.

Commission   The basic fee paid to and earned by a broker for buying and selling securities at your request or to a real estate agent for helping you buy or sell property.

Compound interest   Interest earned on the principal and on interest already earned.

Confirmation   A written explanation of the terms of a trade in securities that is legally required to be provided by a broker or dealer to his or her customer or to another broker or dealer.

Convertible   A bond, debenture, or preferred share that may be exchanged by the owner for common stock or another security, usually of the same company, in accordance with the terms of the issue.

Coupon   The interest rate paid on a debt security, such as a bond. The coupon is set when the security is issued and remains the same until maturity. An 8 percent coupon on a $1000 principal bond would pay $80 annually.

Current ratio   Current assets divided by current liabilities. This ratio indicates a company's ability to pay its current debts. In general, a company with a small inventory that regularly collects accounts receivable can operate with a lower current ratio than a company whose cashflow is less predictable.

Cushion bond   A callable high-coupon bond that sells at a slight premium. Its above-average yield protects or *cushions* it against a decline in price and rising interest rates.

Custodial account   A bank or brokerage account in which the assets are controlled by a custodian rather than by the owner. Custodial accounts, often set up for young people under the Uniform Gift to Minors Act, are also used for people unable to handle their own finances.

Cyclical stock   The stock of a firm whose profits are greatly influenced by cyclical changes in the economy. For example, when the economy is strong, housing and automobile stocks perform well.

Date of record   The date on which a shareholder must own a stock in order to receive its dividend. For example, a company's directors may declare a dividend on September 1, payable on October 1 to all shareholders of record as of September 15. It takes five business days after you buy a stock to become the owner of record.

Day of deposit to day of withdrawal   The time during which interest is earned on a bank account balance, starting from the day funds are deposited up until they are withdrawn.

Day order   A customer's order to buy or sell a security. This order automatically expires at the end of the trading day on which it is placed.

Debt-to-equity ratio   The ratio used to determine a company's solvency. It can be calculated in several ways: total liabilities divided by stockholders' equity, or long-term debt plus preferred stock divided by total stockholders' equity. A 1:2 ratio means liabilities are half of stockholders' equity.

Deep-discount bond   A bond that sells well below face value (often 20 percent or more) because of its low coupon rate or low credit rating. The low rate also makes it less likely to be called than bonds paying higher rates.

Defensive stocks   Those that resist stock market declines, such as electric utility, food, and supermarket stocks. During bull markets, these stocks tend to rise less quickly than more cyclical stocks.

Discretionary account   A brokerage account in which the customer gives the stockbroker the right to buy and sell securities without consulting him or her. The amount of discretion can be full or limited.

Diversification   The spreading of investments among different companies in different fields. Another type of diversification is also offered by the securities of many individual companies because of the wide range of activities.

Dividend reinstatement plan (DRIP)   A system that allows shareholders to automatically reinvest their dividends in additional shares of the same company's stock.

Dollar-cost averaging   The investment of a fixed amount of money at regular intervals, typically monthly, in the same stock or mutual fund. As a result, more shares are purchased when the price is down and fewer when the price is up.

Double taxation   The federal government taxes corporation profits once as corporate income; any part of the profits distributed as dividends to stockholders may be taxed again as income to the recipient stockholder.

Dow Jones Industrial Average   The most popular means of judging the performance of the overall stock market. It measures the price movement of 30 blue-chip stocks traded on the New York Stock Exchange. The Dow is quoted in points and eighths, not dollars.

Earnings per share   A company's net income divided by the number of shares outstanding. It indicates the amount of income a company has, on a per-share basis, to pay dividends and reinvest in itself. A useful tool for comparing the financial condition of companies.

Equity   The ownership interest of common and preferred stockholders in a company. Also refers to excess of value of securities over the debit balance in a margin account. Also, the value of a property that remains after all liens and other charges against the property are paid. A property owner's equity generally consists of his or her monetary interest in the property in excess of the mortgage indebtedness. In the case of a long-term mortgage, the owner's equity builds up quite gradually during the first several years because the bulk of each monthly payment is applied, not to the principal amount of the loan, but to the interest.

Escrow   Money, property, or securities held separately (typically by a third party) until the conditions of a contract are met.

Estate tax   Tax imposed by the federal government (and by some state governments) on the taxable estate of a person who has died.

Excess liability insurance   A policy that protects against loss in excess of coverage provided by another insurance contract.

Ex-dividend   Literally means without dividend. The ex-dividend date refers to a business day before the *date of record* (see above). Investors who buy a stock after the ex-dividend date are not entitled to the most recent dividend.

Executor/Executrix   The person named by the originator of a will to carry out his or her final instructions for the disposal of the estate.

Face value   Also known as par value, the value or principal amount of a bond, note, or mortgage, as stated on the certificate. Although bonds fluctuate in price after they are issued, the face value is the amount that will be paid upon maturity, along with accrued interest.

Floor   The huge trading area of a stock exchange where stocks and bonds are bought and sold. Also, the minimum amount of a transaction cost.

Fundamental analyses   A method of evaluating a stock's likely performance by studying the company's balance sheet, income statement, and other financial measures to determine its basic value. Fundamentalists believe that a stock's price movement is determined by current and future earnings trends, industry outlook, and management's expertise.

Futures contract   An agreement to buy or sell a quantity of a commodity or a financial instrument (such as a foreign currency) at a given price on a particular date. The contract buyer is obligated to purchase the underlying commodity and the seller to sell, unless the contract is sold to someone else before settlement date.

Ginnie Mae or GNMA (Government National Mortgage Association)   A government corporation that buys and repackages mortgages for sale. GNMA certificates, backed by the association and representing interest in a pool of mortgages, are sold in units of $25,000 to institutions and investors. As homeowners make monthly mortgage payments, a part of the principal and interest is passed through to investors. *Caution:* The rate of repayment is uncertain.

Holographic will   One written entirely in the handwriting of the testator. In many states such a will is not recognized unless it is published, declared, and witnessed as required by statute for other written wills.

Index fund   A mutual fund whose portfolio matches that of a stock market index such as the S&P 500. The fund's performance then reflects that of the overall market.

Interest-sensitive stock   A stock that moves in the opposite direction of interest rates—up when rates decline and down when rates rise.

Joint and survivor annuity   An arrangement whereby the owner of the annuity elects to have payments continue to another person after the owner's death.

Joint tenancy   A form of co-ownership whereby each joint tenant has an undivided interest in the whole property. When one joint tenant dies, his or her interest passes to the surviving joint tenant(s). The last surviving joint tenant obtains title to the entire property.

Junk bond   A high-risk, high-yield corporate or municipal bond that is rated BB or lower by Standard & Poor's, or Ba or lower by Moody's. Issued by companies with questionable financial strength, with short track records, or as a means of financing a corporate takeover.

Leading economic indicators   A phrase, often heard in discussing the financial markets, used to identify specific statistics for measuring changes and growth in the U.S. economy. These indicators are studied as they change on a weekly, monthly, or quarterly basis. They are:

- *Prime rate.* The bank interest rate charged to the best corporate borrowers.

- *Discount rate.* The rate at which the Federal Reserve Bank lends funds to banks.

- *3-month T-bills.* Government notes auctioned weekly.

- *6-month T-bills.* Government notes auctioned weekly.

- *10-year T-bills.* Government notes sold at quarterly auctions.

- *30-year T-bills.* Government notes sold at quarterly auctions.

- *Consumer price index.* The average cost of a standard set of goods, such as food, clothing, cars, and housing expenses, determined by the Department of Labor, and measured monthly, quarterly, and annually.

- *Money supply M2.* The circulation of cash in the banking and investing systems.

- *Dow Jones Industrials.* A stock market index of 65 major stocks.

- *Standard & Poor's 500.* A stock market index of 500 publicly traded companies.

- *GNP (gross national product).* The sum total of goods and services and their growth in a year's time in the U.S. economy.

- *Business inventory.* The increase or decrease in products stored, ordered, or shipped as supply and demand grows or declines.

- *Gold.* The fluctuation of prices in various markets around the world; the daily price is usually set in London.

Level premium insurance Insurance in which the yearly premium is the same over the life of the policy.

Leverage The use of borrowed funds to increase the return on an investment.

Limit order An order to buy or sell a stock or other financial instrument at a specific price. If the price or limit is not reached, there is no trade. A limit order to sell is usually set above the current market price, whereas a limit order to buy is set below the market price.

Limited partnership A business organization made up of a general partner, who manages the project, and a number of limited partners, or investors, whose liability for the business's debts is limited to the dollar amount they invest. Limited partnerships typically finance projects in real estate, oil and gas, equipment leasing, the theater, and movies.

Liquidity   Refers to assets that can easily be converted into cash or cash equivalents without significant loss. Money-market funds, most bonds, and stocks with a large number of outstanding shares possess liquidity.

Load fund   A mutual fund with a sales charge (typically 8.5 percent), sold through a stockbroker, financial planner, or mutual fund salesperson. A no-load fund, one without a sales charge or load, is sold directly by the fund.

Lump-sum distribution   The complete distribution of benefits from a pension or profit-sharing plan in a single year.

Management fee   The fee paid to the investment manager of a mutual fund. It is usually about one-half to one percent of average net assets annually. Not to be confused with the sales charge, which is the one-time commission paid at the time of purchase as a part of the offering price.

Margin   The dollar amount an investor must deposit with a stockbroker in order to borrow money from that broker to buy stocks.

Margin call   A stockbroker's demand for sufficient money or securities from a client to bring the value of the margin account up to the minimum.

Master limited partnership   A type of limited partnership with shares trading on one of the stock exchanges.

Maturity date   The date on which the principal or full face value of a bond, note, or other debt instrument must be paid by the issuer to the investor.

Mortality table   A table indicating the number of deaths per thousand at various ages, which has been developed from past experiences by life insurance companies.

Municipal bonds   Bonds issued by states, counties, cities, and their agencies to raise money for projects or ongoing expenses. Interest earned, in most cases, is exempt from federal tax, and from state and local taxes for a resident of the issuing state. However, some bonds, known as AMT bonds, are subject to tax.

Mutual fund   An investment company that raises money by selling shares to the public. This pool of money is invested in stocks, bonds, options, and money-market instruments. The portfolio is then professionally managed, with securities bought and sold at the discretion of the manager.

NASD   The National Association of Securities Dealers, Inc. An association of brokers and dealers in the over-the-counter securities business. The association has the power to expel members who have been declared guilty of unethical practices. NASD is dedicated to, among other objectives, "adopt, administer and enforce rules of fair practice and rules to prevent fraudulent and manipulative acts and practices, and in general to promote just and equitable principles of trade for the protection of investors."

Net asset value   The market value of a mutual fund, arrived at by taking the closing value of all securities and assets, subtracting liabilities, and dividing by the number of shares outstanding.

New issue   A stock or bond sold by a corporation for the first time. These stocks or bonds may be issued to retire outstanding securities of the company, to purchase new plant or equipment, or to raise additional working capital.

Odd lot   Any number of shares that is less than a round lot (100 shares).

Open account   When referring to a mutual fund, a type of account in which the investor may add or withdraw shares at any time. In such an account, dividends may be paid in cash or reinvested at the account holder's expense.

Over the counter (OTC)   Securities not traded on a stock exchange, but bought and sold through specialized dealers connected by computer or telephone.

Par value   See *face value*.

Penny stock   A speculative stock that sells for less than $1 per share, although some experts use $5 as a benchmark. Penny stocks are issued by companies with little or no earnings record, and are both volatile and risky. All penny stocks sell over the counter.

Personal financial planning   The process of coordinating a range of financial services, products, and strategies that are consistent with the client's goals and values. The process must develop and maintain a plan of action to reach the client's personal objectives. The plan must respond to changes in goals and environment, reflect the client's stage of life, and include transfer of wealth at death.

Point   With *bonds*, a point is equal to $10 for each $1000 face amount. For example, if a bond moves two points, it changes $20. With *stocks*, a point is equal to a $1 change in price. For example, a move up or down two points represents a $2 change.

Points   A one-time charge made in connection with a home mortgage. One point equals 1 percent of the loan. Points are often 1 to 3 percent of the total mortgage.

Preferred stock   A class of stock that pays a set dividend and takes preference over common stock with regard to dividend payments or liquidation of the company. Preferreds have high yields and are relatively low in risk, but because the dividend is fixed, their market value fluctuates like a bond—down when interest rates rise and up when rates fall.

Premium   A term that indicates that a *bond* or *preferred stock* is selling above face or pay value. For example, a bond with a $1000 face value selling for $1015 is selling at a premium. With *common stocks*, it's the amount an issue sells for above other stocks in the same industry. With *insurance* or an *annuity*, it's the fee or installment made to buy coverage.

Price-earnings ratio (P/E)   The price of a stock divided by the annual earnings per share. This ratio, also known as the "multiple," indicates how many times a stock's selling price is greater than its earnings per share. Low-P/E stocks tend to have higher yields, less risk, lower prices, and a slower earnings growth rate.

Prime rate   The interest rate a bank charges its top-rated commercial borrowers.

Prospectus   The document that offers a new issue of securities to the public. It is required under the Securities Act of 1933.

Proxy   A written authorization that allows someone else to vote your shares on some or all issues presented at a company's shareholder's annual meeting. Cards authorizing your proxy are usually sent out by mail along with an annual report and an invitation to the annual meeting.

Prudent man's rule   An investment standard. In some states the law requires that a fiduciary, such as a trustee, invest the fund's money only in a list of securities designated by the state—the so-called legal list. In other states the trustee may invest in a security if it is one that a prudent man of discretion and intelligence, who is seeking a reasonable income and preservation of capital, would buy.

REIT (real estate investment trust)   A publicly traded company that purchases and manages property and mortgages. REITs must distribute 95 percent of their income to shareholders, and by doing so are exempt from federal income tax; consequently, many REITs pay above-average dividends.

RELP (real estate limited partnership)   See *Limited partnership.*

Return of capital   A distribution or payment of cash made out of capital rather than out of current or retained earnings.

Right, or stock right   A privilege given by a company to its shareholders to buy more stock, frequently at a discount from the market price, and before it is offered to the public.

Rollover   The nonrecognition of gain or loss when amounts realized are transferred into similar types of property, such as from one qualified plan to another, or from the sale of a principal residence into a new residence.

Round lots   The fixed number or blocks of shares, usually 100, which is the commonly traded unit on the organized exchanges.

Rule of 72   A handy formula for figuring the number of years it takes to double principal using compound interest. Divide the interest rate into the number 72.

Savings bonds   Also called EE bonds, they are issued by the U.S. government at half their face value; that is, a $50 bond is sold for $25. Although you do not receive annual interest payments, you receive full face value at maturity.

Secondary market   Also called the *aftermarket,* this is the place where existing securities (those that have already been issued to the public) are bought and sold. The stock exchanges and the over-the-counter market are the main secondary markets.

Selling short   Selling a stock you do not own because you believe it will drop in price. Stocks for selling short are borrowed from stockbrokers, sometimes for a fee. In order to sell short, you must have a margin account.

Single-premium deferred annuity   An annuity in which the investor makes a lump-sum payment to an insurance company. Proceeds are taxed only when distributions begin.

Spread   The difference between the bid and asked price. (See *Bid and asked price.*)

Stock   A certificate representing ownership in a company. With common stock, one share usually represents one part ownership, plus the right to receive one part of any earnings distributed as dividends.

Stock option   An option to purchase (a call) or sell (a put) a stock, for a stated price, within a certain time period. Options trade on the exchanges.

Stock split   An increase in the number of shares outstanding without an increase in value. After a 2-for-1 split, a shareholder with 100 shares valued at $20 per share would have 200 shares valued at $10 each. When a stock has run up in price, a split is often declared to make the stock more affordable.

Stop order   A request to a broker to buy or sell a security at the market price once the stock has reached a designated price (the stop price).

Tax-exempt security   Certain obligations issued by state and local governments, the interest of which is exempt from federal income tax.

Tender   To surrender one's shares in response to an offer to purchase them at a given price.

10-K   A company's annual operations report required by the Securities and Exchange Commission. It is more detailed, though less graphically attractive, than the annual report.

Term life insurance   Life insurance that provides coverage for a specific period, typically 1, 3, or 5 years. It provides protection only, with no cash buildup or loan provisions.

Total return   The return on an investment that includes price appreciation, dividends, interest, and any tax benefits.

Treasury issues   Bonds, notes, and bills issued by the U.S. government and backed by its full faith and credit. They are considered the safest and highest-quality investments available. *T-bills* mature in 1 year or less; they are issued at a discount from face value; minimum investment is $10,000 with $5000 thereafter. *T-notes* mature in 2 to 10 years; minimum denomination is $1000. *T-bonds* mature in 10 to 30 years or longer; minimum denomination is $1000.

Unit investment trust (UIT)   A fixed portfolio of income-producing investments put together by brokerage houses and sold in $1000 units to investors. UITs invest in municipal bonds, government securities, preferred stocks, or corporate bonds. When the securities mature, are redeemed, or are sold, the principal is returned to the investors.

Universal life insurance   A type of permanent life insurance with more flexibility than whole life. The owner can change the size of premiums, and choose the amount of death benefits. The cash value grows on a tax-deferred basis.

Vesting   The legal right of an employee to share in the company's qualified pension plan.

Volume   The total number of shares traded on any day or for a given time period.

Warrant   A security often issued with a bond or preferred stock, granting the owner the right to buy a share of the corporation's common stock at a certain price for a number of years or forever.

Wash sale   The purchase and sale of a security almost at the same time or within a short time. A wash sale can be executed by one or more investors in an effort to create an artificial market and profit from the activity.

Whole-life insurance   Also known as permanent life, ordinary life, and straight life. The policy stays in force as long as the premiums are paid and the insured is alive. Premiums are the same throughout the life of the policy.

Will   The declaration of a person's wishes concerning the disposition of the person's property after death, the guardianship of the person's children, and the administration of the person's estate. A will is executed in accordance with certain legal requirements.

Yield to maturity   The rate of return paid on a bond or certificate of deposit if held to maturity.

Zero-coupon bond   A bond that pays no annual interest and is sold for less than face value and redeemed at full value upon maturity. (See *Deep-discount bond.*)

INDEX

profit-sharing retirement plans, 270, 282

Protective Industrial Insurance Company of America (PIICA), 173

"Publication 17" (IRS), 87

purchasing-power erosion, 212

"Race and Money" (Updegrave), 11

radio shows offering financial advice, 102, 277

Ram Research Group, 109

Randolph, Joseph, 172

real estate
  financing techniques in, 160-162
  real estate brokers, 158
  success stories in, 159, 162, 170-171
  (See also home buying)

record keeping, 62-70
  categories of, 64
  equipment needed for, 64-65
  in filing systems, 64-67
  marriage and, 53
  in notebooks, 65, 67-69
  overview of, 62-63
  purposes of, 63-64
  in safe deposit boxes, 65, 70
  (See also budgeting)

rent-to-buy options, in home buying, 169

resources, 313-333
  books, 316-319
  free brochures, 323-330
  magazines and newsletters, 314-316
  newspapers, 313-314
  on certified financial planners, 331
  on credit cards, 106, 107, 323
  on debt counseling, 323
  on discount investment brokers, 328
  on general financial information, 328-331
  on insurance, 323-324
  on investing, 326-327
  on-line financial forums, 321
  on money management, 325
  on retirement, 325-326
  on taxes, 87, 327
  on top mutual fund families, 331-333
  software packages, 71, 321-322
  videos, 319-320
  (See also financial education; telephone numbers)

retirement, 261-290
  401(k) plans, 270-273
  403(b) plans, 273
  books on, 319
  calculating financial needs for, 265-266
  defined-benefit pension plans, 269-270, 281
  early retirement, 278-279
  employer-sponsored plans, 269-273, 281-282
  financial goals in, 48
  income sources in, 266-276
  individual retirement accounts (IRAs) for, 273-274, 285-286

inflation rates and, 263-265

Keogh plans, 280-283

overview of, 261-263, 290

personal savings and, 275-276

planning checklist for, 276-278

profit-sharing plans, 270, 282

pursuing dreams in, 289-290

reverse-annuity mortgages and, 288-289

SAR simplified employee pension plans (SAR/SEPs), 283

self-employment and, 279-286

simplified employee plans (SEPs), 283-284

social security benefits and, 264, 267-269

software for planning, 322

starting late and catching up on plans for, 286-288

tax planning and, 86

Retire with MONEY magazine, 316

reverse-annuity mortgages, 288-289

risk:
  conservative investments, 212-213, 244, 271
  high-risk investments, 215, 243-244, 271
  moderate-risk investments, 213, 243-245, 271
  types of investment risk, 210-211
  (See also investing)

Rockefeller, Nelson, 201

Rollins, Frankie, 133

safe deposit boxes, 65, 70

Sanders, Steve L., 12

SAR simplified employee pension plans (SAR/SEPs), 283

saving money, 129-151
  CDs (certificates of deposit), 147-148, 219
  on clothing, 144
  for emergencies and special situations, 138-139
  on entertainment, 143-144
  example of, 129-132
  excuses against, 134-136
  on food, 142
  getting help with, 149
  Mark Griffith and, 141
  guidelines for, 139-145
  income from personal savings, 275-276
  interest rates and, 149-150
  versus investing, 207
  overview of, 132-134
  passbook savings accounts, 147
  on personal care and grooming supplies, 142-143
  purposes of, 137-138
  retirement and, 275-276
  savings rates of African-Americans, 132
  in shopping, 140-142
  St. Luke's Penny Thrift Savers Society and, 145-147

success stories of, 7, 37-39, 136, 261

tips for, 136-137, 151

Truth in Savings Act (TISA) of 1991, 150

U.S. Savings Bonds, 148, 334, 344

where to save, 147-149

(See also spending)

savings and loans (S&Ls), 94

savings bonds, 148, 334, 344

Searles, Joseph, III, 215

sector funds, 244

secured credit cards, 106

secured loans, 100

self-employment, and retirement, 279-286

service and appliance manufacturers, 333-334

setting goals. See financial goals

sharecropping, 8-9

Shepard, James E., 120

shopping, saving money in, 140-142

Shorey, William T., 8

simplified employee plans (SEPs), 283-284

Sivart Mortgage Company, Inc., 170

Sloan, Maceo, 176

Smith, A. L., 130

Smith, Joshua I., 8, 58

Smith, Robert Mason, 56

Smith, Stephen, 152

Social Security Administration, 269, 326

social security benefits, 264, 267-269

software, financial, 71, 321-322

Spark, Anna Maria, 291-293

Spaulding, Charles Clinton, 175

spending:
  African-American patterns of, 4-5
  diaries of, 79
  (See also saving money)

Standard & Poor's 500 index, 237

Stewart, Sallie Wyatt, 159

St. Luke's Penny Thrift Savers Society, 145-147

stocks, 224-239
  versus bonds, 216
  brokerage firms and, 231
  categories of, 226-231
  common and preferred stocks, 228
  dividend reinvestment plans (DRIPs) and, 232-235
  Dow Jones Industrial Average (DJIA) and, 236-238
  how to read financial pages, 235-236
  market indices of, 236-239
  overview of, 224-228, 345
  paying dependable dividends, 230
  (See also bonds; diversified investment portfolios; investing; mutual funds)

student loans, 100, 120-122, 334

success stories:
  of achieving financial goals, 37-39, 43, 56-58
  in advertising, 26
  in armed forces, 11
  in banking, 90-92, 99, 101, 117, 120, 170